PRIDE of the PANTHERS

by Billy Powell

Henchard Press Ltd.

Publisher	Henry S. Beers
Associate Publisher	Richard J. Hutto
Executive Vice President	Robert G. Aldrich
Operations Manager	Gary G. Pulliam
Editor-in-Chief	Joni Woolf
Art Director/Designer	Julianne Gleaton
Designer	Daniel Emerson
Director of Marketing and Public Relations	Mary D. Robinson

Printed in the USA.

Library of Congress Control Number: 2006920166

ISBN: (13 digit) 9780977091287
        (10 digit) 0977091287

Henchard Press Ltd. books are available at quantity discounts with bulk purchase for educational, business, or sales promotional use. For information, please write to:
Henchard Press Ltd., SunTrust Bank Building Suite 320,
435 Second Street, Macon, GA 31201,
or call 866-311-9578.

DEDICATION

First and foremost, I dedicate this book to the glory of God for it was He who called me to write "Pride of the Panthers." I had considered writing this book for over ten years; however, each time I contemplated undertaking the project, I quickly dismissed the idea. The task seemed too daunting and complex, especially chronicling 36 years of Perry High School basketball, 1933 to 1969, and capturing in words the vibrant and unconquerable spirit of the Perry community during that halcyon era. Then one day in early March 2005, God spoke to my heart. I became increasingly convinced that, if someone in my generation didn't write the book, the glory days of Perry High School's basketball dynasty would be lost forever. Thus, I became compelled to write the book so that those living through those unforgettable and cherished times could relive their experiences and so that our children and grandchildren might understand why our hearts are still warmed by remembrances of our glorious past.

Secondly, this book is dedicated to my wife, Beverly Davis Powell, who has edited the manuscript and provided invaluable advice and counsel toward making this book the best product it could possibly be.

Thirdly, "Pride of the Panthers" is dedicated to my two sons, Bill Powell and Tim Powell, who have offered encouragement and constructive suggestions at every step along the way.

And finally, it is dedicated to my grandchildren who have enthusiastically supported their granddaddy in this endeavor:

Ashtyn Powell
Alyssa Powell
Jacob Powell
Eli Powell
Jordan Powell

ACKNOWLEDGEMENTS

This book was compiled from five basic sources: (1) Interviews with former Perry High basketball players, Perry High School students, basketball fans, and local citizens, (2) Perry High School yearbooks, (3) scrapbooks of PHS graduates, (4) old newspaper archives covering the period from 1919 through 1969, and (5) personal eyewitness accounts and memories.

Three Perry High School graduates, who witnessed firsthand the Perry basketball dynasty, volunteered to assist me in writing "Pride of the Panthers" and made significant contributions to the finished product:

Thomas "Boot" Hunt: Researcher

Hunt, a two-time All-State basketball player and captain of Perry's 1959 state championship team, spent untold hours researching and photocopying old microfilm records at central Georgia libraries. He captured all newspaper records of Perry basketball games spanning the Coach Eric Staples' era, 1933 to 1965, and the Coach Paul Hartman years, 1966 to 1969. Boot's unrelenting efforts ensured in-depth coverage of 36 years of Perry High basketball and expedited completion of this book.

William Harrison: Researcher

Harrison, a star Perry basketball player on the outstanding 1955 quintet, made many valuable research contributions, including reconstructing the life of Jim Gooden, Perry's first basketball coach, 1919-1933, and in ferreting out much needed biographical information on Coach Eric Staples before he came to Perry in 1933. William also undertook a host of special assignments to ensure both in-depth coverage and accuracy of the book's contents.

Mary Kathryn Duggan Thornton

Mary Kathryn, a 1955 PHS graduate, former PHS cheerleader, and retired college English professor has made many valuable contributions in providing technical advice and counsel and in suggesting manuscript improvements.

Others who made valuable contributions:

- Sue Lay, PHS librarian: scanning photographs and providing information from old Perry High yearbooks, 1946 to 1969. Many of the photographs she provided are included in "Pride of the Panthers."
- Derry Watson: research on Perry team rosters, 1933 to 1965
- Cheerleader information and photos: Cheryl Richards Conner, Lula Alice Collier Batchelor, Jerry Cater Pierce, Jeanne Pierce Bledsoe, Skeet Chapman, and Billy Gray.
- Team photos, biographical information on Coaches Staples and Gooden and other pertinent data: Skeet Chapman, Horace andNell Woodruff, Willis Harrison, Betty Gooden, Rita Todd Hall, Charles Irby Shelton, Beth Bennett, Jean Martin Davis, Dr. Jack Thornton, Sherry Staples, Caroline Wilbert, and Jeff Pierce
- Transcription of speeches from videotape: Karen Hunt.
- Bobbe Nelson and her history of Houston County, "A Land So Dedicated."
- Advice and counsel: Perry Mayor Jim Worrall, Charlotte Perkins, Gilda Stanberry-Cotney, Dwayne Powell, Bill Powell, Tim Powell, and Beverly Davis Powell.

CONTENTS

FOREWORD

If any coach in high school basketball history was better than "Fessor" Staples, no one should try to convince me, because I will never believe it.

From my first job digging worms in the Staples' backyard worm bed to packing peaches each summer under his direction—from the first grade through Perry's graduating class of 1956—to basketball and golf state championships, I was one of "Fessor's Boys."

Eric P. Staples (known to us as Fessor—short for professor) coached for 38 years, six years at towns in west Georgia and 32 years at Perry High School in Perry, Georgia, amassing a career record of 924 victories and 198 losses. From 1933 to 1965, he established a basketball dynasty at Perry High School. During this era, Perry competed against the toughest teams in Georgia and took on all comers, including the highest classification schools. Fessor's Perry teams won an unprecedented eight state championships and 25 district and region titles. His 82.4 winning percentage was the best in the nation during his era.

What was the formula for Fessor's success? How did he nurture and cajole young men into skilled athletes and diligent students? How did he inspire ordinary basketball players, usually shorter and slower than their opponents, into cohesive, disciplined teams? Why and how did this educator make his teams and his entire community of Perry, in the words of sportswriter Jim Minter "forget their ABCs?" [Perry, a Class B school, routinely defeated the higher classisfication A and AA schools.] How did Fessor turn students and athletes into champions?

Fessor's often repeated admonition, "You've got to be willing to pay the price," not only made me better than I really was on the basketball court, it has stuck with me through life and inspired me to dig deeper for commitment and tenacity in dealing with life's tough challenges.

"Pride of the Panthers" is a story that begged to be told. Billy Powell was one of those Panthers with pride and skill, and he used both to lead Fessor's 1953 team to Perry's third state championship.

Billy also uses both his pride and his skill in writing this labor of love that captures for our children and grandchildren the amazing story of a brilliant coach and his outstanding record of success. If you liked the movie "Hoosiers" and enjoy high school basketball, this book is for you. If you are a former basketball player, cheerleader or fan, you will find this book a walk down memory lane. If you had a teacher or coach who had a profound influence on your life, this book will rekindle your gratitude.

"Pride of the Panthers" is more than a story about a basketball dynasty—it is about a small town's pride and a coach who was a master psychologist, who knew how to tap the hidden potential of every player and mold a group of players with diverse talents into a cohesive and triumphant team.

In recounting the championship years at Perry High School, Billy Powell has captured the essence of this great coach and teacher—his brilliance, his integrity, his example, his ability to snatch victory from defeat and the resulting respect that the state of Georgia held for this Hall of Fame coach.

This book is about the heart of a champion and how champions respond when the chips are down and imminent defeat stares them in the face.

Eric P. Staples' lessons last a lifetime, so I am still one of "Fessor's Boys." So is Billy Powell, and in this book he tells us why.

Sam Nunn
Perry High School Class of 1956
U.S. Senator, 1972-1996

1 Dawning of the dynasty

In 1933, as the country was limping along from the aftermath of the Great Depression and suffering the birth pains of a slowly burgeoning economy, another birth was taking place in the Deep South--the dawning of the greatest high school basketball dynasty in Georgia history. Little did the citizens of Perry, Georgia, expect their sleepy little town would become the epicenter of Georgia high school basketball. In those days, few basketballs were bouncing in Perry backyards, and community interest in the sport was subdued. But, a new coach came to town in August 1933 and changed all that. He was the catalyst who created a basketball dynasty at Perry High School that lasted for 32 glorious years, 1933 through 1965. During this time span, the United States fought in World War II, struggled through the Korean and Vietnam conflicts, and landed a man on the moon.

My introduction to the dynasty came through my grandmother. In 1939, when I was four, I had an insatiable yearning to play ball, but times were hard, and I didn't have a ball. To satisfy my obsession, my grandmother, Delia Ethridge Powell, made for me what she called a "sock ball." Being an excellent seamstress who made dresses and quilts, she collected cloth cuttings from her sewing, stuffed them into an old sock, and stitched the sock into the rounded form of a ball using a pedal-driven sewing machine. Once she made the sock ball, Grandmother Powell played pitch with me in the backyard. Since she never refused to play with me and was willing to interrupt her housework to accommodate my pleas, I spent many glorious days playing sock ball with grandmother.

Later, as a third grader in 1943, I overheard adults speaking in glowing terms about Perry's basketball team, so I asked Grandmother if she would take me to a basketball game. My parents and grandparents lived in the same house and neither owned a car, so Grandmother decided we would walk to the game. The gym was about a mile away, so she clasped my hand and off to the game we went. The night was cold and dark, the only light being streetlights at the major intersections. The long stretch of Gilmer Street was so dark that it was spooky, causing me to move closer to Grandmother. As we crossed at the streetlights, I could see smoke billowing from chimneys as people huddled around their fireplaces to stay warm. The howling of dogs in the distance and the rustling of leaves were the only sounds except our hurrying feet. Soon we were approaching the Perry gym, whose outside lights illuminated its front entrance. In the distance I could see excited fans lined up in the narrow dirt street waiting to buy tickets.

From the opening tip-off, I became enthralled with the game of basketball. Spirited cheerleaders whipping the crowd into a frenzy, fans cheering every play, high arching shots swishing the net, and the deafening crowd roar after every score were spine-tingling sights and sounds I had never experienced. I sat by Grandmother, soaking up the enchanting atmosphere of the old gym, cheering and clapping for the Perry team. During the waning moments of the game, the score was tied. In attempting to get an offensive rebound, a tall and lanky Perry player was knocked to the floor near the foul line. The errant ball magically rolled into his lap. He quickly released a two-handed shot while still sitting on the floor. The ball was in mid-flight as the game-ending horn sounded. Time seemed to slow down as that ball floated through the air and the fans, in utter silence, looked on with nervous anticipation. Suddenly, the ball came swishing down through the net with the classic snap of the nylon chords, causing great jubilation to erupt on the Perry sidelines. Perry had won a thriller over a determined archrival. The fans were ecstatic.

That game set me on fire for the game of basketball. It was an unforgettable moment in my life. Walking back home and reflecting on the game, I asked, "Grandmother, who was the player who made the winning basket?" "Walter Skellie," she replied. "I want to be a basketball player just like him," I exclaimed. As the seasons and years went by, Grandmother continued to take me to the basketball games. I shall never forget those wonderful times, clutching grandmother's hand and walking with her to the games.

L-R: *Billy Powell, Dwayne Powell, age 2, (with basketball) and Kenneth Whipple.*

My brother, Dwayne, was born when I was nine years old. I wanted to impart my enthusiasm for basketball to my little brother, so I built his first goal when he was two years old and began teaching him how to play. The goal stood only three feet off the ground, yet little Dwayne could barely get the ball over the rim. As Dwayne grew stronger and taller, the goals were moved higher and higher. By the time he was 10 years old, the goal was standard height. When he became a teenager, I would play him one-on-one games. To keep his motivation high and not kill his enthusiasm, I would let him beat me from time to time. When he became a senior in high school and later a star player at the University of Georgia, the days of letting him win were something from the past, because I found myself literally fighting for my life in every game we played. The score was always close with every game going right down to the wire. We would play for hours on end. Grandmother would come out of the house from time to time and ask, "What's the score?" Almost invariably the score would be tied. It later became a source of amusement to us that uncannily she never asked unless the score was tied. Our stock answer was always, "The score is tied, Grandmother!" Grandmother lived to see both of her grandsons play basketball for the Perry Panthers.

Both Dwayne and I were fortunate enough to become a part of Perry's basketball dynasty. By the time I reached high school during the early 1950s, Perry High School had been a perennial winner for nearly 20 years, and had consistently received the acclaim of sportswriters and basketball

observers as having the state's premier basketball program. When Dwayne
played a decade later during the early to mid-1960s, the dynasty was at
its zenith, and the Perry coach was receiving national recognition as the
winningest coach in America.

Because of the fervent fan support and strong tradition that winning
produces, basketball was more than a game in the Perry community; it
was a way of life. The citizens of Perry took great pride in their basketball
teams and supported them devotedly. When the Perry teams played at
home, a large portion of the community could be found at the local gym.
When the teams played out of town, local businesses closed early and
caravans of cars motored to the site of the hardwood battle. In this little
Georgia hamlet of 3500 citizens, basketball was king during the decades of
the1930s through 1960s.

There were many parallels between the basketball fervor and
community life in Perry and that depicted in the fictitious town of
Hickory in the 1986 blockbuster movie, "Hoosiers." Hickory represented
Milan, Indiana, a small high school of 161 students, which won the
1954 Indiana "all-classification" state basketball tournament over the
highly favored team from Muncie Central, a much higher classification
school. Having watched the Milan-Muncie game on ESPN several times,
I firmly believe that Perry's state championship teams would have been
highly competitive with both Milan and Muncie. Perry was gifted with
a great coach who knew how to get the most out of every player. His
well-disciplined teams rarely missed an assignment or turned the ball over.
Further, all of his championship teams featured great shooters, something
that neither Milan nor Muncie evidenced in their 1954 Indiana state
championship battle.

Although Perry's basketball dynasty was not officially launched until
1933, its building blocks can be traced back to 1919. That's when James
(Jim) Madison Gooden, a World War I veteran, arrived as the Perry school
principal, in June of that year. Before entering World War I, Gooden
had taught school in Byron, Georgia. First and foremost, Gooden was
an educator, yet one of his first orders of business was to organize a boys'
basketball program. Gooden, who had played basketball while growing
up in Alexander City, Alabama, and later at Mercer University in Macon,

Georgia, was dismayed when he learned there were few basketball goals in town and only a handful of boys who knew anything about the game.

Two weeks before school began in early September 1919, Gooden held tryouts for his first basketball team. Most of the boys were novices at basketball, so it was no small order for Gooden to teach the fundamentals and to whip his top candidates into a cohesive unit.

To provide an outdoor basketball court, Gooden graded an area on the northeast edge of the school grounds. There Gooden installed a dirt court with basketball goals on each end. The full court ran north to south. It was located on the lot adjacent to what is now Watson-Hunt Funeral Home on Main Street in Perry.

By mid-September 1919, Gooden had chosen a roster and scheduled home-and-home engagements with neighboring towns. For uniforms, short pants and V-neck tank tops were worn. These pioneer players chose maroon and gold as the school colors and the Panther as the

Perry's first boys' basketball team, 1919-1920. Front row, L-R: Bunyan Watson, Dennard Skellie, and Marion Houser. Back row, L-R: Coach Jim Gooden, Vernon Wallace, E. A. Murray, and Willie Woolfolk.

mascot. In late September 1919, Perry High School won its first game from Montezuma High School. Little did this bunch of greenhorns, who comprised the 1919-20 quintet, know that they had formed the cornerstone of a future basketball dynasty.

In those days, there were no bleachers where fans could sit. Spectators either brought their own chairs or stood up. During a game, a coach could instruct his team only at the halftime. If the coach had any instructions or advice to impart to his players, he could convey it to them only through a substitute. There was no admission charge to watch the games, always played in the afternoons, but after the game a hat was passed around for contributions. Visiting teams were entertained in local homes, which included meals and sleeping accommodations; transportation was provided by parents. On the day of the games, the entire school held a pep rally under the leadership of the teachers. There were no organized cheerleaders to lead the cheering at the games. Many games had to be canceled due to weather conditions. When inclement weather struck, the

1927 District Champions. Players, L-R: Chester Edwards, Hilt Gray, Earnest (Red) Edwards, Glea Gray, William (Bill) Dorsett, Nick Harper, Ralph Martin, Coleman (Jube) Strother, and Ormond C. (Freck) Skellie. Coach J. M. Gooden and manager James Etheridge are in the center. Not pictured were Ernest Edwards and Benny Hall.

team practiced drills in the school halls.

From 1919 through 1926, Coach Gooden's teams played on dirt courts. Notable players during this era were Marion Houser, Vernon Wallace, E.A. Murray, Willie Woolfolk, Bunyan Watson, Chester Edwards, Earnest (Red) Edwards, William (Bill) Dorsett, Nick Harper, Ralph Martin, Coleman (Jube) Strother, Ormond C. (Freck) Skellie, Dennard Skellie, Elmore McCarey, Raleigh Ward, Wordna Gray, Glea Gray, Hilt Gray, Bowie Gray, Homer Davis (author's father-in-law), Floyd Tabor, Louis Gilbert, Louis Harper, Alfred Edwards, Jake Murray, Alton Rainey, and Emmett Rainey.

In 1927, Perry began playing indoors when a gymnasium was built by public subscription on land donated by Penn-Dixie Cement Corporation. The 1927 team responded by winning the district tournament hosted at Hawkinsville, Georgia.

Perry repeated as district champions in 1928 in a tournament played at the Perry gym, and again in 1929 at Vidalia's gym. Members of 1929 team were Francis Nunn, Bowie Gray, Wilson Martin, Herman Martin, Jim Tharpe, Elmer Wolfe, and Harold Duncan.

Perry continued its winning ways by capturing the district championship in 1930 held at Cochran, and again in 1931 at McRae. In summary, after the gym was built, the Perry teams thrived by winning five consecutive district titles from 1927 to 1931.

Gooden established an enviable overall record, both outdoors and indoors. From 1919 through 1933, his teams won seven district championships, six in the old Twelfth District, and his last in the new Third District in 1933. This was Jim Gooden's last season as coach of the Perry Panthers

On opening night in the 1933 district tournament, the Panthers defeated Columbus Industrial 33-19. In semifinal action, Perry blasted Chauncey, 36 to 16. In the title game, Perry downed Byron 30 to 25 in a hard fought battle. This was Perry's first championship in the new Third District. The box score of the district championship game:

Perry-30	**Byron-25**
Fred Butler-11	Goss-11

Curtis Clark-8   Davis-4
L. C. Todd- 9   English-2
Roger Carter-2   Lineberger-5
Bob Massee   Aultman-2

Subs: Perry-none; Byron: James, Wilder-1

Perry's 1933 team. Front row, L-R: Coach Jim Gooden, Fred Butler, Curtis Clark, Marion Brown, and J. M. (Pepper) Martin. Second row: Allen Martin, Bob Massee, L. C. Todd, Roger Carter, and Bill McKinley-manager.

The 1933 team advanced to the state tournament in Athens and was beaten on opening night, March 2, 1933, by Canton on a last-minute desperation field goal. Perry was leading Canton by one point during the closing seconds of the game, when Canton's star forward Jones fired a lucky shot from center court that ripped through the net and crushed Perry's title hopes.

After that game, with seven district titles to his credit, school superintendent Gooden retired from coaching to devote full time to his administrative duties. To fill the coaching position, he promptly journeyed to Tallapoosa, Georgia, to woo a highly recommended young coach to Perry, a man who was making quite a name for himself in northwest Georgia basketball circles, where his teams at Rockello, Bowdon, and Tallapoosa had won consistently and played championship-caliber basketball. To make the job offer lucrative, Gooden, with the approval of the school board, offered the young coach the position of high school principal in addition to basketball coach, which he accepted. The new coach signed a contract to assume his new positions at Perry beginning in the fall of 1933. Gooden remained as school superintendent through the end of calendar year 1936. Gooden's legacy was establishing a winning tradition for his successor to build upon.

Jim Gooden

On January 1, 1937, Mr. Gooden assumed a position with the department of education in Atlanta as a state school supervisor in charge of 55 southwest Georgia schools. To recap his tenure at the Perry school, Gooden served as high school principal his first year, the 1919-20 school year. He was elevated to the position of superintendent of Perry consolidated schools the following school year, 1920-21, and remained in that capacity for the next 16 years. During Gooden's tenure as Perry's superintendent, he was recognized as one of the state's top educators and school administrators. In the community, Gooden was a highly respected individual and a man of integrity. When it came to school matters, he was a strict disciplinarian and one who stressed the importance of education.

Gooden retired from his state job in 1958 and returned to Perry. He and his wife, the former Stella Wade of Leslie, Georgia, resided on Washington Avenue in Perry for the remainder of their lives. During his retirement years, Gooden was active in civic and church organizations and taught Sunday School at the Methodist Church until he was 90 years old. Their only child, Betty, graduated from Perry High School, where she was a cheerleader.

Jim Gooden was the forerunner, who prepared the way for a young coach who had a date with destiny, a coach who would lead Perry to the Promised Land of high school basketball.

The Panthers' new mentor would become widely known as Georgia's "Mr. Basketball." Late in his coaching career, as his victories accumulated, he would reign as the winningest prep coach in the nation...

2 Georgia's "Mr. Basketball"

A capacity throng of 3500 frenzied fans were screaming and yelling. Every seat was occupied and an overflow crowd filled the aisles and doorways. Every score produced a deafening roar. Macon's City Auditorium seemed to reel and sway on its girders. It was March 14, 1953. The Perry Panthers, of which this writer was a member, were playing the tremendously tall and talented Clarkston Angoras for the state championship of Georgia. Although the Panthers had led by a small margin throughout the game, most basketball observers felt that we were playing over our heads and that the powerful Clarkston team would ultimately prevail.

During the waning minutes of the fourth quarter with Perry nursing a six point lead, Clarkston suddenly sprang a full court press that produced two Panther turnovers and two quick Angora baskets. Clarkston had closed the gap to only two points. The scoreboard read: Perry-59, Clarkeston-57. Only one minute and 40 seconds remained in the contest. The tide had turned. Clarkston had the momentum. Pandemonium and jubilation broke loose on the Clarkston sidelines. The Angora fans were smelling victory. Surprised by the suddenness of the Clarkston press, the Perry team appeared confused and bewildered.

Defeat seemed imminent for a Perry team that had won 33 games, climbing over formidable opponents to gain the state finals. The dream of winning a state championship, which only moments ago seemed attainable, was fleeting from our grasp with the countdown of seconds irreversibly flashing away on the scoreboard clock.

Our coach signaled for a timeout. As we approached the Perry bench, we were met by a coach who in the thick of battle was a model of composure. Any indication of indecisiveness or a slight quiver of his lip could have sealed our doom. In the heat of battle, we drew strength from this giant of a man who exuded confidence. He believed in himself and his approach to the game. He talked to us in a calm manner, a reassuring tone in his voice. He emphasized the importance of controlling the ball and the clock for the remainder of the game. He instructed us to execute a three-man weave beyond the top of the key with the two post men split to the sides to open up the middle. We were cautioned to drive for the basket only if our defender was screened out and the lane opened. Should the lane suddenly close during a drive for the basket, we were told to pass off to the open post man and resume the weave out front. The team walked back on the court, with a renewed determination, resolutely determined to scrap Clarkston to the bitter end. We believed that victory was ours if we followed his instructions. His stratagem worked to perfection as it had hundreds of times in the past. We scored four points during the remaining seconds, held Clarkston scoreless, and won the state championship game by a six point margin, 63 to 57.

The coach who guided his team to victory was none other than the inimitable young coach who school superintendent Jim Gooden brought to Perry High School twenty years earlier, in 1933—the one destined to lead the Perry Panthers to new heights in high school basketball. His name was Eric Staples. His teams over 38 years (one year at Rockelo, three at Bowdon, two at Tallapoosa, and the last 32 years at Perry), won an unbelievable 82.4-percent of their games: 924 victories versus only 198 losses. During this span, his Perry teams (1933-1965) captured an unprecedented eight state championships and 25 regional or district championships. Additionally, Staples' teams were runner-up in state tournament competition on four separate occasions, and in region-district tournaments finished in second place a total of six times. Because he consistently snatched victory from defeat, Coach Staples, during his era, was the winningest high school basketball coach in America, and became a legend in Georgia basketball. He was inducted into the Georgia Sports Hall of Fame in 1957.

Eric Pierce Staples, was born in Roopville, Georgia, in Carroll

Eric Staples

County on October 12, 1905, the son of Pelham and Ola Staples. His association with basketball began his sophomore year when he made the varsity traveling squad on Roopville High School's first basketball team. When Roopville played on the road, the trip was made by horse and buggy. The games were never scheduled so far away that the team couldn't return home by nightfall. Beginning his junior year, he transferred to Carrollton High School and played on the varsity the next two seasons. After graduation from high school in 1923, he played basketball and football two years for Bowdon State Normal and Industrial College in Carroll County. Following junior college, he enrolled at Bowdon College and received his degree in 1927.

Staples was not a star basketball player, but he was an outstanding team player. He fit the mold of most great basketball coaches, who were never stars, but ordinary players who were avid students of the game and knew how to teach the sport and motivate young men.

Staples was, however, a star football player. He starred as a running back at Bowdon State Normal and Industrial College. The local Bowdon newspaper, in 1924, reported on a football game between the Bowdon State Golden Bears and the Carrolton Agricultural & Mechanical College Aggies. Staples, referred to as Eric "Little" Staples in the article, led the Golden Bears to a 13-0 victory over the archrival Aggies. Not only did he "clip off spectacular gains" in rushing yardage, the article stated, but he also returned a kickoff eighty yards. The newspaper account reads: "The second and last touchdown came from a return of a kickoff. A little streak of undiluted greased lightening who totes the name of Eric (Little) Staples snatched the swineskin out of the air and merrily trotted to as glorious and brilliant a touchdown as the gods have seen. The beautiful exhibition of dodging, twisting, side-stepping, and morally 'selling-out' led the fleet little back something like eighty yards. The long run was aided and abetted by as nifty blocking on the part of several teammates as one would care to see. Staples proved to be the outstanding star of the entire game." This newspaper account serves to demonstrate the strong competitive spirit that characterized Staples' entire life as a player, coach, and educator. Staples' nose had been broken so many times playing football that later in life he had to undergo nasal surgery to remove scar tissue.

Staples' coaching career began in the fall of 1927 at Rockelo, a four-teacher weatherboard school in Heard County, where his team played on an outdoor basketball court. Staples told an amusing story about the first game his Rockelo team played indoors at a big warehouse in Hogansville, Georgia. Having always played outdoors, his players couldn't get accustomed to the overhead electric lights. "They said the lights blinded them and wanted to play with their hats on," chuckled Staples.

In the fall of 1928, he transferred to Bowdon as head coach and stayed there for three years. Staples once remarked that, during his first three years of coaching (1927-1930), only twenty-five percent of all high schools had a gym. The remaining seventy-five percent practiced on outdoor dirt courts that were rolled and graded. Since most games were played at schools with indoor courts, schools with outdoor courts scheduled few home games, and schools having a gym rarely played an out-of-town game. All tournament games, however, were played indoors. Those were the days of the center jump after each basket. During that era, players shot field goal attempts and free throws with both hands between their legs in a swinging, underhanded motion. The center jump after each score remained in effect until the 1938-39 basketball season.

In the fall of 1931, he assumed the reigns of head basketball coach at Tallapoosa High School, in northwest Georgia near the Alabama line, where he remained for two years. While coaching at Tallapoosa, he roomed with a young man from Perry, Georgia, whose father happened to be on the Houston County Board of Education. His roommate suggested to his father that the board consider hiring Staples. Realizing that Staples was a promising young coach, the Houston County Board of Education offered him a job to come to Perry in 1932. Since Staples had already signed a contract with Tallapoosa, he told the Houston group he would remain there to honor his commitment, but if they still wanted him the next year, he would come to Perry.

Coach Staples arrived as a new employee in the Perry school system during the fall of 1933. In addition to hiring Staples as basketball coach, Perry school superintendent Jim Gooden also appointed him to serve as principal of the high school. Gooden threw in the additional duty of school principal as an inducement to seal the contract with Staples.

Since Staples had harbored aspirations of becoming a lawyer, having previously taken law courses at the University of Georgia, he continued his law studies at nearby Mercer University School of Law in Macon, Georgia, after coming to Perry. After passing the state bar examination in 1936—after his third season as Perry basketball coach--Staples experienced a strange and compelling change of heart concerning his career plans. The call he had experienced earlier in life to work with young people became so strong he was unable to ignore it; consequently, he made the decision to forego establishing a law practice and to remain in school administration and coaching. To better equip himself as a school administrator, Staples continued his studies at Mercer and received his Master of Arts Degree in 1939 with emphasis in mathematics. Records show that Staples also attended basketball coaching clinics at Mercer University in 1933 and 1934.

From the time basketball began at Perry under Coach Jim Gooden in 1919 until 1927, the basketball teams had played on an outdoor court on the northeast side of the school grounds. A new wooden gymnasium was constructed during 1926 on land donated by the Penn-Dixie Cement Corporation. At the beginning of the 1926-27 school year, Perry began playing in the new gym.

Since Coach Gooden had established an enviable record from 1927 to 1933, winning five championships in the old 12th district, he hired a coach whom he felt could continue Perry's winning tradition. So when Coach Staples came to Perry in the fall of 1933, he became the recipient of a relatively new gym, which was a far cry from the tobacco warehouses where his earlier northwest Georgia teams had played.

Effective January 1, 1937, Mr. Gooden assumed a position with the department of education in Atlanta as a state school supervisor in charge of 55 Southwest Georgia schools. Upon Gooden's departure, Coach Staples, principal of the high school, was elevated by the board of trustees to the position of school superintendent in charge of all Perry schools.

Staples came to Perry prepared to play championship basketball. He patterned his offense after the deliberate style of legendary Kansas State coach, Phog Allen, and adopted the same tenacious, sticky man-to-man defense employed by the Baron of the Bluegrass himself, University of Kentucky coach Adolph Rupp. Staples met both Allen and Rupp at basketball coaching clinics. He received tutoring from both men and on occasion corresponded with them seeking advice. As a result, over the next 32 years at Perry (1933-34 season through 1964-65 season), Staples became the "Alexander the Great" of Georgia basketball. Perry was the most feared name in high school basketball circles across the state of Georgia. Staples' teams took on all comers and routinely played higher classification schools every year. After 38 years of coaching (six before coming to Perry), Staples' teams averaged slightly over 24 wins a year against only 5 losses per season, a truly phenomenal record. Because of Coach Staples' success in producing outstanding teams year after year, sportswriters and fans alike routinely referred to him as "Georgia's Mr. Basketball" and the "Dean of Georgia basketball coaches," distinctions that not even his closest challengers would attempt to deny. In fact, a contemporary of Staples, Coach Jimmy Maffett of Montezuma, Georgia, an outstanding coach himself, who coached basketball against Staples, first at Oglethorpe High and then at Macon County, declared, " In my estimation, Coach Staples was unquestionably the greatest high school coach in Georgia history."

Any team vying for a regional or state title knew somewhere along the way it would have to go through Perry's backyard to advance to the championship. Sportswriter Sam Glassman, of the "Macon Telegraph" during the 1950s, aptly said it when he wrote that when the state tournament started in Macon every year, you could "brush off a bench for the Perry Panthers" because they were expected to be there.

Staples was a distinguished-looking, southern gentleman with slightly graying temples and steel-rimmed glasses. He often wore a hat and was always spiffily dressed. His game attire usually included a starched shirt and tie, dark blue blazer, gray pants, and wingtip cordovan shoes. During the course of a game, he constantly chewed on a cigar that was never lit. As he chewed on that cigar, you could almost anticipate the brain waves that were being generated to determine the best strategy to employ at any given moment in the game.

He was not a coach who bounced up and down on the sidelines, yelling and gesticulating to his players, but was a very cerebral individual who sat quietly on the bench, analyzing every play and thinking ahead as if he were playing a chess game to anticipate his coaching opponent's next move and how best to counteract it with a preemptive ploy of his own.

On offense, his teams ran simple screens and pick and roll patterns that had been practiced over and over until his players had perfected their execution. His teams never raced up and down the court, but played a slow and deliberate control game that looked for the high percentage shot. Passing the ball cautiously to prevent pick-offs was stressed. Throwing the ball across the seams of the hardwood was discouraged. Instead, working the ball quickly around the horn was emphasized as the safest way to get the ball to an open man.

His defenses were a work of art. His teams never played zone defenses, but employed tenacious man-to-man defenses that shifted like an accordion with the flow of the basketball. On defense, he told his teams not to pay attention to a player's feet and arm movements, but to watch his mid-section, for where it went, so did he.

Although the Perry teams never had a man over 6' 3" tall, their strength was on the backboards. Coach Staples stressed blocking out your opponent on rebounding, and never letting him get between you and the basket. He emphasized that the team with the most rebounds had the best chance of winning the game.

When trying to take the ball away from an offensive player on the dribble, his players were taught never to reach down on the ball, but always to tap the ball away in an upward motion, to avoid fouling. When blocking a shot attempt, the objective was to slap the ball to a teammate rather than slam it against the floor or knock it out of bounds.

Perry teams were known for their error-free style of basketball and committed fewer turnovers than their opponents which usually provided

the margin of victory. Staples eschewed turnovers, advising his team
that every lost ball was worth an average of one point to the opposing
team. Make a bad pass, miss an assignment, or fail to get back quickly on
defense, and you would be taken out of the game and set down on the
bench beside Staples. He never scolded or berated a player publicly during
a game for making a mistake, because the player knew what infraction
he had made. Being taken out of the game was punishment enough. You
would, however, feel his wrath at practice. During my sophomore year as
a Perry basketball player, he stayed on my case constantly. Every mistake
I made, he would stop practice and chew me out, never in a cursing or
nasty manner, but forcefully emphasizing what I had done wrong and
explaining how to prevent repeat mistakes. One day, almost in tears, I
went to my confidant, Coach Earl Marshall, the assistant varsity and
B-team coach, and told him that Coach Staples had been getting after
me hot and heavy. "He seems to be singling me out; he doesn't jump on
the other players like he does me," I told Coach Marshall. "He thinks
you have great potential," responded Marshall, "that's the reason he gets
on you. Don't take it personal." Coach Marshall continued, "When you
make a floor mistake, you retreat into a shell; you must learn to shake off
your mistakes and continue playing basketball." Those were magic words
of wisdom by Coach Marshall. He completely changed my outlook
on the game; from that day forward, I began developing into the type
basketball player that Coach Staples wanted me to become.

Capitalizing on free throw opportunities was continually stressed by
Coach Staples. Accuracy at the charity stripe won many close games for
the Panthers. Before concluding practice, a special session was devoted to
improving free-throw skills. His players were encouraged to hit 10 shots
in a row from the foul line before leaving practice. For those experiencing
difficulties, Coach Staples would demonstrate his unorthodox, between-
the-legs method of shooting foul shots—a carryover from his playing
days during the 1920s—that was very accurate; in fact, he could routinely
ring nine out of ten shots. I can't remember any Perry player developing
that style, however, as it looked weird and was anachronistic to the 1950-
60s era when players shot over-handed and often one-handed. Staples
was blessed over the years with great shooters. When he came to Perry

in 1933, he encouraged that basketball goals be built in every backyard. From the time his players entered grammar school until they reached high school, they had perfected their shooting skills in their own backyards. Oftentimes the backyard competition was so keen that if a player could hold his own in a backyard game, he had no trouble in a real game.

Many have wondered over the years why Coach Staples was such a winner. How could any coach capture as many games as he did, engineer so many come-from-behind victories and beat opposing teams who were heavily favored to win? To these questions there are no simple answers. However, as one who had firsthand exposure and a long association with this great coach, I will offer my impression of those qualities which contributed to his success. One of the most important prerequisites to winning is the mutual respect that must exist between player and coach. Coach Staples won the respect and admiration of his players through his exemplary Christian life. Like the preacher whose most convincing sermons are not preached in the pulpit but in the conduct of his daily life, Coach Staples was an "example setter." The most indelible impressions he made on his players were not so much what he said, but how he treated others and by his actions both on and off the court. He never showed partiality and was known for his square dealings and sense of fair play. For example, if you were not a starter on the team, you knew that you had been given every opportunity to prove yourself and that the guy playing ahead of you—for the moment anyway—had outperformed you.

Coach Eric Staples

Coach Staples never used abusive language or tactics with his players, always criticizing constructively and not destructively. Never did he "horseplay" with his players. He was strictly a "no nonsense" coach, always dead serious. He was friendly and joked occasionally with his boys, but always maintained that "critical balance" in the coach-player relationship that told you he was "the boss." I never heard Coach Staples say anything off color or do anything that was demeaning to his character. His interest in his players went beyond the athletic arena. He saw them as human beings with personal strivings and needs other than athletic achievement and was genuinely interested in their welfare. A player will play his heart out for that type coach.

He was a firm believer that hard work was indispensable to success. This equated to practice, practice, and more practice. As a result, his teams were always well coached and fundamentally sound. He imposed strict training rules to keep his players in tip-top condition and meted out discipline when the rules were compromised. Always emphasizing that you had to be willing "to pay the price" to be a winner, Coach Staples demanded excellence and got it. Perry's basketball program achieved the success it did, not because of abundance of superior players or great talent, but because of hard work, dedication and dissension-free teams playing as units—"one for all and all for one." Perry teams never played "free lance" basketball. They always had a system of attack, both offensively and defensively, that was constantly executed. In practice sessions, offensive plays and defensive tactics would be run over and over until they were perfected.

Staples also was a stickler for his players being well conditioned, eating properly, and getting at least eight hours of sleep every night. During school days, he imposed a 10 p.m. curfew; no one was supposed to be away from home after that hour. He encouraged his players to go to bed around 9 or 10 o'clock at night, believing that a well-rested player would practice and play better. He always contended that every hour of sleep before midnight was better than any two hours after midnight. He also encouraged us to take naps during the afternoon before games; a practice he followed himself.

One night during the fall of 1952, James and Olin Logue and I borrowed Dot Roughton's car to travel to Byron to see some girls we had heard about. Once we arrived, we were so enamored with Priscilla Calhoun and several of her pretty high school friends that we lost track of time and didn't leave Byron until 11 p.m. Olin Logue was driving. We reached Perry about 11:30 p.m. and carried Dot Roughton his car. By the time we walked home, it was after midnight. Olin made the mistake of telling someone at school the next morning what a marvelous time we had in Byron the previous night and that we were late getting home. That was a serious mistake, because the word finally got back to Coach Staples, who called us into his office. He asked us if it were so, and we had to say it was. He summarily dismissed us from the team. I immediately went to Mr. Glea Gray, a former 1920s Perry basketball star under Coach Jim Gooden and a confidant of Staples. I told Mr. Gray I would take any punishment that Coach Staples meted out, if he would let me return to the team. "I want to play basketball, Mr. Gray," I pleaded, "Please intercede with Coach Staples for me. I will do anything he asks and never violate a team rule again." Mr. Gray succeeded, and I was permitted to rejoin the team. My punishment was to run extra laps after practice for several weeks. Coach Staples knew I was sincere and wasn't too hard on me. James and Olin Logue also made it back through Mr. Gray's influence. Coach Staples would give players a second chance, if he felt they were sincere and had learned their lesson well.

Coach Staples was a master strategist, always seeming to come up with the best strategy to combat any given situation. Knowing who Perry would likely play in the district tournament, Coach Staples would begin preparing game plans and practicing for these teams months in advance of tournament time.

He also was an accomplished psychologist. He knew what to say and how to say it to get the most out of every boy. He won many games by psychologically preparing his team for the tough games. Not only did he apply his psychology before the games, but he could dispense it during halftime pep talks and in the heat of battle. Many Perry fans have wondered what coach Staples said at halftime to his teams. If we were ahead and playing to his expectations, he said nothing. We just sat in the dressing room and rested while drinking a half bottle of Coke. It was never a whole Coke that might slosh in your stomach afterwards, but a half bottle that gave you the sugar energy you needed and quenched your thirst.

Staples was the consummate community and church leader, and above all, he was a genuinely, good Christian man whose exemplary actions spoke louder than his words. He taught Sunday School at Perry's

Methodist Church for 38 years and served the church in every capacity imaginable. He was actively engaged in a host of civic organizations. He was an outstanding educator and school administrator. During his administration, giant strides were made in both educational achievement and facility improvements at Perry schools. Perry perennially had outstanding literary teams that won many region and state trophies, and was highly competitive in the state spelling meets.

Most Perry citizens referred to him as "Professor Staples." The school students couldn't pronounce the three syllable word "professor" with ease, so they began to affectionately call him "Fessor." Some of the students even applied the shorter term "Fess" in conversational exchanges. So the name "Fessor" stuck. It became not only an endearing term but one of respect and admiration.

The adage "behind every good man is a good woman" was never truer than in its application to Coach Staples. He was truly blessed with an ever-supportive and loving wife, Chloe Traylor Staples, who was active in supporting school and community activities and appreciated by everyone. This union produced one daughter, Sherry, a cheerleader in 1957 and 1958, and two sons, Pierce and Porter, both of whom played on Perry state championship teams: Pierce in 1959 and Porter in 1963.

These are only some of the magic ingredients that made Coach Staples a legend in his own time. Many basketball observers and sportswriters throughout the state considered Staples to be Georgia's greatest high school coach during his era and that Perry was the Mecca of Georgia High School basketball. Staples' greatest accomplishment, however, was not his winning record, but the significant and lasting contributions he made in the lives of countless young people, and the fact that he is still remembered and genuinely loved and respected by all his players, the fans, and the entire community.

In 1969 soon after his retirement, Staples was quoted in the "Atlanta Magazine" as saying: "Any kid who doesn't know the fundamentals has no business playing on a basketball team. It's true this is a team game, but you must develop certain individual skills. I have never had a great player who didn't have a basketball goal nailed to a post in his backyard. Never." The importance of backyard basketball was a philosophy that Staples brought to Perry in 1933...

3 Dynasty began in the backyards of Perry

When Coach Eric Staples began his initial season as basketball coach at Perry High School in the fall of 1933, he was appalled that few students in the lower grades were actively participating in basketball. Most of the kids in town didn't own a basketball, and few homes even had a basketball goal. It had been his experience during his first six years of coaching at Carroll and Haralson Counties that players entering high school and coming out for basketball for the first time were not sufficiently grounded in the fundamentals of the game. For Perry to become a perennial contender for district and state championships, Staples realized that he had to establish a feeder system starting in the lower grades so his players would be ready for serious competition by the time they reached high school. In those days high school began with the eighth grade since there were only eleven grades. To create a feeder system, Staples instituted junior high and B-team basketball, something his predecessor, Jim Gooden, who doubled as school superintendent, didn't have time to coach. This allowed him to generate a pipeline of basketball players and to see his teams of the future developing at an early age. Staples knew it might take time for this system to produce the continuity of championship teams he desired, but he was willing to pay the high price of preparation that success demanded.

Although girls' basketball had existed at Perry High since the early 1920s, Coach Staples, in his new duties as the high school principal, decided to discontinue the sport at the beginning of the 1933-34 school year. He felt that a girl's program would dilute the emphasis on boys' basketball by competing for available gym practice time and prevent his

B-teams from playing the preliminary game prior to the varsity encounter. Staples had the full support of School Superintendent Jim Gooden, who publicly stated he did not approve of girls' basketball, but had allowed it to be played with little fanfare under the tutelage of high school teachers, who were marginally knowledgeable of the game. Gooden felt the sport was too strenuous for women, and he considered school girls too dainty and refined to run up and down a court, dressed immodestly in short uniforms.

Next, Staples had to determine how to get the Perry youth playing at an early age. Unskilled players required a disproportionate amount of practice time to develop fundamentals such as shooting, ball-handling, rebounding, and defensive skills. Rather than teaching fundamentals, he knew his coaching time could be better spent molding teams into cohesive and competitive units. Year-round exposure to basketball was the only solution, so in the fall of 1933, Staples made it known that all aspiring young basketball players should build a basketball goal in their backyards. Soon basketball goals began to spring up all over town. Backboards in that era were not fan-shaped as they are today, but were rectangular in design and made of wood.

There was no football program in those days. The basketball season started in early October and extended to mid-March. Although there were no official team practices during the off-season (March to October), players were expected to continue perfecting playing skills in their backyards. Some players like my brother, Dwayne, and his friend, Bert Bozeman, didn't let sundown deter them. They would continue shooting in the dead of night by flashlight. That dedication paid off handsomely, as the chapters on the state championship teams attest. Coach Staples left the gym keys in a straw basket on his front porch during weekends so designated individuals could pick them up and open the gym. All day Saturday and after church on Sundays, the gym would be full of players participating in half court games.

I wasn't born until October 1935, but by the time I was in the second grade, in 1942, some of my little classmates had goals, and I wanted one, too. The Powell family lived in a two-bedroom, two-kitchen house at 800 Ball Street, two blocks from downtown Perry--my parents on one side and my grandparents on the other. Daddy drove a gas truck for Benny Andrew's Standard Oil distributorship and Granddaddy was the foreman at the cotton gin. Our household didn't own a car, and every Saturday the entire family lugged groceries by the sackfuls from J. W. Bloodworth's downtown store. Those were tough times. The Japanese had bombed Pearl Harbor and the nation was at war. Food essentials like bread, sugar, and butter were rationed. To make ends meet, my family had to cut corners on a lot of household necessities, like substituting soda for tooth paste; we certainly couldn't afford to purchase a basketball goal.

In those days, we learned to improvise. My first goal post was constructed from a pine tree. I was only seven years old at the time. An older boy, Benny Garrett, helped me cut down a pine tree in the nearby woods, a mile from the house. Its trunk was about 24 inches in circumference. It took Benny and me nearly two hours to drag it back home. The next step was to find some boards to make a backboard. Granddaddy had recently replaced the rotted flooring in our bathroom, so I used the best of the replaced boards. For nails, I pulled out the old rusty nails from the boards, straightened them with a hammer and reused them. Of course, Granddaddy helped me with all this. Once the boards were sawed to a uniform length and nailed to the pine goal post, the only thing missing was a metal hoop. In the backyard was an old metal drum that was rusting at the bottom. I figured, if I could cut away the reinforced rim from the drum, it would be thick enough to form a hoop for the goal. Daddy said I could use it and even helped me remove the outer rim using heavy-duty metal cutters. I took the narrow rim, connected both ends to form a hoop, and nailed it to the backboard. All I needed then was a basketball. Grandmother gave me enough money to go up town to Crockett's 5 &10 Cent Store and buy a cheap plastic ball—not a real basketball, but it would do. The plastic basketball worked okay with the make-shift hoop, but the basketball that Santa Claus brought me a few months later was much heavier and would bend the hoop down when it hit the edge. Each time it bent, I had to push the hoop back to a level position before shooting again. The objective became to score without touching the hoop. The goal post lasted about two years.

One autumn day my friends, James and Olin Logue, who lived in the country south of my house, were playing with me in the backyard. James remarked, "Did you hear that crack?"

"No," I responded.

Olin cautioned, "Reckon the goal post has rotted?"

Several minutes later, it was loud enough we could all hear it. Olin shouted to James, standing beneath the basket, "Watch out, the goal's gonna fall."

James scampered out of the way. At the time, I was standing in the coffin corner, 15 feet from the basket, preparing to shoot. As the old goal started its slow descent, cracking loudly as it lurched forward, I fired a low trajectory shot to see if I could score one last bucket before the old goal went to heaven. The ball zipped through the air, and stripped the net just as the falling goalpost reached a 45-degree angle with the ground. Then came the crash and the old goal was gone forever. It had served me well.

The Logue brothers decided to install a backboard with a hoop on the side of their barn. Before the area around the barn became a basketball court, Bobby Logue, the oldest Logue brother and an aspiring baseball pitcher, would tie us to the side of the barn with a plow line around our waists to test his curve ball. Bobby would place a wooden board on the ground representing home plate and make us stand there and swing at his wicked under-handed curveballs. They would come right at you and then abruptly swerve across the plate. If the ball hit you, you better not whimper or cry, or he would frog you repeatedly on the arm or rub your eye sockets hard with his knuckles. Some days I went home black and blue when his curve balls failed to break.

My favorite comic book heroes were Captain Marvel and Superman. James, Olin, and I reasoned we could fly just like our super heroes with the assist of a cape. So we each fastened a towel around our necks with a clothespin, and prepared to slide off the top of the tin barn with a basketball in our laps. The objective was to sail past the goal and shoot the ball at the basket on the way down. James went first, Olin second, and I was last. I started my slide from the top ridge of the tin roof. When I got to the roof's edge, an unnoticed protruding nail took a slice out of my buttocks and ripped a 12-inch tear in my pants. I ran to Mrs. Evelyn Logue. I was so embarrassed. My bottom was stinging, and I feared Mrs. Logue would die laughing, but she didn't and soothed my wounded pride. She doctored my cut and then sewed my pants so I could ride my bicycle back home without the split exposing my derriere. I cried all the way back home, worried that mama would give me a spanking for tearing my pants. I knew my sore rear couldn't handle it.

Over in the Sand Hill community on the south side of Perry, just across Big Indian creek, the neighborhood boys built a goal on the side of a giant oak tree at the home of James and Bennett Mauldin. Boot Hunt and Francis Marshall cut their basketball teeth on that court playing with the older boys. Huge roots projected from the bottom of the tree trunk. James Mauldin could take a running start up the root ledge, leap upward and dunk the goal.

One of the most popular outdoor courts in town was in Tommy Mobley's backyard. Tommy lived on Swift Street in Perry. There was a tree stump at the side of his court from which everyone loved to shoot, especially Bill Holland, a mentally-challenged 40-year old and Perry's most faithful basketball fan. Bill could hit 30-footers from that stump with uncanny accuracy.

Living just up the street was a young lady named Lula Alice Collier, two years older than I and physically larger at the time. She would beat me like she owned me. Lula would have developed into a great player, if Staples had allowed girls' basketball. In later years, when Lula became a cheerleader, a ball rolled in her direction during the half-time of a game. She scooped the ball up and fired a two-handed 30-footer that knocked the bottom out of the net.

Coach Staples was coming out of the dressing room and witnessed the shot. He remarked, "Great shot young lady. I didn't know you could do that."

Lula responded, "Fessor,

William Harrison, star guard on the 1955 Perry Panther team, one of Perry's strongest squads.

when are we going to have a girls' team?"

"We'll have to think about that," said Staples.

Another popular goal was in north Perry at William Harrison's house in Commercial Heights. William and I would play a shoot-around game called "HORSE," in which you could shoot any type of shot, regardless of how unconventional it was. If you rang it, your opponent had to duplicate the shot. If he missed, he was penalized with a letter, the first one being an

Deryle Whipple, "All-State" player on Perry's 1947 state championship team, Coach Staples' first.

H, the next an O, and so forth to E. First man to reach HORSE lost the game. William was unbeatable, a formidable competitor in HORSE. William went on to become one of Perry's finest players.

Deryle Whipple, an older boy, had a dirt court on Washington Street. Many days, I watched in awe as Deryle would put on a shooting exhibition with his classic, two-handed set shot—the shot he carried to the state finals in 1947. Hitting 10 in a row was routine for him. I would go home and try to imitate his shot.

Sam Nunn's backyard goal was a stone's throw from the Perry gym. His court was covered in grass, which made it hard to dribble. Being an older boy, I taught Sam how to perfect his one-handed push shot. I apparently taught him well, as you will read in my account of the 1956 state championship game.

Basketballs were constantly being dribbled on the basketball court in the Powell's backyard. Just ask the former neighbors, who had to listen to the bouncing ball from sunup to sunset. This court was the scene of many basketball wars over the years. The best outdoor court player I have ever seen was Larry Bailey, a schoolmate of my brother's. Larry never tried out for the high school team, but I always chose him first to play on my backyard team. Larry never missed a jump shot in a tight game, and he was impossible to defend. During my high school years, if you could hold your own in a game on the Powell court, you didn't worry about the real game. Over the years, many outstanding basketball players played on that court. Once, Leroy Boswell, a star on the 1940 Perry team, and his young bride, Inez, moved next door. A wire fence, about 30-feet from the goalpost, separated the two backyards. Every time Leroy came out the backdoor, I would throw him the ball for a shot. Leroy would stand at the edge of the fence and shoot those high-arching, two-handed shots that would come crashing down through the net time and time again, as if they were guided by radar. I saw firsthand why many considered him to be one of Perry's all-time greats.

The most unforgettable backyard basketball game was played in the Powell backyard at 800 Ball Street in Perry during early January1963— when my brother was a senior basketball star at Perry High and Lee Martin was a freshman sensation playing at the University of Georgia. My brother, Dwayne, and I usually played on opposing teams; however, when we played together as a twosome we never lost a game. One Friday night, Bobby Mayo and Lee Martin sat around at the Wigwam (local Perry grill and youth hang-out) and plotted how they were going to defeat us; they decided to issue the challenge the next morning. Martin had led Perry to an undefeated season the previous year and was recognized as the best player in Georgia. Mayo's parents had moved to Florida when he was in the sixth grade. Mayo had talent to burn before he left Perry and developed into a truly outstanding player, an All-State basketball player, who starred at Plant City High School in Florida. Had Mayo remained at Perry, he would have played with Martin and Boot Hunt on Perry's 1959 state championship team. That Saturday morning I was awakened to the doorbell ringing at my front door. It was 8 a.m. I was living in Fort Valley at the time. When I answered, Mayo and Lee Martin were standing on the porch steps, a serious countenance on their faces. They had driven all the way from Perry to Fort Valley to deliver the challenge. "Billy, me and Lee want to play you and Dwayne a game of two-on-two," said Bobby. "We sat around talking at the Wigwam last night and decided we could beat y'all."

"Where do you want to play?" I asked.

"Let's play in Perry in Dwayne's backyard," responded Lee.

"Okay, I haven't eaten breakfast yet. What about us meeting at 10:30 in Dwayne's backyard?" I asked.

"We'll be there," remarked Mayo, and as they turned to walk away, Mayo shot back, "You and your brother are going down to defeat today."

After eating breakfast, I drove down to Perry. I will confess that I was worried about the game. Lee and Bobby were two of the very best, and they were so determined to beat us that they had driven from Perry to Fort Valley early in the morning to tell me that a beating awaited me in Perry. I knew, if they won, I would never be able to live it down.

When I arrived, Dwayne, Lee, and Bobby were warming up, shooting baskets. We agreed to play the best three out of five games to 20, each basket counting one point. I huddled with Dwayne to devise our offensive strategy. Knowing I had the greatest shooter in high school basketball on my side, I decided the best advantage we had of winning was to exploit Dwayne's shooting ability.

"Dwayne, I will bring the ball in and then set up down low. Neither Mayo nor Martin can stop me one-on-one, so lob the ball to me on the low post. When they attempt to double-team me, I will flick the ball back to you for an open shot." I knew Dwayne seldom missed within a range of 25-feet from the basket. When Dwayne would lob the ball to me, Mayo, guarding Dwayne, would shift backwards to double-team me. The instant he did, I would fire the ball quickly back to Dwayne. Little brother was deadly; he never missed. The score of the first game was 20-12 in favor of the Powell team, and Dwayne was yet to miss a shot. The score of the second was 20-8 in our favor, and third was 20-10. Dwayne was making 80 percent of the points; my role was that of a decoy to draw Dwayne's defender away and open him up for a clear shot. I don't discount the fact that Martin and Mayo were among the greatest players ever to walk the streets of Perry, but how can you compete with a robot that never misses. Many teams learned this the hard way in 1963 when my little brother led Perry to the state championship, averaging 30 points a game. The 1962-63 season was Perry's first venture into the Class A ranks. The growth of the base at nearby Warner Robins had caused Perry's population to increase, thereby moving the school up a notch in classification from Class B to Class A. The fact that Dwayne and I won this backyard battle didn't make us better basketball players than our opposition. Heavens no. We won because we executed a game plan that accentuated our strengths and attacked their weaknesses. That's the reason Coach Staples won 82.4 percent of his games, not because his teams were better than their opponents, but because he had a superior game plan and often out-smarted the opposing coach.

Because Grandmother Powell was so supportive and took such an interest in our basketball playing, my brother and I named the court "The Delia E. Powell Memorial Coliseum." Today, a storage shed sits on the site of the old court. I cannot stop the tears that well up in my eyes, when I ride by the old home place and look in the direction of that once popular basketball court, where Perry stars of the future learned to compete.

I built so many basketball goals that I became an expert in their construction. People frequently consulted me before they put up a goal. The single most important specification was the height of the hoop. The regulation height in a gym was 10 feet from the floor. Since most backyards have a slightly undulating surface and are not perfectly level, the optimum outdoor hoop height is 9 feet, 10.5 inches from the ground. A mere inch and a half variance, although slight, will make a big difference in a player's shooting accuracy, when going from an outdoor court to the local gym. A player who practiced on a 10-foot outdoor court would often overshoot the basket in a regulation gym. This necessitated that he recalibrate his shooting arch once he entered the gym, which was often the cause of poor shooting on game days.

In 1961, one of the major reasons the Perry team lost the region semifinals to Telfair County, the defending state champs and a squad they beat earlier in the season, was that the hoop at the Mount Vernon gym was 10 feet and one inch from the floor and tilted up in front. This was confirmed by a local Mount Vernon fan, who had measured the hoop and found that it exceeded regulation height. Many out-of-town teams had complained. Most of Perry's shots during the first half of that semifinal game were falling short. During the second half, when the Perry players tried to compensate, they began to overshoot the hoop. Since this was their home court, the Telfair team had adjusted to the goal's height and had no trouble finding the range.

Coach Staples had heard that I knew a secret on the proper height for outdoor goals, so when his two sons, Pierce and Porter, became old enough to play, he asked my advice on building the basketball goal in his backyard. We bolted his hoop to the backboard exactly 9 feet, 10.5 inches from the ground. It worked well for the Staples boys.

Coach Staples was indeed a strong proponent of backyard basketball. It was in the backyards that his players of the future could work on fundamentals year-round and be ready for varsity competition when the time arrived. He felt so strongly about the importance of backyard practice that he even drove around town to see whose backyards had basketball goals and whose didn't.

When Coach Staples stepped aboard as Perry basketball coach in 1933, he wondered what talent he had inherited among the returnees from Coach Gooden's 1932-33 team that won the district tournament, but lost a heart-breaker in the state opener. He was eager to meet the players and scheduled a practice session the first week of school...

4 Thirteen Years of Frustration

In early September 1933, when Coach Staples held his first practice session with his new team, he was pleasantly surprised. The players were better than he had expected, and rightly so, because returning from Jim Gooden's 1933 district championship team were two starters and three extremely talented reserves, who had logged considerable playing time. After subjecting his new players to four weeks of long and intense practice sessions, Coach Staples vastly improved the execution of fundamentals and incorporated his offensive and defensive brand of basketball. When the season began in mid-October, Staples intuitively felt that his first Perry team would be very competitive and, with a little luck, would do well at tournament time. His optimism was confirmed when his 1934 Perry team finished the regular season with an impressive record of 25 wins and only 3 losses. The team won the district tournament after surviving a gargantuan struggle with Fort Valley and then advanced to the state tournament in Athens. By overwhelming Hazelhurst, 42 to 27, the Panthers moved into the state finals to play Canton, a team they had beaten earlier in the season, 29 to 18. The Panthers' good fortunes ran out in the Canton game, however, as they experienced a poor shooting night and lost to the Greenies by a lop-sided score of 42 to 23. Although his Panthers lost the big game, Coach Staples, in his first year as Perry's basketball mentor, sent shock waves throughout the state that his future Panther teams would be a force to be reckoned with for years to come.

As the next season approached, basketball fever took hold in Perry with an enthusiasm and excitement the little hamlet of 3500 people had never experienced. The townspeople had soaked up the success of the previous year and were convinced that Staples was the coach to lead Perry High School to new heights in basketball. By then, every young boy in Perry wanted to become a Perry Panther and play for Coach Staples. Backyard basketball goals began springing up all over town.

Staples' 1935 team went undefeated during the regular season, marched unruffled through the district tournament, and entertained high hopes of winning the state championship. In state tournament play, the Panthers progressively moved up the brackets to the state finals by sequentially defeating three good teams, Dublin-40 to 24, LaGrange-37 to 23, and Canton-34 to 32. The Panthers were one game away from carrying home the coveted state trophy. Only Albany stood in their path. The final day of the tournament, Perry had to play two games: Canton in the afternoon semifinals and Albany that night for the championship. Having survived a hard-fought, double-overtime victory against Canton only hours earlier, Perry's players were physically and mentally exhausted for their championship battle with Albany.   As a result, Albany prevailed 34 to 20, and Perry claimed the state Class B runner-up spot for the second year in a row.

Of the first two Perry teams that Staples coached, the 1935 team had the best chance of bringing home all the bacon. The meltdown of the 1934 team in the state finals was enough of a disappointment, but the fall of a great 1935 team in the final game was not only a great letdown for Coach Staples, but a source of disenchantment for the Perry fans, who felt they were hopelessly jinxed.

Nothing happened over the next four years to reverse the will-o'-the-wisp mentality regarding a state title, as Perry failed to advance beyond the district tournament from 1936 to 1939, claiming third place in the district in 1936, second in 1937, third in 1938, and second in 1939. However, in 1940, Perry assembled one of its best teams in school history and was a consensus pick to capture the state crown. The team won a 36-team, state-wide tournament in January of that year, which was tantamount to a state tournament. The 1940 quintet captured the district title and moved into the state playoffs with high expectations. In the state quarterfinals, star guard Bobbie Holtzclaw sprained his ankle and could not play in the semifinal game against Clarkston. This was a serious blow to the Panthers, who depended heavily on Holtzclaw's rebounding and defensive skills. In a hard fought contest, Clarkston prevailed over Perry, 29 to 23. By then, it was evident to the Perry faithful that its teams were snake-bitten and that a state championship was a quixotic dream never to be realized.

As the 1941 season rolled around, the Panthers again looked like a state championship contender, but lost in the third district semifinals to Fort Valley in a squeaker, 31 to 29. Being knocked out of a title hunt by arch-rival Fort Valley was tantamount to having salt poured on the wounded hopes and dreams of Pantherville.

Staples regrouped his team for another title run in 1942, but lost star center, Leroy Boswell, who became ineligible. After the third district tournament concluded on February 27, 1942, with Perry emerging victorious, Leroy Boswell reached his 20th birthday the next day, on February the 28th, and was ineligible to play in the state tournament. The Perry Panthers, badly crippled by the loss of its offensive leader, faced Cochran in the opening round of the state tournament. Although Perry had defeated Cochran four times during the regular season, the prospects of beating Cochran became a daunting task without the point production of Boswell. Perry came close to scoring an upset, but a last minute rally by Cochran overcame Perry. The final score was Cochran-19, Perry-15. Many observers felt that had Boswell been able to play, the 1942 Panthers may have gone all the way.

The Panthers reloaded for another title shot in 1943. Perry breezed past Fort Valley in the district tournament. In the state opener, the Panthers won a thriller over Reidsville, 19-18. In the semifinals, Perry downed Athens, 26 to 24, a team sporting a perfect record and a state powerhouse that was the consensus pick to capture the state diadem. The championship game pitted Perry against Cochran, a team the Panthers had defeated twice during the year. Cochran refused to be impressed by Perry's sensational win over Athens and soundly defeated the cold-shooting Panthers, 25 to 17. This loss marked the third time, since Staples took the reins as coach in 1933, that the Panthers had a legitimate shot at the state crown and came away second fiddle. By this time, Staples must have felt like Chicken Little.

Hope always sprang eternal in Perry, however, and the 1944 team gave its fans renewed cause for optimism. Perry easily won over the Fort Valley Green Wave to capture the district tournament. The Panthers looked to be on course for another state title game when they edged the favored Gainesville team in a nail-biter, 21 to 20. Next came Rossville in the semifinal game. With a minute to go, Perry was leading, 23 to 22, and in control of the game. A lucky shot by a Rossville player from near center court reversed the lead to 24 to 23 in Rossville's favor. Rossville added a free throw, held on to the ball for the closing moments, and sent the Panthers back home again empty-handed. Rossville became state champs the following night by scalping Decatur 38 to 23.

The 1945 edition of the Panthers never got its basketball express off the runway. They lost the best two out of three games to a strong Americus five in the district tournament and had to settle for second place.

The next year was a rebuilding year, but the 1946 Perry team achieved redemption by recapturing the district crown it had lost the previous year with a stunning victory over Fort Valley. The Green Wave had beaten the Panthers three times during the regular season; however, Coach Staples had his boys ready for tournament play, and they defeated the mighty Green Wave 30 to 27. Off to the state tournament went the upset-minded Panthers. Their hopes were quickly dashed, however, in the state quarterfinals by the tournament favorite, the Canton Greenies, who capitalized on their distinct height advantage and handily defeated the Perry Panthers, 41 to 28.

Recap: Thirteen Years of Frustration

Year	District Finish	State Finish
1934	1st	2nd
1935	1st	2nd
1936	3rd	–
1937	2nd	–
1938	3rd	–
1939	2nd	–
1940*	1st	Lost in semifinals
1941	3rd	–
1942**	1st	Lost in opener
1943	1st	2nd
1944	1st	Lost in semifinals
1945	2nd	–
1946	1st	Lost in quarterfinals

* Lost star guard and great defender and rebounder, Bobby Holtzclaw, to ankle injury in quarterfinals; Holtzclaw unable to play in semifinal game.
** Lost top scorer and rebounder, Leroy Boswell, to age ineligibility following district tournament.

Coach Staples came to Perry with serious intentions of establishing a basketball dynasty. During the 13 years from 1933 through 1946, his teams won approximately 80 percent of their games during the regular season, captured seven district titles, finished second in district play three times and third place three times. In state competition, his teams were runner-up three times and advanced to the semifinals on two other occasions. By any stretch of the imagination, these accomplishments would constitute an outstanding record for which any coach could be proud, but not Staples! He wanted to get the black cat off his back and win a state championship. Nothing less would satisfy him.

To understand Staples is to recognize that he was driven by a relentless quest for excellence, a trait few individuals possess. From an early age, Coach Staples had been a fierce competitor and disliked losing at anything whether it was basketball, golf, or even a game of Parcheesi. When he lost a basketball game, his family said he was hard to live with for several days. Because of his intensity, games took their toll on Staples, and he had to take precautions to moderate that damage. To be fresh for every encounter, he always took a nap the afternoon of the game; the tougher the game, the longer the nap. By supper time, his nervous stomach would be in spasms and churning so badly, he sometimes had to settle for soda crackers and water. Sitting on the sidelines, he chewed on that unlit cigar—he had given up smoking—and oftentimes had the wrong end in his mouth. Sometimes, when one of his players lost the ball or missed an assignment, he would stomp the cigar with his shoe. Later he would reach down, pick up the flattened cigar and put it back in his mouth. If you were a player for Coach Staples, you knew he meant business, and you better give your best efforts at all times, or you would not be a Panther on his team.

In traveling to out-of town games, he finally had to give up driving. He was so engrossed in strategizing about the upcoming game that he would be driving 70 miles per hour one minute and 20 miles per hour the next and absent-mindedly drifting to the outside lane of curves in the road. His players became so unnerved traveling to games with Staples at the wheel that they finally begged him to let one of them drive.

This cigar-chewing, hat-stomping, perfectionist-minded coach was really a nice guy, who was totally and unflinchingly dedicated to excellence and demanded that his players be willing to pay the price for success. He was not a good loser, but when he did lose, he held his emotions in check and always acted the role of a gentleman, exhibiting good sportsmanship. He once told this writer, "A good loser will never excel in competitive sports."

Although 13 long years had elapsed without a state title, there was no diminution in Coach Staples' drive to win that coveted state crown. Something was about to happen, however, that he least expected— something that would change basketball fortunes in Perry forever. Those backyard basketball goals were poised to produce results that would exceed his fondest expectations. The era of the great shooters was beginning to emerge...

5 Era of the great shooters

Championship basketball teams require the assemblage of certain skills that must be melded into a cohesive unit. These skills consist of defensive stalwarts, rebounding wizards, ball-handling and playmaking specialists, and offensive scorers. All of these offensive and defensive skills are essential to winning basketball games, but when opposing teams are evenly matched, the shooters in the offense provide the margin of victory. There are two levels of shooters who play on teams good enough to advance to the state finals. There are good shooters and there are the great shooters. The teams with the great shooters usually prevail.

Great shooters are born. They possess a high level of eye-to-hand coordination and depth perception. After a visual sighting of the basket, they know just the right force to exert behind the ball, based on its distance to the basket. Coach Staples called Dwayne Powell the greatest shooter he had ever seen. Dwayne, according to his family physician, Dr. A. G. Hendricks, had 20-06 vision, which contributed to his phenomenal shooting ability. Those gifted with such inborn talent must first learn the correct technique of shooting the ball, and then practice it for years to perfect their shot. At least ten years of dedicated practice are required to develop a great shooter.

I started my brother, Dwayne Powell, playing basketball when he was only two-years old. He could barely push the ball over the rim of his 3-foot goal. I made sure he learned, from an early age, the correct shooting techniques and didn't develop bad shooting habits. Although he was an accomplished shooter by the time he entered high school, he soon learned that altering his shooting style was necessary to reach the pinnacle of offensive capability. That revelation came to him during his sophomore year, in 1961, when Perry played Telfair County, the defending state Class B champions, in the region tournament. Telfair's "All-State" player, Bonnie Strom, arguably the best defensive man in the state that year, throttled Dwayne in the semifinal game, holding him to 9 points.

After the season ended, I suggested to Dwayne that he attempt to imitate the shooting style of Boot Hunt, a sharpshooter who led his team to the 1959 state championship. Rather than shoot the conventional push shot from shoulder level; Boot released his jump shot with his hands vertically extended above his head. Boot could routinely spring 20-24 inches off the

Panther captain Boot Hunt drills a jump shot in 1959 state championship game.

floor on a jumper and, with the ball released at the highest possible point, was virtually unstoppable. Dwayne took my advice and practiced that technique all summer. By the start of the 1961-62 season, Dwayne could dribble to his left or right and shoot a jump shot uncontested over much taller opponents. His teammate Lee Martin, a two time "All-State" player on the 1959 and 1962 state championship squads, was so quick and evasive that he didn't have to worry about the level he released the ball. When Lee did shoot, he was deadly, averaging 18 points his junior year and 20 points his senior year.

A great shooter is easy to recognize in a hotly-contested game. Every time he touches the basketball and fires up a shot, the opposing fans will wince and silently pray he misses. That's because they know the trajectory of his shot is always on target with the basket. A great shooter is slightly off target about half the time, but his margin of error is so small that a

9.5-inch diameter ball has a good chance of dropping through the 18-inch diameter hoop. A great shooter always wants his hands on the ball in critical game situations. He believes in himself and in his ability to hit the clutch basket. A great shooter is dangerous anywhere within 30 feet of the basket, shooting one at the top of the key with the same aplomb and confidence that he does a lay-up. A great shooter may miss the first five shots he takes in a game, but that won't deter him because he may hit the next seven in a row. In a state championship game, a team featuring a great shooter may fall behind four to six points with little time on the clock, but the sharpshooter can quickly erase that deficit in several trips down the court. As a case in point, Perry's 1964 team was down 14 points in the state title game as the final quarter began, yet walked away with the championship on the strength of its great shooters—Bert Bozeman, Jimmy Dorsett, and Garold Spena. These three sharpshooters did not just get lucky in a game—they had paid the price of spending untold hours in their backyards perfecting their shooting skills.

I, too, was an enthusiastic participant in Coach Staples' backyard basketball program. As a youngster, I had always wanted to become a great shooter like Leroy Boswell, Deryle Whipple, and Mack Peyton, who were my idols when growing up in Perry. In pursuit of that objective, by the time I became a senior at Perry High, I had probably spent more time practicing my offensive skills than any Perry player who preceded me. I became an offensive threat and leading scorer on the 1953 state championship team, because I paid a tremendous price in preparation to reach that level of competence.

I stated earlier that the reaction of opposing fans was a good indicator of the threat a given offensive player posed. A game between Perry and Montezuma in 1953 illustrates that point. During my entire high school career, I fouled out of a game only once and that was the Montezuma game in 1953. The Montezuma squad, featuring such outstanding performers as Ben DeVaughn, John Albert Williams, and Buddy Liggin, represented one of Macon County's greatest teams. The game was played in the Montezuma gym. Coach Bill Martin assigned his best defensive player, "All-State" John Albert Williams, to guard me. Coach Staples realized that Montezuma had a plan to shut me down, using to advantage their little match-box of a gym that restricted movement. As a counter measure, Staples called for a series of picks to screen off my defender. As I attempted to run around the picks, the local referees called fouls on me for charging rather than on John Albert Williams, who constantly bumped me trying to avoid picks set by my teammates.

The contest was extremely close with the lead seesawing back and forth. With four minutes left in the game, the referees called the fifth foul on me, and I was ejected from the game. As I walked off the court toward the Perry bench, the entire Montezuma sideline erupted in jubilation and started beating their Coca-Cola bottles (sold in 8-ounce glass bottles in those days) against the seats. This thunderous and frenetic drumbeat continued after play resumed, disrupting the game and causing the referees to call time out. A referee, using a megaphone, warned the Montezuma crowd that a technical foul would be called if the noise persisted. Although I had fouled out, the Montezuma fans paid me a supreme compliment. With me out of the game, they were sensing victory. My sidekick at guard, the redoubtable Franklin May, scored three baskets from long range during the closing minutes to keep Perry in contention. When the game-ending horn blew, the hard-fighting Perry Panthers had won by one point, 41 to 40.

A similar backhanded tribute was paid Dwayne Powell during the 1963 state championship year. In a regular season game against Perry's arch-rival, the perennially- powerful Warner Robins Demons, Dwayne was clipped and upended while fast-breaking down court. The Demon label aptly describes the conduct of the Warner Robins' fans. Rather than showing concern when Dwayne hit the floor and lay there motionless, they all stood and cheered, as if their mortal enemy had been disabled. Assistant Coach Paul Hartman, thinking Dwayne may have been seriously injured, bolted off the bench and rushed to his fallen warrior. I was sitting in the stands praying. The hard fall Dwayne took could have broken bones and ended his season. To my surprise, my dazed brother got up and, with Coach Hartman supporting him, walked slowly to the bench. Within minutes, he was back in the fray, scoring key baskets in a shootout that downed the mighty Demons and disappointed their unruly fans. Although not intended, the response of the Demon fans was really a compliment to the offensive prowess of Dwayne Powell. He had averaged

18 points per game the previous year, 1962, when Perry went undefeated and won the state championship. In 1963, Perry repeated as state champs, as Dwayne averaged 30 points a game and hit over 50 percent of his shots. No wonder the Demons had exhibited such euphoria when he went down.

State championships cannot be won without great shooting, and it must be consistent. Inconsistency is the reason three Perry teams--1934, 1935, and 1943--finished second in state competition. Each team lost the championship game, because it experienced a cold shooting night in the title game.

The 1940 and 1942 Perry clubs featured great shooters as well as strong supporting casts of defensive players and rebounders, but didn't win the state crown because each team lost one of its top stars at tournament time. In 1940, star defensive player and rebounder, Bobby Holtzclaw, was incapacitated in the state semifinals with a sprained ankle; and in 1942, the high-scoring Leroy Boswell was caught by the age limit and ruled ineligible after his team won the district tournament.

I mentioned earlier that it takes at least ten years to develop great shooters. As the 1946-47 basketball season began, the backyard goals, installed over a decade earlier at the insistence of Coach Staples, were poised to produce their first dividends. Deryle Whipple, who had practiced basketball with a passion on his backyard court for many years, helped lead his 1947 team to Perry's first state crown—Staples' first in 14 years as head coach. Although Perry's offense was spearheaded by Deryle Whipple and Clint Cooper, Billy Bledsoe could shoot from the outside with the best, but saw his role as a rebounder, defender, and floor general. Many outstanding Perry offensive players were content to sacrifice their scoring ability for the good of the team.

A mere two years later, in 1949, it happened again. This time an offensive three-some of Billy Gray, Mack Peyton, and Ed Chapman led the way to Perry's second state title. At this stage in Perry's basketball history, there seemed to be a queuing of great shooters from grammar school to high school. In 1953, with Billy Powell and Billy Beckham providing the offensive fireworks, Perry won its third state championship. Three years afterwards, in 1956, an offensively explosive Perry team with Sam Nunn, Virgil Peavy, and Bennett Mauldin sharing the scoring burden walked out of Macon's City Auditorium with the school's fourth state trophy.

Great shooters continued to roll off the assembly line in the ensuing years. In 1959, with sharpshooters Boot Hunt and Lee Martin providing the scoring punch, Perry won its fifth state title. Then in 1960 came a rash of football injuries to key players that kept Perry from being competitive.

The next year, the 1961 team possessed the shooters, but lacked the maturity of age and experience for a genuine title run. However, the 1961 team, although defeated in the region semifinals, contained the building blocks for a rendezvous with basketball destiny that was totally unexpected. Over the next three years, Perry won three consecutive state championships: 1962, 1963, and 1964. Senior Lee Martin and junior Dwayne Powell led the 1962 team offensively; Dwayne Powell kept the ball rolling in 1963, and an awesome "All-State" trio of Bert Bozeman, Jimmy Dorsett, and Garold Spena astonished the Class A ranks in 1964 with their offensive firepower.

When Coach Staples retired in 1965, his teams had won eight state championships (six in Class B and two in Class A), an unprecedented feat in Georgia basketball during that era. It was the emergence of the great shooters that contributed heavily to Staples' eight state crowns.

The very next year, Staples' hand-picked assistant, Paul Hartman, coached the 1966 Perry team to the school's ninth state crown. This was indeed the icing on the cake, yet 1966 marked the end of the dynasty. The 1966 team had Perry's last great shooter in Joe Martin, who could score 25-30 points on any given night, but after he graduated, the production line of shooters dried up. No longer could you hear bouncing balls in the backyards like the old days. In fact, sociological changes had begun to take place. Potential players were no longer willing to "pay the price" as Coach Staples had preached. Other outlets were vying for their time and energies. Whereas I owned only a bicycle and a basketball and there was no TV in my day, the youth of the late 1960s had personal automobiles and other distractions and simply didn't spend the concentrated practice time required to be champions. They played only during basketball season, and their lack of attention to fundamentals was evident. After practice sessions, they made a mad rush to hit the showers. In my day, we played year round and stayed after practice to improve our game.

In summary, every championship team was a total team effort, offensively and defensively, but the great shooters made the difference when opposing teams were evenly matched. During the 1940s, '50s, and '60s, the basketball exploits of Perry High School placed Perry, Georgia, on the map. This once quiet and sleepy little hamlet of 3500 citizens, located in the center of the state, became the stronghold of the greatest basketball dynasty in Georgia's history.

Earlier in the 20th century, the Vienna Wonder Five had created quite a stir, winning three consecutive state championships in 1927, 1928, and 1929 and going to the national finals each of those years under the coaching wizardry of Colonel Joe Jenkins. The Irwinville Farmers, behind the coaching genius of Wallace "Country" Childs, were the talk of Georgia, going undefeated in 1950 and 1951 and capturing 78-consecutive victories. And the great Class A and AA Lanier teams under Georgia Hall of Fame coach Selby Buck, with a career record of 499 wins and 140 losses, were always among Georgia's best. But Perry, during the Staples' era, established itself as the Mecca of Georgia basketball by virtue of its 32-year dominance of the sport. Every Perry High graduate and every Perry citizen looks back with great fondness on that magical era. Those were the glory days of Perry basketball that may never be duplicated.

A winning tradition produced in Perry a spirit and excitement that was contagious and bonded its citizens together in a community pride unequaled in Georgia basketball history...

6 Basketball Fever Envelops Perry

Perry's passion for high school basketball was lukewarm until Coach Staples arrived as head coach in the fall of 1933. From the time basketball began in Perry in 1919 through the 1932-33 season, only limited fanfare existed for the sport. During the first eight years of that period, 1919-1926, when Coach Jim Gooden's teams played on an outdoor court on the northeast corner of the school ground, fewer than 100 spectators turned out for the games. Since there were no bleachers to accommodate spectators, few people in the community were enthusiastic about dirt court basketball. Fans had to bring their own seats or stand throughout the entire game.

The new 900-seat wooden gymnasium, built in 1926, was expected to generate enthusiasm for the sport and draw large crowds, but it was seldom filled. The townspeople knew that Coach Gooden's first priority as school superintendent was academics and not sports. Splitting his time between school administration and basketball was quite a juggling act. It was evident that basketball would not receive the desired emphasis until a fulltime coach took over the program.

Gooden considered delegating his coaching responsibilities, but no teacher in the school system had sufficient experience to coach boys' basketball. His de-emphasis of girls' basketball was apparent, as he assigned teachers with scant knowledge of the game to coach the girls. In early 1932, a board member suggested to the county school board that a young coach named Eric Staples in northwest Georgia would make Perry High School an excellent basketball coach. The board member's son, who roomed with Staples, had recommended Staples to his father. At the time,

Staples had coached for five years and made quite a name for himself in northwest Georgia. The school board gave Gooden the authority to make Staples an offer. This was music to Gooden's ears. He immediately drove to Tallapoosa, Georgia to meet with Staples. To Gooden's dismay, Staples had already signed a contract with Tallapoosa High School to coach another season. Staples informed Gooden he was obligated to honor the contract, but if Gooden still wanted him the next year, he would be available. The two men made a pact with a handshake. The agreement reached was that Gooden would coach one more season, 1932-33, and Staples would come to Perry to assume the reigns of the basketball program at the beginning of the 1933-34 school term.

When the 1933-34 basketball season began, the townspeople, whether genuinely interested or just curious, turned out in record numbers to see Staples' team perform. They were not disappointed. During the regular season, Staples' first team won 25 games and lost only three. His 1933-34 quintet won the district crown and captured second place in the state tournament. Even better was Staples' second Perry team, his 1934-35 squad. This team, undefeated during the regular season, waltzed through the district meet, and earned the runner-up spot in the state tournament for the second year in a row.

With only three regular season losses in two years plus two district titles and two second place finishes in the state, basketball fever quickly spread throughout the entire community. The new coach was the talk of the town. His demeanor was intense, his competitive spirit contagious, his coaching fundamentally sound, and his integrity irreproachable. Fans came to see Staples coach as much as they came to see the team play. Staples exhibited flamboyance and charisma. He came to the games impeccably dressed in a coat and tie, essentially the same attire he wore teaching Sunday School at the local Methodist Church. He was a man everyone looked up to and respected. Perry fans and supporters were convinced he was the basketball messiah the town had been waiting for. They hoped Staples would be Perry's coach for many years to come. Their only concern was that another school would attempt to steal him away with a better offer. To insulate the school against that possibility, Gooden made Staples the high school principal. In effect, Staples was more of an assistant to Gooden than a principal and could devote his full energies to coaching basketball.

During the Staples' era, basketball became more than a game in the Perry community; it became a way of life. Everything revolved around basketball. When the team played at home, fans would form long lines waiting for the gym to open so they could purchase tickets. When the game was away, local businesses closed early so employers and employees alike could travel to the game. Caravans of cars could be seen leaving town for out-of-town games. The few people that remained in downtown Perry on game day included the three policemen comprising the town's police force. The only time a majority of the community did not attend out-of-town games was during World War II, especially the 1942-43 and 1943-44 seasons when gasoline was rationed.

During the week, clusters of fans sat around dining tables in restaurants sipping coffee and talking basketball. They gathered at Lashley's City Café, Risher's Restaurant, and the New Perry Hotel. There they reviewed the previous game and discussed the upcoming game. It was almost a sin for Perry to lose a game. Perry fans did not cope well with defeat and would be heartsick for days. They would rationalize for hours why the game was lost, how it could have been won, and reason that it wouldn't happen again. Basketball was always a hot topic of conversation at the town's only barber shop where three barbers--B. W. Bozeman, Mr. Stribling, and Mr. Summers—stayed busy cutting hair, especially when long waiting lines formed on Saturdays.

On Saturdays, everyone converged on downtown Perry. They came to buy groceries, fellowship with friends, attend the movie, and yes, talk basketball. During the 1940s, a theater ticket cost 14 cents. A bag of popcorn sold for a dime, a candy bar and a soft drink a nickel each. The old Roxy Theater, managed by Rhett Milan Sr., was located on the east side of Ball Street, about halfway between Carroll and Commerce Streets. On Saturdays, for the admission price, you could watch a western, a double-feature movie, a comedy, a continued serial that kept you dangling in suspense and guessing what would happen from week-to-week, plus a five-minute world news report. The theater had no restrooms. To relieve bladder pressure, the males went outside and walked up a dark alleyway beside the theater. The show opened on Saturday morning and closed at midnight. Parents would drop their kids off at the theater on Saturday morning and come back for them later that night. During the late 1940s, theater employees Bobby Logue and Donald Marshall alternated between ticket attendant and concession stand operator. They were both pranksters. Twelve-years old at the time, I purchased a ticket at the ticket window and entered the lobby. A waiting hand reached to take my ticket. I looked up and there stood a smiling, topless teenager that Bobby and Donald had stationed there to see the expression on my face. They almost died laughing, as I was shocked, speechless, and blushed from ear-to-ear.

On game days, Perry High School was abuzz with excitement and staged pep rallies to release pent-up tensions and to foster team support. The basketball players were heroes among the student body, and every youngster, whether he had athletic ability or not, dreamed of playing basketball for Coach Staples. At the games, the students always sat in proximity to the cheerleaders and cheered wildly. The Perry fans were known as one of the most spirited and strident cheering groups in central Georgia.

A number of unique individuals attended the games. There was O. W. Waddell, a local painter and a mainstay at Mr. Nick Cabero's wine and beer parlor on Carroll Street in downtown Perry. Waddell had been a war hero during World War II. A favorite expression of Waddell was "What the hell Waddell!" He often told the story of being in a foxhole on Laiti Island during World War II. He was a machine gunner guarding the beachhead from Japanese attack. According to Waddell, as the first rays of sunlight pierced the darkness, a Japanese soldier raised his head up over a sand dune and shouted, "What the hell Waddell." That was the battle cry starting the invasion. Waddell said he cut down on the invading soldiers, panning the beach with round-after-round of fire until his machine gun became so hot he could barely hold it. When the sun came up, Waddell said he looked across the beach and all he could see were dead Japanese. He added that his machine gun fire had chopped down coconut trees and sprayed coconut juice all over Laiti. His military record revealed that he received a military citation for killing 140 Japanese soldiers with machine gun fire while protecting a beachhead in the South Pacific.

Once Waddell drank too much wine and fell asleep in the back stockroom of Mr. Nick Cabero's store. Not knowing Waddell was inside, Mr. Cabero closed early that afternoon to go home and get ready to

Billy Powell (R) visits O. W. Waddell (L) in December 1995

attend the basketball game. Waddell awakened later and tried to leave, but couldn't—the front door was locked. He called Mr. Cabero over the phone and asked, "Mr. Nick, when are you coming back down and open up?" Nick, thinking Waddell wanted to get in the store to buy another bottle of sherry, replied, "Waddell, just hang on. I'll be back early in the morning and let you in."

Waddell responded, "Mr. Nick, I don't want to get in, I want to get out and go to the basketball game."

Waddell always stashed a half pint of sherry wine in his hip pocket, but would finish it off before entering the gym. Sometimes he would quaff down the wine so fast, that it would overflow past his lips and trickle down his chin.

Another was "Gunrod" Irby, an ardent supporter of the Panthers, who always sat on the Perry sideline near the back door of the gym. Gunrod was an elderly black man, who lived in the New Hope section of Perry. He shuffled to work everyday on arthritic feet to perform janitorial work at the Bank of Perry. The affable and good-natured Gunrod often sat on the front steps of the bank. He would strike up a conversation with everyone who entered the bank or walked by. Once a tourist pulled up at

the Carroll-Ball Street traffic
light in front of the bank and
asked Gunrod the directions
to Fort Valley. Gunrod said,
"Mister, you don't wanna go
over there, we beat them pretty
bad last Friday night and they's
still fighting mad."

Sometimes individuals
would come to the game
inebriated. A Perry fan,
obviously looped, was watching
a heated game with an arch-
rival. He decided to give the
team some incentive, so he
staggered out of the stands and
weaved a crooked path to the
Perry bench. Coach Staples had
called time out and was giving

*Bill Holland (R) gives Garold Spena (L) a
victory handshake in 1964*

his boys instructions. The drunk stuck his head into the huddle and said,
"Boys, if you win this one, I will set the team up for the best steak dinner
that money can buy." Staples didn't let on that he was aggravated. He
patted the drunk on the shoulder and thanked him for his offer.

Perry's most faithful fan throughout the dynasty years was Bill
Holland, a pleasant mentally challenged, middle-aged man, who always sat
among the cheerleaders and shouted encouragement to the players over a
megaphone. Bill wore a string of rabbits' feet on a chain around his neck
for good luck. Before every game, he let the players rub the rabbits' feet
and gave them a victory handshake with both hands and arms crossed. Bill
tallied Perry's scoring on a small writing tablet. For a field goal, he marked
a numeric "2" beside the player's name and a "1" for every free throw. He
also kept a record on personal fouls. For each foul, he made a short vertical
line beside the player's name. If he crossed four lines with a diagonal, that
was bad news because the player had fouled out. Once, according to Bill's
scorebook, my brother, Dwayne Powell, scored 42 points in a game. The
official scorer had Dwayne with only 41 points. Bill insisted that he was

right and contended the official scorer had given one of Dwayne's points to someone else.

Growing up in Perry, I enjoyed the privilege of playing basketball with Bill not only in the unlocked gym on weekends, but also in practically every backyard in Perry. We played in Tommy Mobley's backyard, where Bill would shoot atop a tree stump 30 feet away and ring the goal repeatedly. We played at Bert Bozeman's house, where he would deliver a twirling 360-degree shot and knock the bottom out of the net. He often came down Ball Street to play with Dwayne and me in our backyard. Many times I have seen Bill shoot a high arching ball that would ricochet off overhanging tree limbs and swish through the net. Bill had an insatiable fascination with basketball. He loved to launch a basketball 25-30 feet from the goal and watch it buckle the net. In backyard games, I always teamed with Bill to set him up for spectacular shots. A big broad smile always broke out on his face when he scored.

Old-timers have told me that back during Bill's school days in the 1930s, the short, chubby Bill would arrive at school early in the mornings so he would have time to shoot on the old dirt courts before the school bell rang. They say that Bill could eat his egg sandwich with one hand, change hands shooting, and never miss a bite.

Perry basketball games would not have been the same without Bill. Certainly, no other fan enjoyed the games more than Bill. Coach Staples appreciated Bill and arranged for him to attend all home games free. Someone would usually give Bill a ride to out-of-town games. If not, he rode the school bus with the cheerleaders and student fans.

Bill thought that nothing could measure up to Perry basketball. One night after a game, assistant Perry coach Paul Hartman was driving Bill home. That happened to be February 20, 1962, the same day that John Glenn became the first American to orbit the earth in a spacecraft. Hartman commented to Bill what an awesome sight the earth must have been to the orbiting Glenn. Bill didn't immediately respond, obviously digesting the spectacle that Glenn must have seen. Then Bill turned to Hartman and remarked very seriously, "Coach, but John Glenn hasn't seen the Panthers play yet."

Another faithful fan of the Panthers was Sheriff C. C. Chapman. In the winter of 1948, Perry was playing the Lanier Poets of Macon,

Georgia, at the local gym. James (Tank) Lawrence was a star Lanier football player, who also was a starter on the basketball team along with such talented players as Claude Greene, Bill Fickling, Bobby Schwartz, Jimmy Holton, and Eric Sauerbrey. During the second half, the Panthers picked off a Lanier pass and executed a fast break down the court to make a quick score. Tank Lawrence, a big hulk of a man, raced toward the lane where Perry's Seabie Hickson was dribbling full speed and clipped him below the waist, knocking him upside down. Seabie came down hard and could have broken some bones. He lay there motionless for a while before being helped up and led to the sidelines. The Perry fans roundly booed Tank Lawrence and the Lanier team. Several minutes later, the same thing happened, but this time Tank Lawrence upended Ed Chapman, the sheriff's son. Ed appeared hurt. His dad, Sheriff C. C. Chapman, with his revolver strapped to his belt, walked out to mid-court. The referees didn't dare say anything to him for coming on the court; they knew the sheriff meant business. Mr. C. C. stood at center court and glared directly at the Lanier bench with a mean scowl on his face for over a minute, then turned and walked off the court. His actions were stronger than any words he could have spoken. The Perry fans cheered. Everyone got the message, especially Tank Lawrence and his Poet teammates, that their rough house tactics would stop and they would stop immediately.

Perry's most vocal fans were C. J. Davis and Riley Young. They loved the Panthers and followed them everywhere they played. They both possessed built-in megaphones. At the games, their deep and resonating voices rose above the chatter of the crowd. They were so boastful of the Panthers that I am sure it incensed opposing fans. And they were bad about rubbing it in, especially when the Panthers beat arch-rivals or highly rated teams. Referees would feel their wrath when questionable calls were made against the Panthers. When C. J. and Riley walked into the gym, you knew it was "show time."

A familiar sight sitting at the official scorer's table during the dynasty years was Wilson Martin, Sr. Martin had been a 5'8" guard on Coach Jim Gooden's late 1920 teams, graduating from Perry High School in 1929. Because of his great love of basketball, he became Perry's official scorekeeper. He kept score at both home and away games. No one has seen more Perry games than Martin and his devoted wife, Una, a constant companion. When Martin retired, he had logged over 40-years keeping score. He was widely known and one of the most respected members of his profession. Many called him the "Dean of Georgia Scorekeepers." He saw firsthand the glory years of Perry basketball, to which his family made significant contributions. His three sons played on Perry state championship teams: Wilson-1959, Lee-1962, and Joe-1966. His daughter, Jean, was a star player on Coach Earl Marshall's Perry girls' teams from 1966-1969. Martin's two younger brothers were star players under Coach Staples: J. M. "Pepper" Martin in 1934 and Allen Martin in 1934 and 1935. On January 21, 1949, when the big fight broke out at the Perry-Fort Valley game, I was sitting directly behind Mr. Martin, who was tallying game results at the scorer's table. The scuffle happened within a few feet of Martin. A detailed account of that fight is covered later in the book.

Perry's five starters were transported to all out-of-town games for many years by Glea Gray, a close friend of Staples, who had been a star player on Coach Jim Gooden's 1925-1927 teams. Mr. Gray, a student of the game, gave inspiring pep talks to the players while driving them to the games. The confidence he exuded was contagious. He expounded on such truisms as "The other team can't score when you've got the basketball." This made a lot of sense, especially considering Staples' possession brand of basketball. Mr. Gray was constantly counseling us to block out our opponent on rebounding and to work the ball around for the high percentage shot. He was a joy to be around and had Perry's players primed and ready to play when they arrived at their destination.

Another great Perry fan was. J. Meade "Cap" Tolleson, a millionaire lumber man. On my way home, I often stopped to chat with Mr. Tolleson. He owned a tourist court in town called the Perry Court. It consisted of 15 cabins and sat directly across Ball Street from the New Perry Hotel. Yankees traveling down Highway 41 enroute to Florida would spent the night at his court. At the front of the court was a gas station. I usually found Cap Tolleson sitting in a chair by the side of the station. We would sit around and talk about basketball, rehashing old games and speculating about upcoming contests. Cap had three sons: Buddy, star on 1939 and 1940 teams; Mell-1951 and 1952 teams; and Buck, a great Perry fan and supporter. One day, Cap conveyed a tidbit of basketball wisdom I shall never forget. He stated, "Billy, when you get close to the basket, never throw the ball back out, keep moving toward that basket." From that day forth, I espoused that philosophy because throwing the ball back out moves the offense back to square one. Continuing to penetrate offers better chances to score or draw a foul. In 1940, when the game-ending fight took place between Perry and Clarkston in the state semifinals, Cap Tolleson took to the court to protect the Perry players from harm.

Once Staples established Perry as a perennial contender, the news media closely followed the team. The "Macon Telegraph and News" covered all of Perry's games. Their sports editors, first Sam Glassman and later Harley Bowers, reported on Perry basketball for several decades and often wrote editorials about Coach Staples and the Panthers.

In the 1959 state semifinal game, Heard County, coached by Don Staples, was ahead of Perry by two points with less than a minute to play. Covering the game was "Macon Telegraph" Sports Editor Harley Bowers. He evidently thought Heard County would prevail, because he had typed a headline to that effect for the morning edition. Horace Woodruff, a member of Perry's 1938 team, sitting directly behind Bowers, easily read the headline. It stated: "Heard County crushes Perry's title hopes" with the subheading "Eric Staples loses to brother Don." Perry miraculously rallied and defeated Heard County 34 to 30. Woodruff said Bowers snatched the page from his typewriter and started retyping.

The "Atlanta Journal and Constitution" also provided excellent coverage of the Panthers at tournament time and when Perry played Atlanta teams. The Perry weekly newspaper, the "Houston Home Journal," published game results on its front page, but in summary form. During the mid-1950s, "Atlanta Constitution" sportswriter Charlie Roberts drove down to Perry to interview Coach Staples. He was astonished at the overwhelming pride expressed by Perry citizens for their basketball team. Everyone he encountered from the gas station attendant to the restaurant waitress to the citizen on the street exclaimed about the accomplishments of the Perry Panthers.

Basketball fervor was not restricted to adults and teenagers. Small children often attended games with their parents. Little kids, from the time they started to school, had heard about the mighty Perry Panther basketball teams. During the halftime of the 1953 state championship game, the team was resting in the dressing room at Macon's City Auditorium. We heard a faint knock on the door. Coach Staples opened the door and there stood L.C. Todd, a star player on Coach Jim Gooden's 1933 team. He was holding his little five-year-old son, Terry. "Come in L. C.," said Coach Staples.

L.C. stated, "Coach Staples, my son Terry wants to meet Billy Powell. He has been crying throughout the first half, saying he wanted to meet Billy. Would you mind if Terry sees Billy, so he will stop crying."

"Certainly," responded Staples. "Bring Terry on in."

L.C. handed Terry to me. I held him in my lap and talked to him. Terry and I had a nice five-minute visit. The second half would be starting soon, so I handed Terry back to his dad and thanked L.C. for bringing Terry to see me. Terry's visit took the game off my mind and allowed me to relax. It also gave me encouragement knowing that a little fellow in the stands was pulling for me. Perry defeated Clarkston that night, 63 to 57, for the state title, and I shot 28 points for Terry. Terry played on Perry's 1966 state championship team and was selected to the All-State team. His sister, Patsy, was one of Perry's top girl basketball players in 1959. His sister Rita, a 1956 Perry High graduate, was one of Perry's staunchest fans.

Coach Staples' basketball dynasty established in Perry a winning tradition, an unconquerable spirit, and a unity of purpose that has never been duplicated in Georgia. That spirit and unity still lives today; it burns brightly in the hearts of Perry graduates and fans, who followed the Perry Panthers during the glory days of old Perry High.

If any town in Georgia had fans whose fervor came close to that exhibited by Perry's fans, it was Fort Valley, a town 12 miles northwest of Perry, which took great pride in its basketball teams. The rivalry between Perry and Fort Valley was one of the fiercest and most intense rivalries in Georgia history...

7 Rivalry between Perry and Fort Valley

Competitiveness in sports between nearby towns is normal and expected, but the rivalry between Perry and Fort Valley has been one of the most heated in Georgia history. The rivalry that exists today between the two towns, only 12 miles apart, pales in comparison to its intensity during the decades of the 1930s-1960s. In those days, death was better than losing to the opposing school. Adding fuel to the rivalry during the 1950s and early 1960s was the fierce competition between the schools generated by opposing coaches whose winning records placed them in the Georgia Sports Hall of Fame—Eric Staples of the Perry High Panthers and Norman Faircloth of the Fort Valley Green Wave. Because of their coaching genius, either Perry or Fort Valley would usually win the Third District championship and advance to the state tournament.

There are several views regarding the origin of the rivalry. History buffs trace its roots to the early 1850s when Fort Valley defied strong opposition from Perry in bringing the railroad to Houston County and, in 1873, completing a spur to Perry. Hard feelings erupted again in 1924 when Fort Valley, by a legislative act, withdrew from Houston County and created a new county named Peach County. Fort Valley's new independence from the Perry county seat fomented ill will; in fact, many citizens in both communities stopped talking to one another for years. Others contend that Fort Valley was slighted by political shenanigans that resulted in Interstate Highway 75 being routed through Perry during the 1960s rather than Fort Valley. While I-75 has brought growth and prosperity to Perry, Fort Valley businesses have suffered from the lack of interstate traffic.

Most observers, however, believe the genesis of the rivalry began with the fistfight in 1937 at the Peach-Houston County line on highway 341 near Bay Creek. Of the six Perry boys who assembled for that legendary fight, only one is still living and he is Dot Roughton of Perry, who was 85 years old on July 4, 2005. Roughton was a star Perry basketball player under Coach Staples during the 1938-1941 seasons. In addition to Roughton, the Perry group that assembled for the storied fight comprised John Webb, Donald Clark, C.A. Boswell, Horace Grimsley, and J. B. Hawkins, who later became Perry's chief of police. Boswell and Grimsley also were players on the Perry basketball team. Only six of the ten Fort Valley boys have been identified: Rudolph Cannon, Biddy Vaughn, Lowell Parks, Yates Crutchfield, King Mullis, and Joe Mullis. Several of the Fort Valley boys were members of the Green Wave basketball team.

Few people except the old timers know what precipitated the fight. Roughton disclosed in an interview that the county line brawl was the direct result of an earlier fight between John Webb of Perry and a Fort Valley boy. Both were trying to woo the same young lady from Fort Valley. Roughton provided this account of the fight: "Only two people fought. The fight occurred on a residential street in Fort Valley. A carload of us were riding around Fort Valley looking for girls. The driver, John Webb, spotted a boy walking down the street who had dated the Fort Valley girl he was sweet on. John pulled the car over to the curb, jumped out and challenged the Fort Valley boy to a fight. I got out of the car to referee the fight. After the fight got underway, it was obvious that the Fort Valley boy wasn't much of a fighter; Webb definitely had the upper hand. The neighbors saw a commotion going on in the streets and called the police. The police arrived and arrested the entire carload of Perry boys. The four of us who got out of the car were fined twenty five dollars each. The story that spread throughout Fort Valley was that a carload of Perry boys ganged up on a single Fort Valley boy."

With the Fort Valley crowd seething over the incident, a contingent of high school boys seeking revenge assembled on the county line and sent word to the Perry group to meet them for a showdown. Roughton said the Perry boys found him in the old Roxy theatre and asked him to join them. Six Perry boys packed into one automobile and headed toward the Bay Creek area near the Houston-Peach County line. When the Perry boys arrived, they were outnumbered, ten to six. Since Fort Valley had a larger group than Perry, they mutually decided to pick one from each side to do the fighting. Roughton, who had fought 16 amateur fights, was chosen to represent Perry. The Fort Valley group sent an emissary to town to bring back Rudolph Cannon, the state golden gloves champion. Roughton and Cannon each weighed about 145-pounds.

When Rudolph arrived, he asked, "Dot, what are we fighting for?" Roughton responded, "I guess it's because you're from Fort Valley and I'm from Perry." "Well, let's get on with it," responded Cannon. Cars were parked with their headlights illuminating the fight area. Biddy Vaughn, the Fort Valley police chief's son, was named the referee. Rules were established that it would be a stand-up 'bare knuckles' boxing match. Wrestling, kicking, gouging, and choking were not allowed. It was a contest of who was the better boxer and who would be the last man standing. Roughton and Cannon squared off and began slugging it out just off the shoulder of highway 341 near a peach orchard located a half mile north of Bay Creek. Both Roughton and Cannon were knocked to their knees numerous times, but each time they got back up to fight with renewed determination. After

Dot Roughton still remembers the fight.

32 minutes of fighting—by the referee's watch--with no man giving any quarter, Roughton caught Cannon with a vicious left jab and a right cross that sent Cannon sailing into the roadside ditch. Cannon's back hit the ditch embankment so hard that he momentarily lost his breath. He was visibly shaken and was slow to get up. As Roughton came in to finish him off, Cannon came out of the ditch and threw a wild haymaker that buckled Roughton's knees and almost knocked out three of Roughton's teeth. Cannon's knuckles and fingers were deeply cut as his fist smashed

into Roughton's teeth. Blood began to pour. Cannon's fist was bleeding so profusely, they decided to discontinue the fight and rush Cannon to a doctor. "Well, if Rudolph can't continue, I'll take Roughton on," said Biddy Vaughn, the referee from Fort Valley. J. B. Hawkins of Perry, its future police chief, looking at an exhausted Roughton, quickly defended his ailing buddy, saying, "No you won't Biddy. You'll have to whip me first. I'll take you on right now." Biddy backed down and, after a little jawing back and forth, the two warring parties quietly drove away. Cannon needed medical attention and Roughton was a bloody mess.

When Rudolph arrived home, his sister, Uldene Cannon Pearson, was shocked to see how bloody and beaten up her brother looked. She said, "My parents were quite upset and, as they examined Rudolph's wounds with great concern, he said, 'You should see the other guy.'" Roughton said, "I was beat up so badly my mother did not recognize me the next morning." Roughton had two black eyes, three loose teeth as well as cuts and bruises all over his face. Yates Crutchfield, the only known Fort Valley survivor, now 83, described the fight as "brutal." "Cannon and Roughton beat the starch out of each other. Neither boy

Marie Anderson of Fort Valley displays painting of her late husband, School Superintendent, Ernest Anderson.

would quit," observed Crutchfield. "No one won that fight," declared
Roughton. "In my life I have fought 67 professional and amateur fights
and won several boxing tournaments, but that was my toughest fight ever.
I would unload on Rudolph with all I had, and he would keep coming."
Roughton reasoned that, had not the two fought instead of all 16-boys,
someone would have been seriously hurt. "Rudolph and I became friends,"
said Roughton. "He was a good man. I liked him and respected him."
Cannon's sister, Uldene, who graduated from Fort Valley High School
in 1937, remembers the event well and will never forget how bloody her
brother was. That incident set the stage for even more intense rivalry
between Perry and Fort Valley.

Over the next decade there were many classic battles between
the two schools on the hardwood, but in 1949 the lid blew off when
a Fort Valley fan and a Perry assistant coach, Bob Shuler, got into an
altercation following a heated basketball game at the Perry gym in which
Perry defeated Fort Valley 41 to 32. A detailed account of that fight is
included later in the book. The Georgia High School Association issued
a stern warning to both schools that a repeat occurrence would result in
banishment from high school sports and a possible loss of accreditation.
Soon after this episode, Mr. Ernest Anderson, Peach County School
Superintendent--and one of the best superintendents in Georgia's history--
made the decision to stop playing Perry during the regular season and only
play Perry, if necessary, in tournament competition. Mrs. Marie Anderson,
Anderson's wife, remarked, "Ernest felt that it would be best to suspend
play until the ill feelings subsided."

Weeks after the altercation in 1949, Perry again had to play
Fort Valley, coached by Ned Warren, this time for the third district
championship at Fort Valley's gym on Riley Avenue. The Perry team,
heckled by Fort Valley's fans certain of victory, came from behind 14-
points at halftime and won on the outstanding play of Mack Peyton, Billy
Gray, Ed Chapman, Seabee Hickson, and Bobby Satterfield.

In 1952, with Coach Norman Faircloth at the reigns, his undefeated
Fort Valley team edged Perry by 2-points on a last second driving lay-
up by Richard Aultman, a great friend of mine, who is now a retired
Methodist minister residing in Byron, Georgia. This writer was a junior
playing in that game for Perry. Fort Valley had possibly its greatest team

that year. Its big guns were Ed Beck, Pat Swan, Jimmy Thompson, Strib McCants, Eddie Merritt, Ted Joyner, and Aultman. They went on to capture the state title and ended the season undefeated.

The next year, 1953, I was a senior on the Perry team. My teammates were Billy Beckham, Franklin May, David Gray, Joe Leverette, Tommy Mobley, James Logue, Jackie Miller, Martin Beeland, John Malone, and Billy Brock, After much speculation that Perry and Fort Valley would meet to determine the district championship, Fort Valley was eliminated by Hawkinsville in the district semifinals, and Perry won an overtime thriller over Hawkinsville to capture the Third District title. Perry's 1953 team advanced to the state finals and emerged victorious.

In 1954, with Fort Valley's giant center, Ed Beck, returning for his senior year, the Fort Valley Green Waves beat Perry in the third district championship game at Fort Valley's gym and two weeks later brought home another state crown, their second in three years.

Two years later in 1955, Perry beat Fort Valley in district tournament play led by Sam Nunn, Virgil Peavy, Bennett Mauldin, Percy Hardy, William Harrison, Jimmy Beatty, and Ed Beckham. A year later, in 1956, virtually that same Perry squad won the state championship. The 1949-1956 era was highly representative of the intense rivalry that existed between the two schools.

Prior to integration, the next and last time Perry and Fort Valley competed in basketball was in the semifinals of the state tournament in 1962. Perry was undefeated. Its squad comprised such top performers as Lee Martin, Dwayne Powell, George Nunn, Dennis Fike, Ronnie Sanders and Ronnie Griffin. Fort Valley was defending state champions, having won the state title in 1961, and were led by Tee Faircloth, Ray Pearson, Dave Hardeman, Dan Harrelson, Tommy Tucker, Ronnie McDaniel, Jody Hardeman, Nim Tharpe, and Herby Smith. Perry won the 1962 game by eight points, 52-44, before a capacity crowd at Macon's city auditorium in the state's first televised high school basketball game. That game concluded the rivalry between the two schools during the Faircloth and Staples' era.

All is well that ends well. Roughton and Cannon became friends. Mrs. Helen Faircloth, stated, "Norman (Faircloth) and Coach Staples were the best of friends." Mrs. Marie Anderson added, "Ernest (Anderson) and

Coach Staples were also good friends." And I became close friends with Mr. Anderson and Coach Faircloth after I moved to Fort Valley in 1959. In fact, Mr. Anderson and I worked together on preparing a nomination package that resulted in Coach Faircloth being inducted into the Georgia Sports Hall of Fame. The day his selection was announced, Coach Faircloth called to thank me.

The county line battle did not stop the Perry boys from dating Fort Valley girls, however, as Perry boys became notorious for stealing away Fort Valley's most beautiful girls and in marriage taking them to Perry to live. Lee Powell did. He married Margaret Braswell of Fort Valley, who became my mother. Billy and Ed Beckham did. Mel Tolleson did. Bill Jerles did. Buddy Andrew did. And I did when I married Beverly, Homer Davis' daughter, except Beverly kept me in Fort Valley. Coach Faircloth was lamenting the exodus of Fort Valley's girls one day in a discussion with several of his Perry friends. Coach jokingly commented, "It is a shame we have lost so many pretty girls to Perry boys over the years, and all we got to show for it is Billy Powell."

Because of Perry's dominance in this long term rivalry, many Fort Valley fans referred to Coach Staples as "the old gray fox"...

8 Crafty Old Fox Outsmarted His Foes

Coach Staples' lifetime record shows that he won 83 games out of every 100 played. More importantly, he found a way to win the crucial games, the outcomes of which either make or break a season. Those who followed Staples' teams over the years contend he coached more come-from-behind victories and won more close games that any other coach in Georgia history. Because of Staples' ability to out-coach his opponents and win the big games, opposing fans referred to him as the "old gray fox." And a crafty old fox he was—a master tactician of the X's and O's, who approached game preparations with the same forethought and anticipation that a world-class chess player contemplates his next move. For every change in game tactics by an opposing coach, Coach Staples countered with effective offensive and defensive adjustments.

Devising a defensive plan to shut down a prolific scorer is a nightmare for any coach; however, in this area of expertise Coach Staples excelled. In some cases, he concentrated on slowing the point production of the offensive ace. In other instances, he conceded to the scoring whiz his customary points, but instead attempted to limit the scoring of his four teammates.

In 1953, the Perry Panthers won the Third District Class B tournament and faced the Class C winner, Oglethorpe, for the overall district championship. Leading Coach Jimmy Maffett's Oglethorpe Eagles was W. C. Jones, who was averaging 25 points a game, but on occasion would explode for 35 to 40 points. For the Panthers to win, Staples knew that Jones' assault on the basket had to be contained. He assigned Franklin May to guard Jones. An excellent choice that was, as May was one of Georgia's finest defensive players. In the pre-game team meeting, Coach Staples sketched on a chalkboard where Jones lined up on the court and stated, "Ninety percent of the time, Jones will drive the baseline to reach the basket. Franklin, you must block the baseline and not let him get by you." Staples continued, "We'll concede to Jones the option of driving in the other direction, but, when he does, I expect three defenders clogging the middle of the court...I want every defensive player to shift toward Jones when the ball moves in his direction." Staples' plan to stop Jones was indeed a coup de maitre. Franklin May held Jones to only 11 points, allowing Perry to defeat Oglethorpe and to capture the Class B and C district crown. The chapter on Perry's state championship teams contains detailed accounts of Staples' defensive strategies.

During my senior year at Perry High in 1953, Coach Staples had me performing the strangest practice routine. Every afternoon at study hall for about six weeks, before the regular team practice session, he sent me to the basketball gym to practice shooting. Staples sent along my friend, Ken Barrett, a ninth grader, to retrieve my shots and throw them back. I was instructed to shoot exclusively from the coffin corner and from no other position. The coffin corner is the area where the side line and the end line meet. This is the hardest shot in basketball. The front of the backboard is not visible to judge distance, and the lone net, dangling in thin air, plays tricks with depth perception. I would shoot several hundred shots from the coffin corner every practice session. I wondered why Coach Staples had me doing this, but I knew he had his reason and didn't dare ask. The answer to my question came in the last game of the season—the state finals against Clarkston, the tallest team we had faced all season and a squad that many sportswriters had picked to win the state title. In his pre-game talk to the team before the title game, Staples drew on the blackboard a play he called the "Button Hook." At the guard position where I played, I was instructed to bounce-pass the ball to forward, David Gray, who exchanged positions with me. Once I moved to the forward slot and Gray passed the ball to the other guard, Franklin May, I ran quickly to the opposite side of the court, screening my defender off Billy Beckham, positioned on the low post. David Gray quickly fed the ball to the other forward, Joe Leverette, who vacated the corner to open it up for me. Leverette fired the ball to me the instant I arrived in the coffin corner, and there, for a split second, I had a 20 to 25-foot shot at the basket. After I had hit five in a row, I knew then what Coach Staples had in mind when he sent me to the gym to practice every day. I had practiced the coffin corner shot so many times, I could hit it in my sleep. We beat Clarkston for the state crown, and I scored 28 points—a majority of them from the coffin corner.

Coach Staples considered every possible angle when readying his teams for tournament competition. In 1953, the Perry team had won the third district championship and was preparing for the state tournament. Toward the end of practice, Coach Staples sent Sam Nunn in to guard me. I was a senior. Sam was a freshman and a starter on the B-team. The first time down the court, Sam elbowed me. On the next series his fingernails drew blood as I shot the ball. When I tried to get offensive position, he would push me away. Several plays later, he tripped me as I drove toward the basket, and I went sprawling. Nobody was calling his obvious fouls. I looked sharply at Sam. On his face, I saw nothing but determination and seriousness. I wondered to myself, "What is Sam trying to do? This is so uncharacteristic of him. We are supposed to be friends. I even taught him how to shoot the ball. Is this ninth grader trying to show me up and make an impression on Coach Staples?" Next time down the court he bumped me again, very hard. That was the last straw. Being a larger boy at the time, I grabbed Sam by the shoulders and shoved him into the front row of seats in the old gym.

When I did, Coach Staples rocketed off the bench like a fire-breathing dragon. He abruptly stopped practice, walked directly toward me and, with a stern expression, yelled at me, "You did exactly what I thought you would do. Don't be mad with Sam. I told him to go in there and make you mad. You failed the test, and you failed it miserably. When we enter the state tournament in Macon, some unscrupulous coach might send in a hatchet man to make you mad. If you retaliate, the referee will eject you from the game. We don't want that to happen. Let this be an object lesson to you, son. Never lose your temper or your composure. If someone tries to provoke you, let me handle it." My eyes met Sam's. He had a wide smile on his face. Spontaneously we shook hands and everything was okay.

This valuable lesson was put to use two weeks later in the state championship game against Clarkston. A player, 6 feet 5 inches tall, very strong and muscular, lined up next to me. At the center jump, he elbowed me so hard in the solar plexus that I went down hard. I was still lying flat on my back as Clarkston scored an opening lay-up. I immediately remembered what Coach Staples had taught me, so I gathered my wits and concentrated on playing basketball the Staples' way.

Another way Coach Staples prepared his teams was through superior conditioning and proper nutrition. He felt it was important that his players ate a proper meal at least three hours before the game; consequently, before tournament games, the team always ate at his home where Mrs. Staples cooked sumptuous meals. Her chicken was the best I have ever eaten. It was slow cooked in butter in a frying pan and then placed in the oven for baking. Her mashed potatoes, butter beans, white creamed corn, iced tea, and desserts were meals the Perry teams will never forget. And if I were ever crushed to death, I trust it would be under an avalanche of Mrs. Staples' mouth-watering rolls.

Coach Staples discouraged his players from drinking carbonated drinks and eating junk food such as candy and popcorn. One day during the off-season, I had stopped by the old Roxy Theater in downtown Perry to buy a bag of popcorn. I started walking down Ball Street eating the popcorn on the way home. Man, was it tasty. As I approached the New Perry Hotel, along came Coach Staples in his car. He stopped and offered me a ride. When I got into his car, he said, "What are you eating, son?" I replied, "Popcorn." He responded, "Don't you know that basketball players are not supposed to eat popcorn?" I looked sheepishly at him and answered, "Yes sir, I remember your telling us that." He then said, "Give me the bag." I did so. He started eating my popcorn and was still enjoying it as he put me out at home and drove away.

Perry's basketball program received a strategic shot in the arm during the 1950s when Coach Staples hired Frank Holland as assistant coach. Coach Holland was a winning coach in his own right and had produced outstanding teams during the 1930s and 1940s, first at Byron, and later at Chauncey. He came to Perry as assistant coach in 1952 and retired from coaching in 1960. During that span, Perry won three state championships: 1953, 1956, and 1959. Coach Holland was known for his famous "Little Black Book," so legendary in basketball folklore that the Georgia Sports

Hall of Fame wanted it for display, but the book has not been found. This book contained detailed scouting reports on opposing teams and notes regarding the strengths and weaknesses of individual players. In pre-game team meetings, Coach Holland often referred to his book, turning from page-to-page as he addressed the Perry team on specific offensive patterns to expect from the opposing team and how best to defend against a given player. Opposing teams and their coaches were apprehensive about the "Little Black Book" and considered it a secret weapon in Perry's arsenal. Holland was a man of small stature, who usually wore a dark suit and dark hat and walked in short, choppy steps with his head down, as if he were in deep thought. He looked the role of a Scotland Yard inspector, who had investigated the deep, dark secrets of the other team. Teams felt that Coach Holland had X-rayed their innermost secrets and would use this

Coach Holland (center) scribbles in his "Little Black Book"
during game as Coach Staples (R) watches play on the court.

knowledge to defeat them...and he did.

Staples was such a smart coach that you could never count the Panthers out in a close game, regardless of how many points they were behind and how little time was left on the clock. A Cochran fan said it best: "You don't know you have beaten Perry until they turn out the lights, lock the gym door, and you are on the school bus heading out of town."

Reflected in the table below are the winning percentages of the nine state championship teams. The overall winning percentage of 91.9 percent is evidence of Coach Staples' wisdom in encouraging the placement of basketball goals in every Perry backyard.

Won-Loss records: Perry High School State Championship Teams

Year	Wins	Loses	Winning Percent
1962	35	0	100
1956	29	1	96.7
1953	34	2	94.4
1966*	31	2	93.9
1963	30	3	90.9
1964	32	4	88.9
1947	31	4	88.6
1959	27	4	87.1
1949	33	5	86.8
Totals	282	25	91.9

Coach Staples retired following 1965 season. The 1966 team was coached by Paul Hartman, Staples' former assistant.

Perry won its first state championship in 1947...

9 Championship Years

Epitome of Teamwork: 1947 team

1947 Perry team. Kneeling, L-R: Jack Watts, Ed Chapman, Ed Thompson, Deryle Whipple. Mack Peyton, Seabie Hickson, Bubber Riley. Standing, L-R: Coach Eric Staples, Charles Whitworth, John Blue Calhoun, Billy Bledsoe, James Matthews, Clint Cooper, Bobby Sutton-manager and Jimmy Connell-manager. Not pictured: Billy Gray

Black cat stalks Perry's basketball fortunes

With the loss of all-state player Carlton (Bubber) Pierce and his classmate Richard Ogletree to graduation, the 1947 team opened its season with only three returning veterans: Clint Cooper, Billy Bledsoe, and Ed Thompson. Another top prospect was Deryle Whipple, who lost

valuable playing time during the previous season when he came down
with mononucleosis and was incapacitated for several months. When
Perry's starting lineup was announced before the season opener in October
1946, no player stood over six feet tall:

Deryle Whipple: forward--5' 7"
Clint Cooper: forward—5' 9"
John Blue Calhoun: center—5' 10"
Ed Thompson: guard—5' 5"
Billy Bledsoe: guard—6' 0"
Jack Watts (sixth man)—5' 7"

With such a small squad, the season did not bode well for the
Panthers, particularly against taller and more physical opponents. To
make matters worse, in order to win the district title, Perry would have
to prevail against Warner Robins and its 7-foot center, Bill Spivey, who
already had the eye of college coaches throughout the country. This would
be a Herculean task because Spivey camped around the goal—whose foul
lane was only six feet wide in those days—and would take a lob pass from
his teammates and stuff it into the basket. He was a devastating force on
offense and virtually unstoppable.

No Perry team had ever won a state basketball championship.
Although the '47 quintet would be competitive, no one in his wildest
imagination expected this team to win the district, much less the state.
The state championship had proven to be an elusive aspiration during
Staples' first thirteen years at Perry that started in the fall of the 1933-34
season. Although a perennial contender in the 3rd district, Perry had won
seven district tournaments and three second place finishes in the state
tournament, but never a state title. Certainly, this team with its small size
and limited experience was not projected to get the black cat off Staples'
back. As history unfolded, however, this Perry team proved it possessed an
ingredient that could not be measured—it had heart. Each of its players
possessed the heart of a champion and a fierce determination to win.

Season begins

In its season opener at the local gym on October 20, 1946, Perry got the year off to a great start by beating the Montezuma Aztecs, who over the years had always produced great teams:

Perry-25	Montezuma-14
Cooper-10	Kinman
Whipple-11	Batton-2
Watts	Souter-6
Thompson-2	Deal-2
Bledsoe-2	Easterlin-2

Subs: Perry: Calhoun, Matthews, Gray, Hickson, M. Peyton; Montezuma: Bailey-2, Folks, Nelson
Officials: Lassiter and Braddock

Thirteen straight victories by mid-December 1946

On December 17, 1946, Perry cruised to its 13th consecutive win of the season, a 31 to 20 victory over Byron, who traditionally had fielded strong teams. Clint Cooper and Deryle Whipple both pitched in 8-points, Jack Watts-6, Billy Bledsoe-4, Ed Thompson-3, and John Blue Calhoun-2. Keys, English, and Clark led Byron with 8-points, 7-points, and 4-points respectively.

First defeat and redemption

On January 3, 1947, Perry suffered its first defeat of the season, losing to Montezuma in a struggle that went right down to the wire with the Aztecs prevailing by a margin of only two points, 28 to 26. Deryle Whipple did not suit up for this contest due to a sprained wrist he suffered over the Christmas holidays.

A month later, on January 31, 1947, Perry redeemed itself in the third meeting between the schools. Perry's offense produced a balanced attack with a 42 to 30 win over Montezuma: Clint Cooper-14, Deryle Whipple -11, Billy Bledsoe-7, Ed Thompson-6, John Blue Calhoun-2, and Mack Peyton-2.

Arch-rival Fort Valley

During the regular season, Perry beat arch-rival Fort Valley four times: 31-12, 45-30, 35-25, and 23-15. Fort Valley, only 12-miles up 341 Highway, was Perry's greatest rival; in fact, the rivalry became so heated in past years that gangs of Perry and Fort Valley players had assembled for fist fights at Bay Creek, a midpoint between the two towns.

Perry's third win over the Green Waves was played in Perry with Deryle Whipple, Clint Cooper, and Ed Thompson leading the scoring. Billy Bledsoe, Jack Watts, John Blue Calhoun, Billy Gray, Mack Peyton, and Charles Whitworth all turned in superb performances.

Perry-45	**Fort Valley-30**
Whipple-13	Swan
Cooper -13	Bartlett-10
Bledsoe-3	Hutto-4
Thompson-8	Cannon-7
Watts-3	Mullis-5

Subs: Perry: Calhoun-2, Gray, M. Peyton, Whitworth; Fort Valley: Wilder, Whitley, and McDaniel-2

Almost sneaked up on Poets in their own backyard

The second and third losses of the season were to the Lanier Poets, who were coached by the legendary Selby Buck. Lanier of Macon, Georgia, was a Class A school, the highest classification in that day, which represented 8-10 of the larger schools in the state. These larger schools like Boys High of Atlanta, Columbus High, and Lanier usually had four or five times the student body of the Class "B' schools from which to draw its players.

The Lanier Poets barely beat the Panthers in Macon. The Panthers almost sneaked up on the Poets in the final minutes of the game, but finally succumbed to their taller adversaries by a score of 30 to 27.

Because of their excellent showing in the first game on the Poets' home court, the Panthers hoped to avenge their earlier loss in the return engagement. The second game was played at the Perry gym before a crowd of 900 spectators, mostly partisan fans; however, Lanier, the taller, more physical team with greater bench depth, controlled the backboards and prevailed again by a score of 40 to 27.

Perry-27	**Lanier-40**
Cooper-16	Beasley-10
Whipple-9	Schwartz-5
Calhoun	Greene-13
Bledsoe-2	Veal-5
Thompson	Williams-3

Subs: Perry: M. Peyton and Watts; Lanier: Moody-4, Lawrence, and Bates
Officials: Lassiter and Braddock

Fourth and final loss of regular season

The fourth and final loss of the regular season came at the hands of the Middle Georgia College 'B' team in Cochran on February 10, 1947. Perry had beaten this same team earlier by a score of 42-30 with Clint Cooper and Deryle Whipple leading the scoring with 23 and 11 points respectively. Billy Bledsoe pitched in 6 points and Ed Thompson 2.

In the second game, the Middle Georgia College Bees won by a narrow one point margin 29 to 28, a hard fought game in which the lead constantly changed hands and the game remained in doubt until the final buzzer. Clint Cooper and Deryle Whipple led Perry with 12 and 9 points respectively. Other scorers were John Blue Calhoun-2, Billy Bledsoe-2, and Ed Thompson-3.

Regular season record: 24 wins, 4 losses

The regular season concluded with Perry's won-loss record at an enviable 24 wins against only 4 losses. Perry had beaten two of the teams it lost to: Montezuma and the Middle Georgia College 'B' team. Only the larger Class A school, Lanier, had escaped defeat by the Panthers.

District tournament begins

Now it was tournament time. This was what the season was all about. Winning a tournament is contingent upon satisfying two prerequisites: a team has to be good and it has to be lucky. As teams approach the semi-finals, the caliber of the competition gets better and better and, to emerge victorious, Lady Luck must smile on a given team when a critical defensive play or a last second shot can determine the outcome of a game.

The 3rd district tournament started in Perry's gym on February 18, 1947. Perry received a bye the first night. In the second round of play, Perry beat Cuthbert 34 to 19. In the semi-finals Perry outlasted Baker Village of Columbus by a margin of 39 to 23 and would face Warner Robins for the district championship. Bill Spivey, Warner Robins' 7-foot center, had scored 34 points when Warner Robins defeated Cordele 46 to 28 in the first round, 16 points when his team downed Fort Valley 28 to 22 in the second round, and 16-points when they downed Hawkinsville 29 to 27 in the semi-finals. Spivey had scored roughly two-thirds of his team's points during the tournament. To stop Warner Robins, it was evident that a defensive strategy had to be devised to contain Spivey.

David vs. Goliath

Weeks in advance of the tournament, Coach Staples, who had scouted Spivey heavily, came up with a defensive attack. "Fessor devised a plan," said Billy Bledsoe. "He brought a stool about 18-inches tall to the practice session. He placed Billy Gray on the stool to represent Spivey." Bledsoe continued, "Fessor would have someone lob the ball to Billy Gray, standing on the stool, and the defender, positioned in front of Gray, would try to jump up and knock the ball away before it reached Billy's out-stretched hands. That was done to emphasize that a player standing in front of Spivey would have to leap only 18-20 inches to flick the ball away. If Spivey got the ball, however, it was over with, because he would simply turn toward the basket and dunk the basketball."

So at game time, Coach Staples placed John Blue Calhoun, a muscular, rugged 5' 10" individual, directly behind the 7-foot Bill Spivey and stationed Billy Bledsoe, 6' 0" guard, in front of Spivey. When the Warner Robins team would lob a high, arching pass into Spivey, Calhoun would hold his ground against Spivey, preventing him from backing into the basket, and Bledsoe would jump as high as he could, tipping the ball away. The batted ball would be scooped up by Ed Thompson, Clint Cooper, or Deryle Whipple, who would lead a fast break down court for a quick score. These three players were lightening fast, great ball-handlers, and knew how to execute a fast break. Thompson and Cooper could shoot well on the run, and Whipple was a deadly outside shooter.

The Perry gym was packed to capacity. Over 1200 fans had come. Before game time, the ticket lines had stretched all the way up the block. This writer was a 6th grader at the time and remembers sitting under the east goal of the gym—the playing floor was situated west-to-east in those days. This was the original gym built in 1926 that sat across from the high school, before it was moved down the hill in 1948 beside the agriculture building. The aisles were packed and the sidelines were so crowded the teams could hardly bring the ball in—the referees were constantly asking people to back away from the court and give the players room. Fans, standing atop ladders placed against the outer gym walls, were watching the game through the gym windows that were located near the rafters at the top of the building.

Perry's players were not in the best physical condition. Clint Cooper played despite a sprained ankle, Billy Bledsoe had a sore back, and Deryle Whipple was recovering from a severe cold, but you would never have known it by the way they played.

"Spivey got so accustomed to John Blue and me double-teaming him that when he came down to set up, he would automatically try to edge between us," said Billy Bledsoe. Deryle Whipple observed, "Had Warner Robins tried to pass the ball to Spivey on a more direct line and not a high-arching pass that was descending when it approached Spivey," they might have been more successful." Ed Thompson agreed with Whipple's assessment.

The game was hard fought. The noise level was deafening. I had never seen the Perry fans in such a frenzy of excitement. With each blocked pass to Spivey or a Perry score, their anticipation of victory over Warner Robins moved closer and closer to reality.

The game proved to be a classic struggle between David and Goliath, but Perry outscored Warner Robins in the final quarter and gradually pulled away, winning by an unexpected eight-point margin, 37 to 28. Clint Cooper hit his peak in the game, hitting the hoops for 23 points. Billy Bledsoe, John Blue Calhoun, Deryle Whipple, Ed Thompson, and Jack Watts all played outstanding defensive games and virtually error-free basketball on offense. Spivey was held to only 12 points, thanks to the heretofore unused and gambling, defensive stratagem employed by Coach Eric Staples. This was vintage Staples. He was the master strategist. He knew how to get the most out of his boys and how to minimize the awesome offensive potential of the 7-foot giant.

Mythical Class B and C championship

Next came the mythical 3rd district Class B and C tournament played February 25 at Cochran, Georgia. Perry had won the Class B title and Montezuma had captured the championship among the Class C schools in the 3rd district.

The "Macon Telegraph", in its coverage of the game, stated: "Perry, king of the Class 'B' schools in the district, had dropped one verdict to Montezuma, winner of the Class 'C' title, during the regular season but had trimmed the Aztecs in three other encounters. Tonight's battle, on a neutral court, was arranged to settle the all-division title. The game was a nip and tuck battle all the way, the lead changing hands constantly. Montezuma was off to a fast start and held an 8-4 lead at the end of the first quarter. At halftime, however, Perry had overcome the deficit and was on the long end of an 18 to 17 count. The Panthers held this one-point edge throughout the final frame, leading 30-29 as the final quarter began. The accuracy of Deryle Whipple with his long shots played a major factor in the Panthers' efforts to turn back the battling Montezuma kids, as Perry edged a strong Montezuma quintet in a close contest, 38 to 35. Clint Cooper bagged 11 points for runner-up honor for the winners. Souter, the Aztec center, paced Montezuma with 12 points, while Kinman contributed nine markers. The game was played in Middle Georgia College's gymnasium before a capacity crowd."

Perry-38	Montezuma-35
Cooper-11	Kinman-9
Whipple -18	Taylor-2
Calhoun-4	Souter-12
Thompson	DeVaughn-6
Bledsoe-5	Easterlin-6

Subs: Perry: M. Peyton and Watts; Montezuma: Nelson

Officials: Morris and Matt.

State championship at Mercer's Porter Gym

The Class B state tournament was held during early March 1947 at Mercer University's Porter Gym in Macon, Georgia. In the first game, Perry prevailed against Rossville 25 to 23.

"Atlanta Journal" staff writer, Dan Magill Jr., wrote this account, dated March 8, 1947, of Perry's 36-18 victory over Canton in the second round of play: "Perry fans apologized for the play of little forward, Deryle Whipple, as he scored only four points in the Georgia High School Class B quarter-finals Thursday (Rossville game). But they almost burst the roof off Porter Hall with an earth-quakening ovation here Friday night when the five-foot-eight wizard left the game late in the final period after his superb all-round play had sewn up a 36-18 victory over Canton. Whipple sprained his ankle Tuesday trying to run down a trapped bird in the Perry gym, and it was not until Friday night that he felt like running at full speed. He put on so much speed Friday, though, that the official scorekeeper had great difficulty keeping tab on him, not to mention the Canton Greenies. Whipple sank seven field goals—quite a feat against the big Canton club, three-time state tournament champions and a participant in the state tournament more times than any other Georgia school. He was the ring leader of Eric Staples' typical Perry outfit—the tallest man, Billy Bledsoe, only 6-feet tall—but everyone was a dead shot, ball-hawk, and fast as a whippet."

Deryle Whipple led Perry's scoring against Canton with 14 points closely followed by Clint Cooper with 13 points. John Blue Calhoun added 5, Ed Thompson-3, and Jack Watts-1.

While Perry was winning its bracket, the Valdosta Wildcats emerged victorious over Thomaston in the other bracket and would face the Panthers for the state championship. In the Thomaston game, Valdosta's backcourt standouts, James (Sonny) Stephenson and Billy Grant were scintillating. This virtually unstoppable duo staged a two-man riot in the final quarter to rip their opponents 33-26 and gain the Class B finals.

Perry vs. Valdosta for state crown

So the stage was set for the state title, the Panthers would take on the Valdosta team led by the dynamic duo of Stephenson and Grant and coached by the legendary Wright Bazemore.

"Macon Telegraph" Sports Editor, Sam Glassman Jr., wrote: "Perry, coached by Eric Staples has reached the state tournament 13 previous times, but runner-up twice was the best it has ever done."

Could Panthers slow Valdosta's dynamic duo?

Would the Panthers falter again? Would they be able to slow down the prolific scoring machine of Sonny Stephenson and Billy Grant, who could really light up the scoreboard?

An estimated 2,200 spectators crowded into Porter gym. The "Houston Home Journal" reported that 99 percent of Perry was there to cheer their team to victory. Several hundred fans, refused admission due to lack of seats, were on the outside of the gym receiving shouted play-by-play details on what was going on inside. The game had a slow start with each team playing a possession game and working for the good shot. Valdosta led 5-2 at the end of first quarter. Perry moved ahead at halftime by a narrow one-point margin, 10-9. Although Perry and Valdosta played a slow-down game, Sonny Stephenson was hot as a firecracker when he got open, hitting from all angles. During the second half, Perry progressively pulled away, scoring 19 points while Valdosta scored 11. The final score was Perry-29, Valdosta-20. Perry had captured its first state championship!

Although Valdosta's Sonny Stephenson tallied 15 points, the decisive factor in the game was Perry's great defense holding Billy Grant to only one point during the entire game and the remaining Valdosta team to only 4 points. Deryle Whipple led the Panthers offensively with 15 points, matching Stephenson point-for-point. The same tenacious defense that beat Warner Robins and Bill Spivey in the district was in full sway throughout the Valdosta game. Ed Thompson contributed 6 points, Clint Cooper-4 and John Blue Calhoun-4. Billy Bledsoe turned in a fine performance at guard. He and John Blue Calhoun controlled the backboards during the second half and Ed Thompson, the floor general, ran the offense with precision throughout the game. Clint Cooper played one of his finest games on both sides of the court. Perry subs contributing to the victory were Jack Watts and Ed Chapman.

Coach Staples was so happy he personally hugged each player as he congratulated them after the game. Perry had now won that elusive state championship. There would be seven more to follow during the Staples' era.

All-State team
The Class 'B' all-state team comprised:

> Clinton Cooper-Perry
> Deryle Whipple-Perry
> Billy Bledsoe-Perry
> Edwin Thompson-Perry
> Sonny Stephenson-Valdosta
> Billy Grant-Valdosta
> Abner (Sonny) Dykes-Cochran
> Hugh Radcliffe-Thomaston
> Jimmy Lumpkin-Thomaston
> John Duke-Albany

Comments on Coach Staples:

Billy Bledsoe: "Coach Staples was the most innovative coach in Georgia history. He was the consummate psychologist. He knew how to handle and motivate young people. He didn't rule with an iron hand either. Although he was always in full control, he had a way of making his players think they were performing on their own."

John Blue Calhoun: "He was the quintessential coach. He built a team around what he had to work with. He knew how to get the most out of every player and how to mold a winning team with the talent he had."

Ed Thompson: "Coach Staples was demanding and innovative. He was a master strategist who knew how to respond to any given situation in a ballgame. His strategy won many games for us."

Deryle Whipple: "What a psychologist, a master motivator! He could take a boy with a terrible temper, or a slow learner, or one without a father, and create in each of them a winning spirit. He crossed all barriers as he brought out the best in all of us. Above all, Fessor Staples was a winner!"

Nemesis of the Green Wave: 1949 team

1949 Perry team. Front L-R: Bubber Riley, Edward Chapman, Mack Peyton, Bobby Satterfield, Billy Gray, and Seabie Hickson. Back L-R: Coach Bob Shuler, Pete Carlisle, Bobby Sutton, Charles Whitworth, Herschel Lawhorn, Herschel Thompson, and Coach Eric Staples. Not pictured: Buddy Batchelor and Rhett Milan.

Previous season, 1947-48, was a rebuilding year

After Perry won its first state championship on March 8, 1947, the following season was a rebuilding year. All five starters on the 1947 team (DeryleWhipple, Clint Cooper, Billy Bledsoe, Ed Thompson, and John Blue Calhoun) four of whom were all-state selectees, were lost to graduation. So Perry began the 1947-48 season with substitutes who had played sparingly on the 1947 state championship team. These former subs started slowly but by mid-season had matured into a competitive unit. Perry's 1948 team advanced to the finals of the district tournament, but lost the championship game to Fort Valley by a lop-sided score of 37 to 17, as Green Wave stars Charles Bartlett, Norris Mullis, and Billy Cannon were too much for the young Panthers.

Perry opens 1949 season with veteran team

As the chapter closed on the 1947-48 season, only one player was lost to graduation: Howard Peyton, a scrappy competitor and defensive standout. Consequently, the entire1948 starting squad (Mack Peyton, Ed Chapman, Billy Gray, Bobby Satterfield, Seabie Hickson) and sixth man Bubber Riley, now more experienced, returned to begin play for the 1948-49 season. Two top reserves, Charles Whitworth and Bobby Sutton, also came back for another year. Elevated to the varsity were former B team players: Buddy Batchelor, Rhett Milan, Bobby Sutton, Herschel Thompson and Herschel Lawhorn. If ever a Perry team opened the season with a shot at the state title, it was the 1948-49 squad.

Won 15 of first 16 games

With a veteran team, Perry won 15 of the first 16 games, its only loss to the strong Irwinville quintet coached by a future Georgia Sports Hall of Fame inductee, Wallace "Country" Childs. The game was played in Irwinville on December 10, 1948, with Irwinville winning by three points: 30-27.

Perry had beaten Irwinville three weeks earlier on November 24 at the Perry gym. In the earlier game, Perry, behind 20 to 16 at the halftime, rallied during the final two minutes to come from behind in a gut-wrenching thriller, 35 to 33. During the final half, Gray and Peyton hit from all angles as Perry outscored their opponents by six points, 19 to 13, offsetting Irwinville's four-point halftime lead and providing a slim two-point margin for victory. Perry's victory was significant as these Irwinville players formed the nucleus of a team that would win back-to-back state titles in 1950 and 1951, winning 78 consecutive games without a defeat.

Perry-35	Irwinville-33
Riley-5	Gentry-12
Peyton-13	Dove-6
Gray-17	Reeves-2
Chapman	Hester-2
Hickson	Register-9

Subs: Perry: Satterfield, Whitworth; Irwinville: Gordon-2
Score at half: Irwinville-20, Perry-16
Officials: George and Lasseter

Panthers knock-off unbeaten Canton

As the season progressed, the Panthers were gaining momentum in every game. On January 24, 1949, at the local gym, Perry toppled Canton, one of the best teams in Georgia—touting a string of 15-consecutive victories—from the ranks of the unbeaten by a score of 35 to 34. The defense was spearheaded by Ed Chapman, who held Canton's high scoring guards in check while sinking back in the zone defense and constantly double-teaming Canton's pivot man. Billy Gray scored 14 points with smart faking around the basket. Mack Peyton's shots were not falling in the first half, but he found the range in the last stanza and wound up with 12 key points down the stretch. Seabie Hickson did an outstanding job on the backboards until he fouled out late in the third quarter. Bobby Satterfield played his usual smooth game as floor general, setting up Perry's offense and passing the ball to the open man. Also performing well were Bubber Riley and Bobby Sutton.

Sweet Revenge

The Panthers, smarting from an earlier two-point loss inflicted by Fort Valley at Fort Valley's gym, met the Green Wave for a return engagement two weeks later in Perry on January 21, 1949. Perry gained sweet revenge on Fort Valley, walloping the Green Wave 41-32. Ed Chapman and Billy Gray led the scoring with 13 points each. Rounding out the offense were Bobby Satterfield with 6 points, Seabie Hickson-5, and Mack Peyton-4.

A major factor influencing the outcome of the game was the absence of Fort Valley's big center, James Hutto, during much of the contest. He ran into foul trouble early in the game, committing four fouls before the end of the second quarter. Coach Ned Warren pulled Hutto out of the action and didn't return him to the fray until the final quarter. Within two minutes after Hutto reentered the game, he made his fifth foul and fouled out. Without Hutto, Fort Valley lost its rebounding edge which had been the difference in the first game. Adding to Fort Valley's woes was the fact that mainstays Billy Cannon and Gordon McDaniel also fouled out. With three Green Wave starters fouling out, Fort Valley's fans became very vocal, complaining about the officiating and booing the referees. Shouts were heard accusing Perry of "home cooking" at their local gym and paying the referees.

Perry-41	Fort Valley-32
Peyton-4	Mullis-2
Satterfield-6	McDaniel-2
Gray-13	Hutto-4
Chapman-13	Cannon-10
Hickson-5	Young-3

Subs: Perry: Riley, Sutton; Fort Valley: Strickland-3, Hopkins-6, Rowland-2
Officials: George and Hutto

Fight Erupts After Game

Still savoring an earlier 20 to 18 win over Perry on January 7, Fort Valley fans had packed into the Perry gym that night, January 21, expecting to see their Green Wave beat the Panthers again. Fort Valley fans felt they had a legitimate shot at the district and state titles, especially with big James Hutto at center and a strong supporting cast of shooters and ball-handlers. Yet they knew that arch-rival Perry stood in their path. A lot of bad blood was evident at the game. Every call by the referees was met with a chorus of boos. Losing to Perry was the worst possible fate, and the Fort Valley fans felt the referees were taking the game from them.

When the hotly contested game ended with Perry on the long end of a 41 to 32 score, the animosity in the stands reached a fever pitch. Fans from both sides spilled onto the playing floor and began milling around. They were jawing at one another; some were shoving. This author witnessed the entire spectacle. Being a 13-year old, eighth-grader at the time, I was scared to death and fearful a big brawl was going to erupt. For my personal safety, I contemplated crawling out one of the gym windows at the top of the stands.

Sitting directly behind the Perry bench about four seats up, I watched the Perry team and its coaches being led through the crowd and toward the dressing room by two state patrolmen who had attended the game. Suddenly, I saw a Fort Valley fan, a blond-headed man in his 20s, heading straight toward Assistant Perry Coach Bob Shuler. As he ran up to Shuler, he shouted a demeaning epithet right in Shuler's face. I can't repeat what he called Schuler but you can imagine. Shuler, without thinking, flicked a right hand lead, so hard that it would have knocked over a mule. The guy went down as if he had been struck by a bolt of lightening. He wasn't moving. Several Fort Valley fans rushed to his side. The cold-cocked fan couldn't walk on his own steam, so they carried him off the court and out of the gym. The report came back that they were rushing him to the hospital with a possible broken jaw.

L-R: Ed Chapman (9), Seabie Hickson, Billy Gray (2), Mack Peyton, and Coach Staples (facing away with hat) make their way to dressing room following heated game with Fort Valley.

Some Fort Valleyans contended that Shuler hit the fan with a sucker punch, but there is nothing further from the truth. I was there and witnessed the incident less than 20 feet away. Shuler was clearly provoked. The entire Perry community rallied around Coach Shuler. Although the incident infuriated the Fort Valley faithful, the Perry folks felt that Shuler was justified in defending himself.

Shuler was the last man anyone should want to provoke. He was about 6' 1" and weighed 195 pounds; not an ounce of fat, very strong and muscular. He could throw a discus almost the length of the school house, and no one in the high school could out-distance him in the shot put. He had been a star basketball player at Mercer University, and, being an accomplished student of the game, was able to teach Perry players the finer points of offensive and defensive basketball.

Georgia High School Association investigates the fight

The Sportsmanship Committee of the Georgia High School

Association (GHSA) investigated the incident. Serving on the committee were Charley Rogers of Lanier, GHSA president; John (Stooge) Davis of Rome High School; W. P. Pickett, superintendent of schools at Winder; Harold McNabb, principal of Albany High School; and Sam Burke, GHSA secretary.

Evidence gathered by the committee substantiated that Shuler had struck the Fort Valley fan after an exchange of words. The report disclosed that several Fort Valley fans, including the one struck by Shuler, resented the officiating of referee Bill McDavid, and had shouted insults at him during the game.

The "Macon Telegraph", dated February 19, 1949, reported that the Fort Valley fan hit by Shuler suffered "three jaw fractures and the loss of six teeth." The GHSA committee placed Bob Shuler on probation for one year. The "Macon Telegraph" article further disclosed that Fort Valley was also placed on probation because "the committee felt the Fort Valley fans' conduct was primarily the responsibility of Fort Valley High School officials and the abusive language was the primary cause for the disturbance." The committee recognized the fact that Shuler

Bob Shuler in 1949

"was subjected to abusive language, but as a school official should have controlled his temper." The committee commended Coach Eric Staples of Perry and Ned Warren of Fort Valley for their efforts in controlling the situation which was termed "full of dynamite" by the GHSA report.

GHSA secretary Sam Burke issued this statement: "Any misconduct on the part of players, school officials or spectators from either of the offending towns will mean that their school will be barred from high school competition and might also mean the loss of their accredited standing."

Following the GHSA sanctions, Fort Valley School Superintendent

Ernest Anderson made the decision unilaterally that Fort Valley would not play Perry except in tournament competition. This meant the two schools would never again meet during the regular season. Mr. Anderson felt that the tensions were too great between the schools and did not want to risk disqualification from high school athletics. In view of the possible consequences of a repeat incident, Anderson made a good decision. His ruling remained in effect throughout the 1950s and '60s with the two schools playing each other only in district and state tournaments.

Combat Ace

Coach Shuler was born January 3, 1920, in Griffin, Georgia, where his father was the school superintendent. After attending college for a while, World War II broke out and Shuler joined the Army Air Corps where he served as a combat pilot flying P-38 and P-40 aircraft. Shuler flew 138 missions and logged more than 300 combat hours. He was officially credited with destroying seven enemy aircraft, Japanese Zeros, in the Pacific Theater, becoming a renowned "Combat Ace." He also downed seven more enemy planes unofficially and miraculously survived three crashes, two at sea and one on an airstrip. On one occasion he downed four enemy planes in a single aerial dog fight.

When discharged in 1945, Shuler was a highly decorated officer, holding a Distinguished Flying Cross with an Oak-Leaf Cluster and an Air Medal with 18 Oak-Leaf Clusters. After the war, he completed his education at Mercer University where he became a star basketball player.

Bob Shuler came to Perry High School in the fall of 1948 as a science teacher and assistant basketball coach. He was loved by the student body and was an invaluable assistant to Coach Staples. Shuler was recalled to active duty in September 1949 as an F-51 instructor pilot and stationed at Craig AFB, Alabama. Perry High student, Charles Bledsoe, wrote this glowing tribute to him in Perry's "Home Journal": "Mr. Shuler has gained the admiration of every student and faculty member with whom he has been associated. Perry High regrets, indeed, that we have to lose one of our most valuable assets to our school, but at the same time, wish to Mr. Shuler and his family the best possible luck."

When the Korean War erupted in late June 1950, Shuler was transferred to Pusan, Korea. During the next year, he flew 100 extremely dangerous low-altitude close support and interdiction missions, destroying enemy troops, arms, and equipment. When he left Korea, he had accumulated 238 combat missions in two different wars.

He retired from the Air Force in 1973 with the rank of full colonel and moved to Dublin, where he resided until his death on March 9, 2001, following an extended stroke-induced illness. His wife, the former Barbara Fay Bedingfield, still lives in Dublin. During the night of the fight, January 21, 1949, Barbara said she wasn't at the game, but Shuler's brother Harold was. Barbara had to stay at home to care for her little son, Lucien Bennett Shuler, who was running a fever. The Shulers had two other children, Barbara and Susan.

The Fort Valley Fan

Nothing can be gained by mentioning the name of the Fort Valley fan involved in the fight. He is now an upstanding citizen, has raised a fine family, and is well respected in his church and in his community. In later years this writer had an opportunity to talk with Bob Shuler about the incident. Shuler stated, "I wish I could have had the presence of mind to ignore the insult, but I was young at the time and felt the need to defend myself, especially since the threatening insult was unexpected and completely caught me off guard." In the wisdom of years, the fan, no doubt, has learned that competitiveness can spill over into unbridled anger, and Shuler, by his own admission, acknowledged that he should have exercised more self-control. It would be unfair to single out these two men for censure, for few in attendance at that game were faultless in their conduct. To be realistic, the fight was inevitable. The bad blood between the two schools had been at the boiling point for many years. Had the fight not happened on January 21, 1949, it would have happened sometime down the road.

District tournament looms ahead

Perry finished the regular season with an impressive record of 24 wins and only 5 losses, splitting with three teams it had lost to: Irwinville, Canton, and Fort Valley. In each case, Perry won on its home court and lost on the opposing team's court. There were two losses to Lanier, a large Class A school and defending state Class A champions. The Poets outdistanced the Panthers 47-30 in Perry and squeaked by the Panthers in a close encounter in Macon, 39 to 34.

Northern Division Tournament: February 14-16 at Perry

Beginning February 14, 1949, the Northern Division of the Third District Tournament began in Perry. On the first night, Perry eliminated Eastman by a score of 54 to 34. On the second night of the tournament, Perry met Warner Robins, who was picked by some observers to upset the Panthers. But the Panthers came through with a smashing 53 to 19 victory to eliminate Warner Robins in the semi-finals. On the final night of the tournament, Perry met the dreaded Fort Valley team and prevailed by a score of 40 to 35 to take the Northern Division title.

The game was incident-free as both schools knew that the fight was under investigation by the Georgia High School Association and that any misconduct would be dealt with harshly.

Southern Division Tournament: February 14-16 at Cuthbert

The Southern Division of the Third District was played in Cuthbert, Georgia. Cuthbert emerged as the division winner by defeating East Crisp.

Third District Tournament, February 18-19 at Fort Valley

The first and second place teams from each division met in Fort Valley—a double elimination tournament—to determine the Third District champion.

Perry, winner of the Northern Division, took on East Crisp, the Southern Division runner-up. Fort Valley, runner-up in the Northern Division, was pitted against Cuthbert, the Southern Division champs.

Perry trounced East Crisp, 61-19, and Fort Valley thrashed Cuthbert, 45-20. The former game was such a runaway that Perry regulars did not play the entire game against East Crisp. The scoring was balanced with many of the reserves enjoying significant playing time. Leading Perry was Billy Gray with 13 points, followed by Ed Chapman-9, Buddy Batchelor-8, Herschel Thompson-7, Rhett Milan-7, Mack Peyton-6, Bubber Riley-6, Pete Carlisle-4, and Bobby Satterfield-1.

The stage is set: Perry to meet Fort Valley for district title

Although the Panthers had split with Fort Valley during the regular season, and had beaten the Green Wave in the Northern Division playoff, they would have to replay them to lay claim to the Third District title.

Fort Valley had a strong team. If its big center, James Hutto, did not get into foul trouble, he could virtually control the boards as well as the outcome of the game. If that happened, Perry's prospects of winning would be seriously diminished. To make matters worse, the game that was supposed to be played in Perry was shifted to Fort Valley. This move was necessary to provide seating for the expected large crowd that Perry's gym could not accommodate. During the regular season, the Green Wave had edged the Panthers 20 to 18 in their first meeting in Fort Valley. Since the second game of the regular season (won by Perry) as well as the Northern Division playoff (won by Perry) were both played at Perry's gym, the Panthers had not beaten the Green Wave in Fort Valley. The entire state watched this game with keen anticipation.

Fort Valley's new $80,000 gym (built by my future father-in-law, Homer Davis) could seat more than twice as many as Perry's gym, which at capacity could hold 1200 spectators. It was agreed that Perry would furnish the referees, the ticket takers, and ushers while Fort Valley would be the visiting team on its own court.

Before the game, a public announcement was made asking the fans to observe the rules of good sportsmanship. This announcement was directed by the Georgia High School Association following its investigation of the fight at Perry on January 21. A repeat incident of that nature would be grounds for disbarment from high school athletics.

No one from Perry, including this writer, an eight grader at the time, figured the game would start off like it did. Perry fell behind early. Fort Valley, with its big, physical center controlling the backboards, seemed invincible. By halftime, Fort Valley had jumped out to a 12-point lead, 27 to 15, that seemed insurmountable. The Fort Valley fans must have thought so, for at halftime they all stood up and counted in unison from 1 to 27, then cheered mightily. The thousand or so Perry fans sank deeper into their seats in pained silence. It appeared that defeat was inevitable unless Coach Staples had something up his sleeve. We knew that Staples would make some offensive changes, but would these adjustments be enough to overcome the 12-point lead and compete with this partisan crowd that was smelling victory and poised to taunt us even more as the game progressed?

Coaching genius and a miracle finish

Perry returned to the hardwood for the second half with a completely revised offensive plan. Billy Gray, who normally played under the goal, was moved out to forward and positioned near the corner of the court. Mack Peyton and Edward Chapman were instructed to set-up on a double post.

Since Fort Valley's big center, James Hutto, was guarding Gray, this pulled Hutto out from under the basket. Staples' strategy placed the Fort Valley coach in a catch-22 predicament. If he permitted Hutto to go outside to guard Gray, Hutto could no longer defend the center lane and the area around the basket. If he didn't follow Gray outside, Gray being a great shooter, would be mismatched against a much smaller defender and would wreak havoc on the Green Wave's defense.

Within a matter of minutes, things began to happen. Perry's guards began feeding the ball to Peyton and then to Chapman on the posts. Peyton, who had failed to get loose in the first half, cracked four straight field goals from around the foul line, and Perry moved within four points. Then Ed Chapman went on a rampage, faking his defender one way, then spinning the other and driving down the middle for lay-ups. With Hutto remaining on the perimeter guarding Gray, Perry's guards, Satterfield, Hickson, and Riley, continued passing the ball to Peyton and Chapman.

At the three-minute automatic time out, the score was knotted 37-37. During the ensuing play, Chapman drove around his defender and scored a lay-up. He was fouled in the process and cashed in on the free throw. The score was now Perry-40, Fort Valley-37. With 60 seconds left in the game, Fort Valley's McDaniel connected on a field goal to move the Green Wave within one point, 40 to 39. Perry tried to freeze the ball, but the Green Wave's smothering defensive play forced two quick Perry turnovers. On their first possession after Perry's turnover, Fort Valley attempted a 25-footer from the corner, but it fell short. On its second possession, with less than 5-seconds on the clock, Fort Valley fired again from the outside for the winning basket. Perry's Mack Peyton, anticipating the shot, jumped high in the air and batted it down. The horn blew and the game was over! Perry had defeated the Green Wave and won the district championship! Now, it was Perry's time to count. One thousand cheering Perry fans stood and counted in unison from one to 40. This was Staples' 11th district championship in 16 attempts. Again, the game ended without incident as both schools were aware of the consequences of violating the terms of the probation.

Perry-40	Fort Valley-39
Satterfield	Mullis-7
Peyton-12	McDaniel-4
Gray-9	Hutto-16
Chapman-15	Young-2
Hickson-2	Cannon-1

Subs: Perry: Riley-2; Fort Valley: Roland-6, Strickland-3
Score at half: Fort Valley-27, Perry-15

Third District Class B and C tournament

Montezuma, the defending Class C state champions, won the Class C district crown for the second year in a row, so Perry had to play Montezuma, for the Class B and C district title. The game was played in Montezuma on February 26, 1949. Although Perry had defeated Montezuma three times during the regular season with victory margins ranging from a low of 7 points to a high of 38, these lop-sided scores were no indication how close the B and C championship game would be. Coach Bill Martin's Aztecs put up a fierce fight, the lead constantly changing hands with every basket, but Perry pulled away at the end with a 45 to 42 victory. The difference in the game was Perry's edge in foul shooting. Perry hit 9 of 12 attempts while Montezuma connected on only 6 of 12. Nelson led Montezuma with 23 points. Perry provided a more balanced scoring attack as the box score indicates.

Perry-45	Montezuma-42
Peyton-12	Bailey-9
Satterfield-9	Peaster-4

Gray-7   Nelson-23

Chapman-10   Sawyer-2

Hickson-5   Joe DeVaughn-1

Subs: Perry: Riley-2; Montezuma: Linton DeVaughn-3

State Class B Tournament: 3-5 March at Macon City Auditorium

Perry, employing a tenacious defense and strong rebounding, waltzed right past its first two opponents in the state meet, blasting Fulton High, 57 to 38, and outplaying LaGrange in a ball-control game, 34 to 26.

Valdosta, defending state champions, favored to win

The only team now standing in Perry's path for the state crown was the Valdosta Wildcats, defending state champs, who had beaten a strong Cochran quintet 44-42 in the semifinals in what many considered to be the hardest fought contest of the tournament. In comparison, Perry had played the Cochran Royals earlier in the season, winning by 6 points on its home court and 5 points in Cochran, both being close games. Although Perry had won one game and lost one against the powerful Irwinville Farmers, Valdosta trounced Irwinville by a 10 point margin to win the Eighth District tournament.

Two years earlier, Perry had defeated Valdosta in the state finals, but sportswriters across the state felt that Valdosta, led by all-state Carl Jones and coached by the venerable Wright Bazemore, was vastly improved and had the edge on Perry. Up to this point in the tournament Perry had won with relative ease over its first two opponents, but the Valdosta game had every indication of posing an uphill struggle for the Panthers. Did the Panthers have one more miracle finish left in Coach Staples' playbook?

Macon's City Auditorium was packed with over 2,500 screaming fans. The game started with Mack Peyton drilling a long one-hander from the side. This signature shot by Peyton brought the Perry fans to their feet. With Valdosta playing a collapsing defense around the goal to keep Billy Gray from reaching his previous night's high of 16 points, Staples ordered Chapman, Satterfield, and Hickson to crack down from the top of the circle. This they did with amazing accuracy and the Panthers moved ahead by a 12-6 margin at the end of the first quarter. With the Perry team playing a stingy defense, Valdosta couldn't seem to find the net. As the second quarter started, Valdosta gambled that Perry could not maintain its torrid shooting pace and opted to stay in its tight zone defense around the basket. To the Wildcats' dismay, Perry continued to score effectively from the outside, increasing its lead to 13 points at halftime. The score stood Perry-24 and Vadosta-11.

Although leading by 13 points, Perry could ill afford to let up in the second half because Valdosta's tall and burly center, Griffin, had been a terror on the boards and, should Valdosta come back after intermission and start connecting, the Panthers might find themselves in deep trouble. Perry's fans knew it was too early to get their hopes up since the Wildcats had won the tournament the previous year and returned several starters, including all-state forward Carl Jones.

During the second half, Valdosta matched Perry basket-for-basket, but could not overcome the halftime deficit. Perry lost three starters via the foul route: Bobby Satterfield going out late in the third quarter; Seabie Hickson and Ed Chapman in the closing minutes of the fourth quarter. Bubber Riley filled in superbly for Satterfield and played an excellent floor game. Bobby Sutton and Rhett Milan played well as replacements for Hickson and Chapman. When the game-ending horn sounded, the score stood Perry-42, Valdosta-30. Coach Staples had won his second state crown in three years. By capturing the state crown in 1947 and 1949, Perry joined Vienna and Canton as the only schools to win the State Class B title more than once. Vienna and Canton, however, had each won three state titles.

Perry (3rd dist) -42	Valdosta (8th dist)-30
Chapman-7	Jones-5
Peyton-10	Hill-3
Gray-16	Griffin-15
Hickson-2	Mote-2
Satterfield-6	Wallace-5

Subs: Perry: Riley, Sutton-1, Milan; Valdosta-Alderman

1949 Class B All-State team

Billy Gray-Perry

Ed Chapman-Perry
Mack Peyton-Perry
Horace Bellflower-Cochran
Robert Manning-Cochran
Freddie Wimberly-Cochran
Carl Jones-Valdosta
Archibald Griffin-Valdosta
Charles Hipsher-Marietta
Theo Hampton-LaGrange

Perry's 1949 season at a glance:

Home Games

Opponent	Date	Score	Winner
Warner Robins	15-Oct	61-22	Perry
Montezuma	29-Oct	30-23	Perry
Cochran	5-Nov	60-32	Perry
Warner Robins	23-Nov	41-23	Perry
Irwinville	24-Nov	35-33	Perry
Montezuma	30-Nov	63-22	Perry
Cochran	3-Dec	50-44	Perry
Conyers	31-Dec	43-25	Perry
Conyers	1-Jan	41-18	Perry
Spalding High	11-Jan	72-20	Perry
Canton	14-Jan	35-34	Perry
Fort Valley	21-Jan	41-32	Perry
Lanier	25-Jan	30-47	Lanier
Albany	1-Feb	54-33	Perry
Hawkinsville	4-Feb	61-27	Perry
Adel	11-Feb	50-36	Perry

Games Away

Warner Robins	22-Oct	44-19	Perry
Montezuma	12-Nov	45-25	Perry
Cochran	19-Nov	39-35	Perry
Warner Robins	7-Dec	51-40	Perry

Opponent	Date	Score	Winner
Irwinville	10-Dec	27-30	Irwinville
Adel	11-Dec	25-15	Perry
Cochran	17-Dec	45-31	Perry
Lanier	5-Jan	35-39	Lanier
Fort Valley	7-Jan	18-20	Fort Valley
Hawkinsville	18-Jan	64-28	Perry
Canton	28-Jan	33-37	Canton
Spalding High	29-Jan	64-20	Perry
Albany	12-Feb	54-32	Perry

Regional Meet

Eastman	14-Feb	54-38	Perry
Warner Robins	15-Feb	53-19	Perry
Fort Valley	16-Feb	40-35	Perry

District B Finals

East Crisp	18-Feb	61-19	Perry
Fort Valley	19-Feb	40-39	Perry

3rd Dist B & C

Montezuma	26-Feb	45-42	Perry

State Meet

Fulton High	3-Mar	57-38	Perry
LaGrange	4-Mar	34-26	Perry
Valdosta	5-Mar	42-30	Perry

Best team in 20 years: 1953 team

Perry' 1953 team. Standing, L-R: David Gray, Billy Powell, Jackie Miller, Olin Logue, Joe Leverette, Billy Brock, Billy Beckham, Martin Beeland, John Malone, James Logue, Franklin May, and Tommy Mobley. Kneeling, L-R: Larry Elder-manager, Coach Eric Staples, and Assistant Coach Frank Holland

Would Staples have to eat his words?

Before the 1953 team played its first game, Coach Staples was quoted in the newspapers as saying, "This is the best team I have coached here in 20 years." Eric Staples began coaching at Perry in 1933. Since I was a member of the 1953 club, my teammates and I could not believe that Fessor, usually conservative in his praise, would go out on a limb like that. He always had his reasons for his assertions, but trying to figure them out was impossible as he sometimes dealt in psychological subtleties. He was indeed a sly old fox and you never knew what he was up to; in fact, rival towns referred to him as the "Gray Fox." Maybe he was trying to motivate us. Who knows? One thing I do know, however, is that his public assessment placed us under extreme pressure from the day he uttered it. The 1953 team was one of Perry's tallest teams and it had depth. If the starters weren't doing the job, Coach Staples had plenty of bench strength to rely upon.

A year earlier, the 1952 team fought gallantly and came within two points of upsetting Fort Valley in the third district tournament, played at Fort Valley's gym. The undefeated Fort Valley team, featuring twin towers Ed Beck and Pat Swan and such outstanding players as Richard Aultman, Jimmy Thompson, and Strib McCants, captured the state title in 1952 and was considered to be the best team in Fort Valley history.

Harris Satterfield and James Mauldin, sparkplugs on the 1952 squad, and Dick Hardy were lost to graduation. Perry returned David Gray, Joe Leverette, Billy Beckham and Billy Powell from the 1952 squad with a capable group of reserves. Adding to the team's height going into the season was the acquisition of Billy Brock, a 6' 3" forward who had moved to Perry from Lafayette, Georgia. Billy's father, a state patrolman, had been reassigned to the Perry patrol station. Other outstanding prospects were James Logue, Olin Logue, Franklin May, Tommy Mobley, Jackie Miller, Martin Beeland, and John Malone.

Adding to Perry's fortunes was Coach Frank Holland, who joined the Perry staff as assistant coach. Holland had been head coach at Chauncey and Byron and was considered one of the best basketball minds in Georgia.

Fourteen straight victories without a loss

By Christmastime Perry had won 14 straight basketball games, averaging 55 points per game and holding its opponents to a 34 point average. At this stage in the season, it was obvious that Perry had a high-powered offense that could light up the scoreboard and a tough defense that had shut down some top teams.

Lanier Poets and Perry Panthers to clash in Macon

The game was scheduled for Wednesday night, January 7, 1953. "Macon Telegraph" sports editor, Sam Glassman, wrote in his editorial: "Staples has been coaching almost as long as (Selby) Buck has at Lanier, and has won 13 district championships, two state titles, and state runner-up twice. His teams are considered among the best coached year in and year out in the state. For the first time in many years the Panthers will have some height and they possess one of their strongest benches." Glassman observed, "A keen rivalry has been built up over the last eight or ten years between Lanier and Perry. It has been a good, clean rivalry and even though the Poets are in a higher classification, and have won most of the games, the games during the past years have been close and exciting. Both teams are well coached and their play is of the highest standard."

The Poets were coached by Selby Buck, who was considered one of the best basketball coaches in Georgia. Buck was inducted into the Georgia Sports Hall of Fame three years later, in 1956. The game had every indication of being a battle of the titans. Since Lanier was a Class AA school and had a decided advantage over Perry, a smaller Class B school, the motivation to defeat the Poets was always strong. The largest crowd ever to witness a Perry-Lanier game, approximately 2,000 fans, came to Macon's City Auditorium—about 1,000 of them from Perry.

Was this the team Staples said it was?

The Poets started out with a fast break and worked their offensive patterns with precision, running up a quick 9 to 1 lead. When the quarter was over, Lanier had moved out front by an unbelievable 21 to 5 margin. The Perry team looked bewildered. Any lesser team would have folded its tents; however, with Coach Staples substituting freely and making defensive adjustments, the Panthers fought back to pull within four points, 48 to 52, with 90 seconds left to play. The Poets froze the ball the remainder of the game and, by cashing in on fouls committed by Perry, emerged victorious, 54 to 48.

The bubble had burst. Lanier coach Selby Buck was quoted in the "Macon Telegraph" as saying, "by their play the Panthers did not look as strong as some of the other quintets to come out of Perry....But they are a fine ball club and are going to get rough. The fact that they did not fold up after that sensational first quarter by our boys stamps them as a fine basketball team."

Perry loses second game of season

The Perry Panthers, after suffering its first defeat of the season, an embarrassing loss to Lanier on January 6, 1953—especially the humiliation of being down 21 to 5 at the end of first quarter—journeyed down to Hawkinsville on January 13.

Billy Powell had respiratory flu and, although he started the game, he could play for only short intervals without rest. He was unable to finish the final quarter of play. The Hawkinsville Red Devils led by their two big men, Jim Eaton and W. L. Rewis, downed Perry 44 to 40 in a very physical and hard-fought game. The Red Devils big men, Eaton and Rewis, controlled the backboards and scored 11 points each. Hawkinsville's scoring was balanced with stars Bobby Joe Goode and Ben Lee both garnering 9 points, and Ellis Smith bagging 4.

This was Perry's second loss in one week's time. Was this really Coach Staples' best team in 20 years?

Defeat Avenged

Two weeks later on January 27, Hawkinsville met Perry in the famous Panther den located 22 miles up the road on Highway 341. Perry trailed the hustling Hawkinsville five, 11 to 10, at the end of first quarter, 16 to 14 at halftime, and 30 to 28 after the third quarter, but exploded for 20 points in the final quarter. A key factor in the victory was the strong rebounding of Joe Leverette and Billy Beckham against Hawkinsville's two big men, Eaton and Rewis. David Gray, Franklin May, and Tommy Mobley played outstanding defense and excellent floor games against the talented Hawkinsville's backcourt of Goode, Lee, and Smith. Billy Powell caught fire in the fourth quarter and led Perry's scoring with 25 points.

Perry-48	Hawkinsville-40
Powell-25	Smith-11
Leverette-6	Rewis-8
Beckham-5	Eaton-9
Gray-9	B. Lee-6
May-3	Goode-6

Subs: Perry: Mobley; Hawkinsville: Dunn
Score at half: Hawkinsville-16, Perry-14

Return engagement with Lanier

A month later, on February 10, 1953, the Panthers had a chance to redeem themselves against the Lanier Poets. A capacity crowd of 1,200 fans occupied every bit of seating space at the Perry gym and practically overflowed onto the playing floor. Some spectators were hanging from ladders outside the gym windows.

Another display of coaching genius

After Perry played them in early January, Lanier had developed a full-court press that was devastating. Many teams couldn't get the ball past center court. Utilizing the press continuously, Lanier would crush some teams by halftime and play substitutes during most of the second half. It was pitiful to watch the way Lanier's press would destroy teams.

Coach Staples devised a strategy to cope with Lanier's stifling press. Before the Lanier game, we practiced it over and over. When Perry brought the ball in-bounds, usually after a Lanier score, Franklin May was instructed to pass the ball to me under the basket. At the same time, Billy Beckham, our 6' 3" center, would line up near center court. Once May passed the ball to me, Beckham would break toward me as if he were looking for the outlet pass. Once he reached the foul line, he would quickly reverse directions and speed down court toward the Perry basket. Coach Staples told me to dribble the ball toward the corner to draw the Lanier defenders. After the second dribble, Staples instructed me to launch the ball two-handed—not one-handed mind you—up through the rafters of the Perry gym so it would drop on the foul line of the opposite goal. I had practiced that maneuver so much that I could drop the ball on the distant foul line with regularity. Staples said the two dribbles were necessary, not only to draw two or more Lanier defenders who would attempt to tie me up, but to allow Beckham time to come toward me, then reverse directions, and streak toward the distant foul line on the dead run. Beckham would catch the ball in full stride, the Lanier center dangling all over him, and lay it in the basket. Every time Beckham scored the crowd noise was deafening. I had never heard it so loud in Perry's gym. After Beckham had made five baskets and scored 10 points on that one play, Lanier Coach Selby Buck called time out. You guessed it. Lanier dropped out of its full-court press and met us at half court the remainder of the game. This play developed by Coach Staples was coaching genius at its best.

Lanier was ahead at halftime 26 to 25. Perry continued to score from both inside and outside and led 36 to 34 at the end of the third quarter.

With five minutes to go in the fourth and final quarter, Lanier was trailing 39 to 37. Then with a volley of baskets, the Panthers moved ahead, 48 to 38, with less than two minutes to play. As Perry went into a slow-down, possession game, the game became very rough when Lanier in desperation made some hard fouls. When the horn sounded, Perry had won over the Poets, 51 to 46. There was great jubilation in Pantherville.

Perry-51	Lanier-46
Powell-21	Crawford-5
Leverette-4	Mason-6
Beckham-19	Greene-9
Gray-3	Middlebrooks-6
May-3	Johnson-9

Subs: Lanier: Gibson-9, J. Kitchens-2; Perry: Mobley-1,
Score at half: Lanier-26, Perry-25

Regular season ends with a flourish

During the final eight days of the regular season, February 6 through February 14, Perry beat Lanier once (51-46 in Perry), and two Atlanta AA schools in home and home engagements, Sylvan High (55-30 at Sylvan and 77-41 at Perry) and Brown High (51-47 in Perry and 50-35 at Brown). Over the years Perry fans always received immense gratification when Perry beat the larger Atlanta schools.

The Panthers ended regular season play with a record of 26 wins and only two losses (to Lanier and Hawkinsville). Both losses were avenged.

Third District Tournament: February 24-27 at Perry

Most sportscasters predicted that Fort Valley and Perry, who had lost to Fort Valley in the district tournament the previous year, would meet in the finals of the district tournament. Both Fort Valley and Perry had split with Lanier during the regular season.

Fort Valley, with its top guns returning from its 1952 state championship team, was the odds-on favorite to win the tournament. Standing in Fort Valley's path, however, was the Bobby Gentry-coached Hawkinsville squad who would play the Green Wave on the first night of the tournament. This Hawkinsville team had snapped Fort Valley's 45-game winning streak during the season, and its big men, 6' 8" Jim Eaton, and 6'5" W. L. Rewis, matched up well on the backboards with Fort Valley's 6'7" Ed Beck and 6'5" Pat Swan.

Fort Valley De-throned

Not unexpected, Hawkinsville became the giant killer by upsetting the defending Class B state champions, Fort Valley, 39 to 34, on the strength of superior rebounding by Jim Eaton and W. L. Rewis and the shooting of Bobby Joe Goode who scored 17 points for the night, 12 in the second half.

Perry defeats Marion County in quarterfinals and Buena Vista in semifinals

Perry received a bye the first night and on the next night thrashed Marion County, 56 to 32. In the semi-finals Perry would face a strong Buena Vista quintet led by the high scoring Joe Lowe, who scored 35 points in Buena Vista's defeat of a good Warner Robins team, 67 to 35. Lowe posed a significant offensive threat to Perry as he equaled the scoring for the entire Warner Robins' team.

Franklin May holds high-scoring Joe Lowe to eight points

Perry's outstanding defensive star, Franklin May, held Buena Vista's Joe Lowe to just 8 points as Perry surged past Buena Vista, 54 to 37. Billy Powell led Perry's scoring with 20 points. Billy Beckham and David Gray tallied 13 points apiece. With Hawkinsville nosing by Sycamore 45 to 38, this meant the Red Devils would face the Panthers for the district crown.

A thriller in the making: Perry vs. Hawkinsville

The Perry-Hawkinsville match-up lived up to its pre-game speculation. Perry's gym was packed to capacity with fans cheering wildly throughout the contest. The doors were closed after 1,200 fans had poured into the gym, but this did not stop the most zealous fans. Some climbed up to the lofty gym windows using outside ladders and clung to the window sashes. Others, after reaching the window, shinnied over to the gym rafters and hung there.

With Hawkinsville's Jim Eaton controlling the boards, Perry was getting one shot and one shot only at the basket. The big and physical 6' 8", 250-pound center was cleaning the backboards on every errant shot by Perry. The game turned into a slow-down, possession battle with each team working the ball around for the high percentage shots. The game was very tight. Perry had a one-point lead at the end of the first quarter and held a slim 16 to 14 halftime advantage. At the end of the third quarter Perry moved slightly ahead, 25 to 20, but Hawkinsville was not to be denied; with four minutes left to play, the score was tied 30 to 30. With three minutes to play, the score was still knotted at 32-all.

With less than two minutes remaining, Hawkinsville went into a deep freeze, waiting for the final shot, but the Panthers, being careful not to foul, stayed a safe distance away. With 10 seconds on the clock, as Hawkinsville made its move for the winning score, Perry's Joe Leverette stole the ball, passed to Billy Beckham, who in turn hit Billy Powell crossing the centerline. With Red Devil defenders swarming all around Powell, he released a jump shot at the top of the key that rimmed out as the buzzer sounded.

Overtime

Perry got possession after the center court tip-off and began playing ball control. David Gray, a great clutch foul shooter, was fouled. He received a one, if one, free-throw opportunity and sank both shots. Perry moved ahead 34 to 32. The next time down the court, Perry resumed its stalling tactics. Again Gray was fouled by the same Hawkinsville player. He calmly walked up the line and drilled both gratis tosses. Time ran out and Perry prevailed 36 to 32. This was a thriller for the ages.

Perry-36	Hawkinsville-32
Powell-10	Rewis-7
Leverette-4	E. Smith-8
Beckham-7	Eaton-11
Gray-9	B. Lee-6
May-6	Goode

Subs: Perry-none; Hawkinsville-none

Score at half: Perry-16, Hawkinsville-14
Officials: Smith and Summey

David Gray: Hero of the Game

David Gray, playing his last game before the home crowd, was the hero of the contest. There never was a more pressure-packed moment in Perry basketball than when David Gray sank those four consecutive foul shots in the overtime period. After the game, David told me that, before the referee handed him the ball and he took his first shot, he gazed toward the fans standing against the wall behind the basket and spotted Aldene Lasseter, a star player on Perry's 1935-37 teams. David said Aldene's face looked "pale and ashen," indicating Aldene was vicariously involved in this hard-fought game and feeling the pressure along with the rest of us.

What happened between the regulation game and the overtime period?

Everyone was so excited on the Perry sidelines. Waiting for the overtime to start was stressful. We didn't know what to do. One of the team members suggested we pray, so we prayed the Lord's Prayer together.

Lady in wheel chair forgets broken leg

Cooper Jones, the owner of a Perry pecan business, stated that his wife, who had been using a wheel chair since she broke her leg, got so excited over the radio broadcast of the game that she got up out of the wheel chair, hobbled across the room, and sat in a rocker.

Third District B and C championship game

Perry would play Oglethorpe for the Class B and C district title. The game was played on March 3 at Fort Valley's gym with 1,500 fans in attendance. Coach Jimmy Maffett's Oglethorpe Eagles had soundly defeated Coach Bill Martin's powerful and talented Montezuma five to capture the Class C district crown.

How would Perry stop Oglethorpe's W. C. Jones?

To win, Perry would have to find a way to stop the great W. C. Jones, one of Georgia's most prolific scorers. Jones, averaging 25 points a game, was virtually unstoppable. Perry's top defensive player, Franklin May, was assigned to guard Jones. Coach Staples instructed May to play Jones (Oglethorpe's forward) heavy on one side and not to let Jones drive down the baseline where he was so devastating. When Jones elected to drive toward the foul lane, other Perry defenders, employing a shifting defense, would clog up the middle, stopping Jones' forward progress.

May Held Jones to eleven points

Franklin May held Jones to 11 points and Perry outscored the Eagles 48 to 40 in the championship tilt. Franklin May's outstanding defensive play will be long remembered by Perry players and fans. Billy Powell led Perry's scoring with 21 points. Joe Leverette added 10 followed by Billy Beckham with 7, Franklin May-5, David Gray-3, and Billy Brock-2

Perry-48	Oglethorpe-40
Powell-21	W. C. Jones-11
Leverette-10	Head-3
Beckham-7	Lowe-11
Gray-3	Hunter-9
May-5	M. L. Jones-6

Subs: Perry: Brock-2; Oglethorpe: Kitchens
Score at half: Perry-24; Oglethorpe-17

State Tournament: March 11-14 at Macon's City Auditorium

First game: Perry vs. North Habersham

Perry jumped out in front of North Habersham 18 to 6 at the end of the first eight minutes of play and was never threatened for the remainder of the game. The final score was Perry-54, North Habersham-35.

Billy Beckham and Joe Leverette were standouts on the backboards. Franklin May and David Gray played outstanding defensive games. Also playing good floor games were Billy Brock-2 points, Martin Beeland, and Tommy Mobley. Billy Powell led all scorers with a 28 point outburst, followed by David Gray with 13.

Quarterfinal game: Perry vs. Thomson

Against a Thomson team that had won 19 games and lost only two during the regular season, the Panthers charged out to a quick 20 to 6 first quarter advantage, and increased its margin to a comfortable 37 to 11 halftime lead. Perry's defense was its strong suit as it held a Thomson team that had averaged 65 points a game to only 11 first-half markers. The Panthers, playing a sharper game than they did the previous night, blistered Thomson in the quarterfinal game, 76 to 41.

Coach Eric Staples essentially retired his starting five after the half and used every one of his reserves during the last two quarters. When ninth grader, Percy Hardy, the tournament's smallest player at 5' 1", sank a long, one-handed shot from the outside as the third quarter horn sounded, the crowd gave him a standing ovation.

Joe Leverette and David Gray led Perry with 13 and 12 points respectively. Billy Beckham and Billy Powell each scored 10, and Franklin May hit for 6 points. Other Perry players contributing to the win were Billy Brock-2, John Malone-2, Percy Hardy-2, Martin Beeland-4, Tommy Mobley-3, Jackie Miller-5, William Harrison-1, Sam Nunn, Virgil Peavy-2, and James Scarborough-4.

Semifinal game: Perry vs. Homerville

"Playing as calmly as though walking their dates down Washington Avenue in Perry on a Sunday afternoon, the Eric Staples – coached Panthers, crashed into the Class B finals with a convincing 59 to 46 win over Homerville," the "Macon Telegraph" reported. "The Panthers, who won 29 while losing only two during the regular season, went about the business of winning in as workmanship-like a manner as would a bookkeeper getting a trial balance. Showing very few expressions on their faces beyond a smile and a handshake for their opponents after the game, the Panthers were never threatened."

Panthers' Board of Strategy

The Macon newspaper aptly described Perry's defense: "The Panthers' board of strategy which consists of Staples and Frank Holland, a veteran hoop coach in his own right who put out outstanding teams at Chauncey not too long ago, figured how to stop the big man, (Homerville's) Benny Gene Leviton. How well they did this can be seen from the fact that Leviton scored 30 points against the strong Cassville team Thursday, but got only 10 against the Panthers."

Throughout the game Perry played possession basketball–passing and dribbling until one of the Homerville players was screened off and then driving for the basket. The final score was Perry-59, Homerville-46.

Perry's starting five had a balanced offensive attack: Billy Powell-19, Billy Beckham-12, David Gray-10, Franklin May-8, and Joe Leverette-6. Gray along with May played smart in Perry's shifting man-to-man defense. Leverette and Beckham led Perry's rebounding. Reserves Billy Brock, Martin Beeland-4, and Tommy Mobley fit perfectly into Perry's game plan.

State championship game: Perry vs. Clarkston

The largest crowd of the tournament came to see the championship game. Approximately 3,500 excited fans, taking up every available seat in Macon's City Auditorium and many standing in the aisles, came to see the Perry Panthers take on the highly rated Clarkston Angoras, who many observers felt had the superior team. Coach Staples for the first time unveiled a play called the "button hook" that was designed to counter Clarkston's outstanding defense with multiple picks and screens and rotating offensive players from one side of the court to the other. The play worked to perfection as Perry led the tall and talented Clarkston Angoras 16 to 14 at the end of the first quarter and 29 to 22 at the half.

Perry held a 39 to 27 lead midway the third period, but Clarkston crept back to move within two points, 39 to 37. At this point Franklin May, Billy Beckham, and Jackie Miller scored in rapid succession to increase Perry's lead by ten points, 50 to 40, as the third quarter ended.

Staples calls for freeze with 1:40 on clock to protect lead

In the fourth quarter, with 1:40 remaining in the game, Clarkston had outscored the Panthers, and moved to within two points, 59 to 57. At this point Coach Staples called timeout. He instructed his team to install a three-man weave out front and to freeze the ball to draw fouls by Clarkston players trying to steal the ball. This strategy worked exactly as Staples had planned. During the last 45 seconds of the contest, two Panthers were fouled and dropped in four clutch free throws: Joe Leverette dropped in two, then David Gray—whose clutch foul shooting won the third district title—followed with two more to seal the victory.

A squad Coach Staples had called "the best team I have coached here in 20-years" before the season even opened had narrowly defeated a truly great Clarkston basketball team coached by Jim Owen by a score of 63 to 57.

Powell led all scorers with 28 points. Also leading the Panther attack were Franklin May, who connected for 14 points, Billy Beckham tallied 7, Joe Leverette-5, Jackie Miller-5, and David Gray-4. A decisive factor in the game was the strong rebounding of Joe Leverette, Billy Beckham, and Jackie Miller against their much taller opponents.

Sports editor Sam Glassman, in his lead story in "The Macon Telegraph" the next morning, commented on Powell's scintillating offensive display: "The largest crowd of the tournament, taking up every seat and with fans standing in every bit of available space, was treated to the greatest one-man shooting exhibition of the meet by the black-haired Billy Powell of the Panthers. This dead-eyed sharpshooter from anywhere within 30 feet of the basket scored 28 points as he paced the Panthers to their third Class B title...Perry High has had some great basketball stars down through the years in Billy Gray, Mack Peyton, Walter Gray, and Allen Martin, but this brilliant performance by Powell will live forever in the memories of the large contingent from Houston County."

Glassman added, "Coach Eric Staples tabbed his Perry High Panthers 'the best team I have coached here in 20 years' before the season even opened, and the veteran and most able mentor had nothing to detract after his charges had defeated Clarkston's Angoras, 63 to 57, for the Class B Georgia High School championship last night before approximately 3,500 excited fans."

Perry's third state title

This was Perry's third Class B state championship, placing the school in a tie with Vienna and Canton, who also had won three state Class B crowns.

Perry-63   **Clarkston-57**

Powell-28   DeFoor-4

Leverette-5   Cottingham-16

Beckham-7   Martin-17

May-14   Armistead-10

Gray-4   H. Williams-10

Subs: Perry: Miller-5; Clarkston: C. Williams, White

Score at half: Perry-29, Clarkston-22

Officials: Moore and Wolfe

All-State team

Billy Powell, Perry-team captain *

Billy Beckham-Perry

Leo Holland-Cochran

J. B. Bearden-Cassville

Robert Lassiter-Cochran

Charlie Martin-Clarkston

Eddie Minson-Homerville

Billy Armistead-Clarkston

Earl Tidwell-Cassville

Howard Warren-Ludowici

*Named state tournament's most outstanding performer. Although playing sparingly in runaway contest against Thomson in quarterfinals, Powell scored 85 points in four games

Honorable mention: David Gray, Franklin May, and Joe Leverette, all from Perry

A Coach's Dream: 1956 team

1956 Perry team. Seated L-R: Coach Eric Staples, Jimmy Beatty, Bennett Mauldin, Virgil Peavy, Sam Nunn, Percy Hardy, and Assistant Coach Frank Holland. Back row, L-R: Ed Beckham, Marvin Griffin, Terry Griffin, Ralph Dorsett, and Horace (Chance) Evans-manager.

Lady Luck wasn't smiling in 1955 state semi-finals

The 1955 team defeated Fort Valley for the district crown on a last minute field goal and advanced to the state semi-finals, losing to Hahira by only two points. With only seconds left and Hahira leading 61 to 59, Perry sharpshooter Sam Nunn took the final shot to tie the game and send it into overtime, but it rimmed out just as the buzzer sounded.

There are two requisites to winning a state championship: skill and luck. Lady Luck obviously wasn't smiling when Perry's all-state forward, Sam Nunn, took that last-second outside shot—from the spot where he had been so deadly all season. His shot was a perfect trajectory and heading straight toward the basket, but it brushed the inside of the rim and spun out. The following night, Lakeland beat Hahira in the state finals. The Panthers would have to wait until next year and hope that Lady Luck would smile on them should they return to the Macon City Auditorium for redemption in 1956.

All 1955 starters return except Harrison

Perry's 1956 basketball team was loaded with talent when the season began. Although Coach Staples didn't publicly say how good his 1956 team was as he did in 1953, he knew his returning squad had the potential to repeat as Third District champions and to make a strong bid for the state crown.

All starters on the previous year 1955 team, which won the district and lost in the state semi-finals, were juniors except William Harrison, its lone senior, a superb guard, playmaker, and team leader. Two other seniors on the 1955 quintet were lost to graduation: Dick Doll and Harvey Clarke. The regular season record for the 1955 club was 24-4, three of the losses being to Class AA teams. The 1955 squad did, however, beat four larger classification schools: the Lanier Poets twice: 64-50 and 54-50, Northside of Atlanta: 58-33, and Middle Georgia College B-team: 77-51.

Veteran players returning for the 1956 season were Sam Nunn, Virgil Peavy, Bennett Mauldin, Percy Hardy, and Jimmy Beatty. Nunn and Peavy had been selected to the all-state team in 1955. Top reserves from 1955, Ed Beckham and Marvin Griffin, also returned. Terry Griffin and Ralph Dorsett also moved up to the varsity.

1956 team opens season

The 1956 Perry team opened the season as a team to be reckoned with. In its first game, the Panthers recorded an impressive 54 to 50 victory over a strong Vienna quintet--the eventual Class C champions in 1956-- and won the next six games over formidable opponents.

Perry's Nemesis: Lanier Poets

Next came the Lanier Poets, the perennial nemesis of the Panthers. The Poets were a Class AA team while Perry represented a smaller Class B school. The game was played in Macon's City Auditorium before 1,250 screaming fans who saw the lead change hands 13 times and the score tied 9 times. The Poets raced out to a 13 to 11 lead at the end of the first quarter, and 24 to 21 at the half. At the end of the third period, Lanier still maintained a one point lead, 37 to 36. Perry outscored Lanier in the final stanza 17 to 14 points, which provided the margin of victory for the Panthers to ease by the Poets, 53 to 51.

The Poets outscored Perry from the floor, 19 to 18 field goals, but lost the game from the foul line. Although Perry's foul shooting percentage was only 56 percent compared to Lanier's 75 percent, Perry made more shots on 19 of 34 attempts while Lanier sank 15 of 20 gratis tosses.

Perry's scoring was led by Percy Hardy-14 points, Sam Nunn-12 points, and Virgil Peavy-12 points. Virgil Peavy was a bulwark under the boards, picking off nine rebounds. Bennett Mauldin, Jimmy Beatty, and Ed Beckham played tenacious defense in the hard-fought contest.

Perry-Lanier rematch: Poets gunning to end Perry's 18-game winning streak

Perry entered the rematch with Lanier with a serious disadvantage. Bennett Mauldin was sidelined with an ankle injury, and 5' 6" Percy Hardy, just out of the sickbed, dressed out for the game but wasn't expected to play.

The game, played at Perry's gym, was a defensive battle from the outset. Lanier led at the half 26 to 24. During the first three quarters of the game, the score changed hands 11 times and the score was even on 6 occasions. As the final period started with Lanier leading 27 to 26, Ed Beckham, who scored eight points in the game and tied with Virgil Peavy for rebounds with nine, dropped in two free throws. Virgil Peavy followed with a field goal, and the Panthers were never headed. With 2:32 left in the contest, Lanier lost forward Jimmy Chapman on personal fouls, and with him went any chance of catching the Panthers, who were ahead 38 to 35 when he exited the game. The Panthers scored 22 points in the final period while the Poets could garner only 9 points. Percy Hardy, a gutsy player still recovering from the flu, led the charge as he contributed seven of his 11 points in the fourth quarter. The final score was Perry-49, Lanier-35. This was Perry's 19th straight victory.

Virgil Peavy led Perry's scoring with 15 points followed closely by Percy Hardy with 11. Sam Nunn and Ed Beckham hit for 8 apiece. Jimmy Beatty scored 7 points and played his usual outstanding defensive game. Marvin Griffin also fit perfectly into Coach Staples' game plan.

Perry-49   **Lanier-35**
Beatty-7   Squires-4

Beckham-8	Chapman-6
Peavy-15	Cole-2
Nunn-8	Buck-18
M. Griffin	Veal-5
Hardy-11	Sheppard

Score at half: Lanier-26, Perry-24
Officials: Thornton and N. Moore

Class B Panthers battle Class AA Atlanta schools

Perry soundly defeated four larger classification Atlanta schools during the season:

Perry-62	**Southwest-46**
Perry-41	**West Fulton-35**
Perry-56	**Smith-42**
Perry-61	**Murphy-52**

Typical of the Panthers' domination over the larger Atlanta schools is evidenced by the box score of the Southwest game played in Atlanta on December 15, 1955. Although Southwest towered over the smaller Panthers, the scrappier Perry boys controlled the backboards throughout the game. Perry's "Mr. Inside," Virgil Peavy exploded for 31 points while Perry's long-range bomber Sam Nunn swished the nets for 16 points. Percy Hardy and Bennett Mauldin contributed seven and six points respectively, and reserve Ed Beckham scored 2.

Perry-62	**Soutwest-46**
Peavy-31	Callahan-7
Beatty	Gore-10
Mauldin-6	Sims
Nunn-16	Archer-23
Hardy-7	Forward-2

Subs: Perry: Beckham-2, M. Griffin; Southwest: Davis-4, Malone
Score at half: Perry-32, Southwest-20

Perry vs. Murphy

A game that Perry was not expected to win was against the strong Murphy five from Atlanta, who were touted to win the AA state championship. Murphy brought to town a tall and talented AA team that was rated as one of the strongest quintets in Atlanta and north Georgia. The game was close until Perry spurted ahead mid-way through the fourth quarter and went on to win 61 to 52. Nunn led all scorers on both teams with 21 points. Virgil Peavy chipped in 13, followed by Jimmy Beatty-11, Percy Hardy-8, Bennett Mauldin-6, and Ed Beckham-2.

Perry never learned its ABCs

The 1956 edition of the Perry Panthers produced the second undefeated regular season (first was 1935 Perry team) since Staples became coach in 1933 with an impressive record of 23 consecutive victories. The most impressive aspect of the season was Perry's eight wins over Class AA schools: four Atlanta schools, Griffin twice, and two victories over Lanier of Macon. Jim Minter, sportswriter for the "Atlanta Journal" wrote that "Perry is a basketball team that has never bothered to learn its ABCs. Or respect for the big city." Minter was implying that Perry being a smaller Class B high school routinely beat the larger Class AA Atlanta schools.

Third District Tournament Begins: Perry vs. Cuthbert

Perry drew an opening round bye in the Third District Tournament held at Fort Valley's gym, but in the second round of play on February 15, 1956, came within a whisker of being eliminated. The Panthers held an 18 to 15 lead at halftime, but Cuthbert, playing smart and aggressive basketball, moved out front by five points with time running out in regulation play. Miraculously, the Panthers came from behind and tied the score just as the buzzer sounded, sending the contest into overtime.

Would Free-throw by Cuthbert eliminate Panthers?

With three seconds left in the first overtime period, and the score tied 42-all, Cuthbert center Taylor Marchman had a one-and-one free throw opportunity, but missed the first attempt. Had Taylor sunk the shot, the game would have ended and the Panthers would have been eliminated—rendering their 23 consecutive, regular season victories for naught. Lady Luck, who frowned on the Panthers in a state semifinal game the previous year, was now smiling on the Perry team.

Brilliant Coaching Snatches Victory from Defeat

Before beginning the second and sudden death overtime, Coach Staples made an unusual change in the Panthers' alignment for the center court tip-off. Since Cuthbert's 6' 4" center, Taylor Marchman, had consistently out jumped 6' 0" Jimmy Beatty of Perry and tipped the ball to the Cuthbert forward on the right side, Coach Staples told Beatty not to jump at all, not to even touch the ball. He instructed the other four Panthers to shift immediately to the right side when the referee threw the ball up and attempt to tie up the ball after it was tipped.

This stratagem worked perfectly as Sam Nunn tied up the Cuthbert forward who received the tip. Another jump ball was called. This time Nunn and the Cuthbert forward had to jump at center court. On the tip, Sam Nunn batted the ball over the heads of the Cuthbert defenders, and Virgil Peavy picked up the ball on the dead run and went in for a lay-up. Peavy was grabbed and fouled in the process of shooting by a Cuthbert defender. Peavy calmly walked to the foul line and dropped in two free throws. Perry had dodged defeat and won the sudden death overtime, 44 to 42, on the strength of sheer coaching genius. And Lady Luck was smiling broadly!

District Semifinals: Perry vs. Sycamore

Perry played Sycamore in the semifinals of the third district tournament and emerged victorious, 56 to 43, running its undefeated string to 25 straight. Perry's scoring was led by Sam Nunn with 18 points. Virgil Peavy dropped in 14 points, Bennett Mauldin-10, Jimmy Beatty-8, Percy Hardy-4, and Ed Beckham-2.

Battle Lines Are Drawn: Perry vs. Fort Valley for District Championship

Perry would meet the Fort Valley Green Wave Friday night, February 17, 1956, for the district championship. Since athletic relations had been severed, except for tournament play after the notorious fight in 1949, the two teams had not faced each other during the regular season. Fort Valley had ample motivation to upset Perry and send the Panthers packing. The Panthers had beaten the Green Wave a year earlier on a last minute field goal to win the third district tournament. Now Perry was coming to town undefeated in 25 previous engagements. Fort Valley, by all accounts, had the team to beat Perry. Its team had suffered only a few losses, improving dramatically during the year and beating schools that earlier had beaten them. Fort Valley also had demonstrated its strength by knocking off a number of Class AA teams, including Lanier. Since both teams had held normally 60-point teams to 35 to 40-point totals, a defensive battle was brewing. One dimension of Perry's offense that may have haunted Coach Norman Faircloth of Fort Valley in his game preparations was the fact that the Panthers did not bank on one man to do the scoring. At one time or the other during the season, all five Perry starters had carried the scoring load, and this was an opposing coach's nightmare.

Approximately 3,000 spectators squeezed into the Fort Valley gym that would seat only 2,000. Screaming fans were sitting everywhere, standing everywhere, and three deep around the court. The noise was deafening. There was barely enough room for a team to bring in the ball and the referees were constantly urging the fans to move back from the sidelines. The Green Wave started the game with a flurry of baskets. The Fort Valley fans were smelling victory. By halftime, the Panthers edged forward to hold a slim 16 to 14 lead. By the end of the third quarter, Perry's offensive machine had cranked up and rolled out to a 34-22 margin. In the final period, the Green Waves were held to a meager six points while the Panthers rallied for 18 markers. Perry had decisively defeated Fort Valley 52 to 28 and chalked up its 26th consecutive victory. Virgil Peavy and Sam Nunn scored a combined 37 points, nine more than the entire Fort Valley team. Bennett Mauldin chipped in 11. Jimmy Beatty did a yeoman's job on the backboards and on defense while Perry's "Mr. Hustle," Percy Hardy, played an excellent floor game. Ed Beckham came off the bench to grab rebounds and play tough defense. Russell Vennes paced Fort Valley with 10 points.

Perry-52   **Fort Valley-28**
Peavy-19   Vennes-10

Mauldin-11   Brand-1
Beatty-2   Hutto-3
Nunn-18   Wheaton-4
Hardy-2   Harper-4

Subs: Perry: Beckham; Fort Valley: Young-2, Anthoine-4, and Sutton
Score at half: Perry-16, Fort Valley-14
Officials: Satterfield and Wolf.

Third District B & C championship game: Perry vs. Vienna

The Perry Panthers, Class B champs, and the Vienna Cubs, the
Class C winners, were paired to play for the Third District B and C
championship. Perry had defeated Vienna twice during the season, a 54
to 50 win in the first game of the season played at the Vienna gym on
November 23, 1955, and 62 to 58 in the return engagement at Perry's
gym three weeks later.

The Vienna Cubs almost upset the Panthers in the second game
at Perry. They led the Panthers most of the way; however, with only 50
seconds remaining in the contest Perry tied the score 58 to 58. Then Sam
Nunn hit a two-pointer for Perry to take the lead. Percy Hardy added two
more points for good measure, and Perry emerged with a 62 to 58 win.

Was Panther's bubble about to burst?

The B and C championship game was played at Fort Valley's gym.
The Panthers, sporting a 26-game winning streak including two wins over
Vienna, apparently were looking beyond Vienna to the state tournament
starting in a mere three days. Perry started playing its usual aggressive
game, moved quickly to a 14 to 8 lead at the end of the first quarter, and
held a 28 to 24 halftime advantage. Late in the third quarter Perry was still
leading 42 to 40. From this juncture until the end of the game, Vienna's
offense heated up, scoring 15 points, while Perry's offense grew strangely
cold, mustering only 5 points. The final score was Vienna-55, Perry-47.
Sam Nunn scored 16 points in a losing cause followed by Virgil Peavy-10,
Jimmy Beatty-9, Percy Hardy-7, and Bennett Mauldin-5.

The following week the upset-minded Vienna quintet marched right
through the state tournament and captured the Class C championship.

Its coach was Glenn Cassell, one of Georgia's finest high school basketball coaches. In later years Cassell was enshrined in the Georgia Athletic Coaches Association Hall of Fame.

State Tournament play begins

Perry entered the state tournament played at Macon City Auditorium with a 26-1 record. Before the tournament began, Jim Minter, "Atlanta Journal" sportswriter, described the strengths and versatility of the Perry team: "Coach Staples has been molding his Class B boys into state powers so long it seems he was around to meet General Sherman....This time he doesn't have height to burn, but he has a bunch of jack-in-the-boxes who can jump with any of them...and a basketball seems to attract them like a magnet, to say nothing of their ability to find the basket. His Perry boys may be outranked but seldom outclassed.... Staples has them smartly coached and well-disciplined. They look almost lazy, but really it is superb drilling....As a warning to future opponents, don't try to stop Peavy—a big man but not a skyscraper—and stop Perry. Concentrate on him and his four teammates will beat you quickly. Sam Nunn, Percy Hardy, Bennett Mauldin, Jimmy Beatty, Ed Beckham and the rest were in there often enough to prove that."

At this stage in Coach Staples' career—his 23rd year as head coach—he had brought 13 teams to the state tournament. The Panthers had won state titles three times: 1947, 1949, and 1953. When Perry won its first state championship in 1947, Staples' teams had been to the state tournament eight times, losing in the state finals on three occasions before capturing the elusive state title.

Quarterfinals: Perry vs. Cochran

The Cochran Royals, winner of the sixth district and coached by Shelly Hayes, played a torrid pace during the first half in which the score was tied five times and the lead changed hands three times. Cochran enjoyed its widest lead 28 to 22 just before the close of the first half, but two field goals by Sam Nunn and one by Peavy enabled the Panthers to tie the score 28 to 28 as the half ended. Peavy got two quick buckets to open the second half and the Panthers were never headed, leading 41 to 36 at the three-quarter mark. With 4:59 left in the game, the Panthers started delaying tactics which worked against them as the Royals pumped in five points to reduce the margin of Perry's lead to four points, 45 to 41. At this point, Jimmy Beatty drilled a free throw and Bennett Mauldin added two field goals, and the Panthers held on to win the game 55 to 48.

"I definitely think the defensive job that Bennett Mauldin did on John Harris in the second half was the difference," said Perry coach Eric Staples. "That fine job and our fine defense turned the trick. We had to stop Harris." Harris, Cochran's high-scoring center, picked up 13 points in the first half, but was held by Mauldin to only six points in the second half, two of them being free throws. Virgil Peavy led Perry's scoring with 20 points. Other Perry Panthers scoring were: Bennett Mauldin-10, Percy Hardy-10, Sam Nunn-7, Jimmy Beatty- 6, and Marvin Griffin-2.

Semifinals: Perry vs. Nahunta

Nahunta, who entered the tournament with a 22-10 record, raced to an early 8 to 4 lead before the Panthers scored 13 straight points and were off and running, never to be headed. Perry had a 23 to 12 lead at the end of the first period, and although Nahunta outscored them 20 to 17 in the second quarter, Perry was ahead at halftime 40 to 32. With Bennett Mauldin, Virgil Peavy, and Sam Nunn hitting the nets in rapid succession, Perry raced to a 49 to 33 lead. From this point to the end of the game, the Ronald Luke-coached Wildcats lost ground by another four points and could never catch Perry. The Panthers, who made only one substitution in the earlier Cochran game, used two substitutes who both played all of the fourth quarter: Ed Beckham-5 points and Marvin Griffin. When the final horn blew, Perry had smashed Nahunta 69 to 49, and earned the right to advance to the state championship game.

State Championship Game: Undefeated Valley Point stands in Perry's path

The Valley Point Pointers, who fell to Lakeland 80 to 78 in a thrilling overtime, semifinal battle the previous year, had amassed an impressive season record of 30 wins and no losses during the current season. Coach Charles Acree's Valley Point five was led by Billy Pelfrey, a 6' 2" forward, who was scoring between 30 and 40 points a game. He was virtually unstoppable. With talented players at every position and a strong bench,

Valley Point was picked by most basketball observers to beat Perry in the finals.

The game began true to form as the Pointers with Pelfrey leading the way moved out to an early lead and topped the Panthers 16 to 13 at the end of the first quarter. The scoring between Perry and Valley Point was virtually even during the second quarter with Valley Point leading 32 to 30 at halftime. Valley Point had been red hot during the first half, scoring on 50 percent of its field goal attempts. In comparison, Perry hit only 36 percent as Valley Point employed a tight zone defense that kept the Panthers shooting from the outside. If the Pointers maintained this hot-shooting pace, Perry's title hopes were in serious jeopardy.

Staples' Famous Halftime Pep Talk

During intermission in Perry's dressing room, Coach Staples, as usual, addressed his team's mistakes and made adjustments for the second half. He first pointed out a glaring weakness in Valley's Point's zone defense. Staples noted that Valley Point's defense always retreated for rebounding position after Perry executed its patented pick-and-roll play. He told his team how to exploit Valley Point's defensive tactics by moving into an open slot in the zone. On a blackboard, Coach Staples identified the exact place where the open slot would develop—between the foul line and the outer circle. Sam Nunn was instructed to move into the open slot after the pick play and the second pass. The third pass was to go to Nunn.

Having played a slow-paced, possession game up to this point, Staples further encouraged his team to push the ball down court quickly and not allow Valley Point time to set up its defense. He also changed defensive assignments and instructed the lanky but quick Bennett Mauldin to guard Valley's Point's chief offensive threat, Billy Pelfrey, during the second half.

As Staples looked around the room at his exhausted players whose confidence may have been lagging as they had played to their limits, but still could not slow down the Valley Point scoring machine, he said something very strange and uncharacteristic of this normally fiery coach--something that no coach would even consider in the heat of battle, yet Staples was the master psychologist who always had a motive up his sleeve. He said, "Boys, you've had a great year. We're probably going to lose this game. They're too big, they're too strong, and they're too quick. You probably can't beat them, but I'm proud of you anyway," and he walked out of the dressing room. In effect, Staples had mildly insulted their egos to fire them up, but left open the possibility of victory if they performed to their capabilities. As Perry teammates looked quizzically at each other, the more they thought about what Staples had said, the more determined they became to prove him wrong. They vowed then and there to go back on that court and play with every ounce of energy and purpose they could muster. This game was for all the marbles, and when it was over they wanted to know in their hearts that they had played to the extent of their abilities and had left no unexpended effort on the court.

Second Half Fireworks

During the third quarter, Coach Staples' psychology began to pay big dividends. The Panthers exploded for 19 points while holding Valley Point to only two free throws. Staples' defensive adjustments also were working to perfection as Bennett Mauldin, one of Georgia's top defensive players, had shut down Valley Point's Billy Pelfrey.

Did Perry take advantage of the hole in Valley Point's zone defense?

Perry's offensive fireworks continued during the fourth quarter with Sam Nunn hitting six consecutive baskets from the hole in the zone defense that virtually buried Valley Point in an avalanche of two-pointers. When the final seconds ticked off the clock, Perry had blasted the previously undefeated Valley Point quintet by a whopping 29-point margin, 81 to 52.

A Team Effort

"Macon Telegraph" sportswriter, Ben Griffith, described the game thusly: "It was Nunn, Mauldin, and Peavy who led the Perry quintet in scoring, but it was a five-man ball club, and the efforts

At right, Sam Nunn, Nr. 11, drives around a pick set by Bennett Mauldin, Nr. 15.

of Percy Hardy and Jimmy Beatty cannot be measured in their two points apiece. Both played superb floor games, jumping on loose balls like ducks and fitting in smoothly with Staples' deceptive passing plays. Sam Nunn was the leading scorer with 27-points, made mostly from the one-hand push shot from the outside. Bennett Mauldin, who got his share of the rebounds as well as 25 points, and Virgil Peavy, who was a key man at the pivot and hit for 21, were indispensables in the Panther attack." Marvin Griffin came off the bench to hit 4 points and Ed Beckham played strong on the backboards. With this team effort, the Perry Panthers earned the honor of being the first team to win the State Class B championship four times.

Perry-81	Valley Point-52
Peavy-21	Wilson-6
Beatty-2	Jones-4
Mauldin-25	Pelfrey-19
Nunn-27	Holland-6
Hardy-2	Collins-17

Subs: Griffin-4, Beckham; Valley Point: Dixon, Frazier
Officials: Jones and Burns

All-State team
Sam Nunn-Perry *
Virgil Peavy-Perry**
Bennett Mauldin-Perry

*Sam Nunn was also selected to the All-State team the previous year, 1955. Further, in the Georgia North-South All-Star game later that year, Nunn was a starter and top scorer for the South team coached by Coach Staples
** Virgil Peavy was named the "Most Valuable Player" in the state tournament. He also was selected to the All-State team in 1955

Honorable Mention: Jimmy Beatty* and Percy Hardy.

*Jimmy Beatty was the only junior on Perry's starting five. He was selected to *the All-State team the next year, 1957, and also played on the South Georgia All-Star team in 1957.*

Perry's 1956 Season Record

Opponent	Winner	Score
Regular Season		
Vienna	Perry	54-50
Wilco	Perry	41-40
Hawkinsville	Perry	53-20
Hawkinsville	Perry	46-45
Warner Robins	Perry	75-41
Cordele	Perry	63-28
Middle Ga. College B-team	Perry	49-40
Montezuma	Perry	68-47
Roberta	Perry	79-41
Vienna	Perry	62-58
Montezuma	Perry	70-54
Southwest (Atlanta)-AA	Perry	62-46
West Fulton (Atlanta)-AA	Perry	41-35
Lanier-AA	Perry	53-51
Hawkinsville	Perry	75-32
Roberta	Perry	69-32
Griffin-AA	Perry	41-37
Warner Robins	Perry	53-35
Lanier-AA	Perry	49-35
Wilco	Perry	47-37
Griffin-AA	Perry	46-34
Smith (Atlanta)-AA	Perry	56-42
Murphy (Atlanta)-AA	Perry	61-52

3rd District Tournament

Cuthbert	Perry	44-42
Sycamore	Perry	56-43
Fort Valley	Perry	52-28

3rd District B & C Championship

Vienna	Vienna	55-47

State Tournament

Cochran	Perry	55-48
Nahunta	Perry	69-49
Valley Point	Perry	81-52

Never A Team With More Heart: 1959 team

1959 team. Front row, L-R: Tommie Sandefur-manager, Frank Holland, Jr., Wilson Martin, Derrell Davis, Lindy Evans, Jerry Wilson, Bob Malone-manager. Standing, L-R: Assistant Coach Frank Holland, Pierce Staples, Thomas (Boot) Hunt, Francis Marshall, Charlie Etheridge, Derry Watson, Lee Martin, and Coach Eric Staples. Not pictured: Larry Walker.

New Gym dedicated

Before Perry's home opener against Cochran on December 5, 1958, a new $135,000 gym was dedicated behind the high school on North Avenue. Speaking at the dedication ceremony was Jim Gooden, who organized basketball in Perry in 1919 and served as school superintendent and coach until Eric Staples took over as basketball coach in the fall of 1933. Gooden's teams had played on outdoor courts until Perry's first gym was erected in 1926. Perry's new 1958 gym was built because its first gym, a wooden structure, had been used for 32 years, was outmoded, and was not large enough to accommodate the growing fan base. When Gooden came to Perry in 1919, there were slightly more than 100 students at Perry. Some of Gooden's players on his early teams had sons on the current team. The new building, a combined gymnasium and auditorium, could accommodate 1,600 fans. It was equipped with a large stage and spacious dressing rooms.

Following the dedication ceremony, Perry split with the visiting Cochran teams. Perry's boys defeated the Cochran Royals, 60-41, and were led by Boot Hunt who topped all scorers with 25 points. This was a significant win for the Panthers as the Cochran Royals went on to capture the Class A state championship in 1959. The Perry girls lost to the Cochran lasses by a score of 47 to 30. Patsy Todd paced the Lady Panthers with 13 points. The 1958-59 school year marked Perry's first return to girls' basketball following an absence of almost 30 years. Formation of a girls' team came to pass after 300 local women petitioned the Perry school administration to organize girls' basketball. Some area schools had fielded girls' basketball a decade or more before Perry. In prior years, Perry had enjoyed such a dynasty in boys' basketball that no thought was given to instituting a girls' program. School officials and townspeople alike feared it might dilute the emphasis on boys' basketball.

Would this be the year?

Since winning its first state championship in 1947, Perry had won four state titles in nine years: 1947, 1949, 1953, and 1956. The Panthers had come up short in 1957 and 1958—both years winning the district, but losing in the state tournament. In 1958, Perry lost to Forsyth County in the state semifinal game, 37 to 35, on a last second field goal by Forsyth County's Harold Whitt. A year earlier, in 1957, the Panthers lost in the

state semifinals to Nahunta, 54 to 45. The 1959 Panthers didn't want
to get bogged down in the state semifinals for a third consecutive time;
consequently, the 1959 club could only achieve redemption by bringing
home a state crown. But did the Panthers have the team to do it?

Although top performers Terry Griffin and Eddie Livingston were
lost to graduation, four of Perry's regulars were returning for the 1958-59
season. Coach Staples, the high school principal and now into his 26th
year of coaching at Perry, stated his current squad was "the best we have
had here since 1956."

In Boot Hunt, a rising senior, Perry had one of the top players in
Georgia, both offensively and defensively. The previous year, in 1958,
Hunt had been selected to the state Class B all-state team. Hunt, a
forward, had a jump shot that was virtually unstoppable. Once airborne,
he released the ball with his arms fully extended and could score with
uncanny accuracy anywhere within a radius of 25 feet from the basket.
Freshman Lee Martin, a guard who played on the B team the previous
season, was already receiving rave notices as a player who would lead the
Panthers to new heights before he graduated. Little did anyone expect
what a great year this freshman would have.

Oak Tree Goal at Sand Hill

At starting center was 6' 2" senior Francis Marshall. Marshall grew
up as Boot Hunt's neighbor in a settlement south of Perry called Sand
Hill. They learned to play basketball on a goal and backboard nailed
to the side of a huge oak tree. During Marshall's junior year, he was
encouraged by Hunt to come out for the team. Hunt saw in Marshall
a fierce competitor and someone who could hold his own with anyone
under the boards.

Coaches' Sons

At the other forward post was 5' 11" junior Pierce Staples, son of
Coach Eric Staples. The point guard was 5' 8" senior Frank Holland, Jr.,
a cat-quick defender and ball handler, and son of assistant coach Frank
Holland. Both Pierce and Frank, Jr. were not only blessed athletically but
benefited from the great basketball minds of their dads. Perry boasted

of strong reserves in Wilson Martin, Derry Watson, Jimmy Smallwood, Derrell Davis, Charlie Etheridge, Jerry Wilson, Larry Walker and Lindy Evans. The potential to win a state championship was there, but the team would face a number of tests early in the season that could either make or break them.

Panthers fail their first test

The Panthers' first real test came in the fifth game of the season when Heard County came to town on Friday, December 19. Heard County, coached by Coach Staples' brother, Don Staples, was the consensus pick of sports pundits to advance to the state tournament with a good possibility of taking home the championship trophy.

It was evident the Panthers were not yet ready for the likes of Heard County as Coach Don Staples' charges soundly defeated Perry, 56 to 48, in the Panther Den. The high-scoring Roy Aubrey led Heard County with 26 points. Boot Hunt paced Perry with 15 points, and Lee Martin added 14 in a losing cause. Serious doubts began to emerge about the strength of the Perry team, but an entire season lay ahead, and Perry had a great coach who would ensure that his team profited by its mistakes and improved as the season progressed.

Test number 2: the Lanier Poets

The Panthers had less than 24 hours to regroup from the loss to Heard County, for the next day, Saturday, December 20, they would play the Class AA Lanier Poets at Macon's City Auditorium.

Death of the beloved Sam Glassman

The occasion of the Panther-Poet match-up marked the death of "The Macon Telegraph's" famous sports editor, Sam Glassman, who had passed unexpectedly Friday morning, December 19. The vacant seat at the scorers table stood as a silent reminder of Mr. Glassman's untimely death and of the high esteem in which he was held. One official was quoted as saying, "It just isn't right without Sam Glassman here at the Lanier-Perry game."

It looked like the Panthers were going down to defeat again as Lanier jumped off to a 9 to 3 lead at the end of the first quarter and were still leading at halftime, 18 to 14. The Panthers came onto the floor after the half with instructions from Coach Staples to tighten up the defense and to work for the high percentage shot on offense. With 7:11 remaining in the third period, Perry tied the score, 18 to 18. Pierce Staples, son of Coach Staples, scored a field goal to break the deadlock. As the third quarter ended, the Panthers led by six points, 29 to 23. The Poets' and Panthers' offenses matched point-for-point in the final period, each scoring 13 points; thus, the six-point third quarter carryover lead was the final margin of victory for the Panthers, 42 to 36.

Boot Hunt led Perry's scoring with 17 points, aided by Frank Holland, who pitched in 12 tallies. Perry center, Francis Marshall, was the top rebounder with nine. In defeating the larger AA classification school, Perry had passed its second test with flying colors. The Panthers didn't seem like the same club that had lost decisively the night before to Heard County.

Perry-42	Lanier-36
Hunt-17	Giles-15
Staples-5	Hall-4
Marshall-5	Howell-2
Holland-12	McBryant-4
L. Martin-3	O'Neal-5
W. Martin	Carr-4
Smith	Kite
	Sanders-2

Score at half: Lanier-18, Perry-14
Officials: John Goldston and Barney Dixon

Test number 3: Crawford County

Perry's next major test would be the Crawford County Eagles coached by legendary coach J. B. Hawkins. Going into the game, his Eagles were sporting a 17-game winning streak, having marched over a number of formidable opponents.

Crawford County moved out to a 10 to 2 lead at the first quarter mark and was still ahead at the intermission, 25 to 17. When the third stanza ended, Perry had moved within two points, 38 to 36. During the final quarter, Perry forged ahead, scoring 21 points while Crawford County could muster only 10 points. The final score was Perry-57, Crawford County-48.

Although the high-scoring John Mathews of Crawford County put on a spectacular offensive show, hitting for 28 points for the night, the difference in the game was Coach Staples' strategy to concentrate defensively on the other four Eagle starters and limit their scoring. Frank Holland zipped the nets for 13 points to lead the Panthers' attack while Boot Hunt racked up 12.

Experimental Tournament

The Georgia High School Association staged an experimental tournament at the Perry gym with four teams participating: Class B Perry, Class C Vienna, Class A Cochran, and Class AA Warner Robins. It was called Perry's Christmas Invitational Tournament. Two new rule changes under consideration were tested at the tournament: the 24-second shot clock and two-shot penalty for all fouls committed in the backcourt. In the first round of play, Perry defeated Warner Robins, 59 to 53. Boot Hunt led Perry with 21 points and Pinky Pinckney totaled 21 for Warner Robins.

In the championship game, Perry trounced Vienna, the previous night's winner over Cochran, by a score of 78 to 65. Perry's Boot Hunt exploded with an incredible 39 points, hitting from all conceivable angles and scoring exactly half of the Panthers' points. Hunt connected on 13 of 25 field goals and hit 13 consecutive free throws. Herb Peavy paced Vienna with 18. In the consolation contest, the Warner Robins Demons trimmed the Cochran Royals, 66 to 41. Odel Davis scored 23 for the Demons, and Johnny Mullis racked up 14 for the Royals.

The coaches were divided in their assessment of the proposed rule changes. The 24-second rule would prevent a team from freezing the ball during the waning minutes of the game and give the lagging team a chance to catch up. The two-shot foul rule would slow the game down and give an advantage to the best free throw-shooting team.

Lanier Poets Invade Perry

Coach Tom Porter's Lanier Poets came to Perry seeking revenge for an earlier defeat. Perry starter Pierce Staples could not play because of an injured knee. A furious but late rally by the Poets fell five points short as the Panthers prevailed by a 41 to 36 score. Only 17 fouls were charged in the close, hard-fought contest: 10 against Lanier and seven whistled against Perry.

Perry's red-hot freshman guard Lee Martin led the way for Perry with 15 points and hauled down 10 rebounds for good measure. Wilson Martin hit for 8 points, followed by Boot Hunt with 7, Frank Holland-7, and Francis Marshall-4.

Coach Goot Steiner's upset-minded Wolverines

Perry defeated Dudley Hughes Vocational School of Macon at Perry's gym in a thriller that went right down to the wire. The Panthers were leading, 25 to 19, at the end of the half, but during the third period, the Wolverines scored 17 points while holding the Panthers to 10, thereby moving ahead, 36 to 35, as the third quarter ended. The lead changed hands several times in the next four minutes, and with 4:16 left, the score was tied, 41 to 41. Perry's fluid-motion guard, Lee Martin, went to work and stole the ball twice, scoring four points and putting Perry out front to stay. Martin made all of his six points in the last two minutes of the torrid final quarter. Perry won the hard-fought contest, 49 to 43.

Boot Hunt was Perry's top scorer with 20 points. Other Panthers ripping the cords were Francis Marshall-11, Frank Holland-7, and Pierce Staples-5.

Perry-49	**Dudley Hughes-43**
Hunt-20	Cheek-14
Staples-5	Moore-5
Marshall-11	Churchwell-12
Holland-7	Spires-10
Lee Martin-6	Shores-2

Subs: Perry: Wilson Martin
Score at half: Perry 25, Dudley Hughes-19

Regular season in review

Perry ended the season with 19 victories against only four defeats: to Heard County, Warner Robins, Montezuma, and Cochran. The Panthers split with the latter three teams during the year, but had played only a single game against Heard County.

The Panthers had soundly beaten three Macon teams: Lanier twice, Dudley Hughes twice, and Willingham twice. They had broken Crawford County's 17-game winning streak and beaten Wilkinson County twice. In summary, Perry appeared to have a squad superior to every team on its schedule with the possible exception of Heard County, coached by Don Staples, Coach Eric Staples' younger brother. The possibility existed that the two brothers would meet again, but only if Perry and Heard County won their respective districts and advanced to face each other in the state tournament.

Region 2B-1 Tournament: February 16-17 at Perry

Perry vs. East Laurens

The Perry Panthers trounced Coach Hugh Hill's East Laurens' five, 65 to 48, as Lee Martin blistered the nets for 27 points, primarily with his deadly push shots from the outside. Boot Hunt contributed 18 points, Francis Marshall-9, Pierce Staples-6, and Frank Holland-5.

Perry vs. Dudley Hughes

Perry downed Goot Steiner's excellent Dudley Hughes quintet for the third time during the year, 49 to 39—this time for the Region 2B-1 championship. Boot Hunt led Perry's offense with 14 points. Lee Martin was close behind with 13 markers. Rounding out Perry's scoring were Francis Marshall-10, Pierce Staples-6, Frank Holland-5, and Wilson Martin-1

Region 2B: February 19-21 at Mount Vernon

Perry vs. Vidalia

Eric Staples' Panthers had little trouble with Vidalia in the opening round of the region 2B tournament; in fact, the contest turned into a blow-out. Perry was hitting from all angles, and Ralph Parsons' Indians never knew what hit them. Boot Hunt led the steady barrage on the basket with 22 points as Perry smothered Vidalia, 75 to 44. Lee Martin added 18 points to the victory cause, followed by Pierce Staples, Frank Holland, and Francis Marshall with 6 points each. Reserves coming off the Panther bench and playing exceedingly well were Wilson Martin-8, Derrell Davis-5, Derry Watson-2, Lindy Evans-2, Larry Walker, and Charlie Etheridge. Perry's reserves proved they could compete on even terms with Vidalia's varsity. A number of them would have been starters on other teams in the area.

Region Semifinals: Perry vs. Portal

The Portal game was by far the most difficult test for the Panthers in the tournament. Perry led by only two points, 22 to 20, at the half; however, Boot Hunt, heavily defended by Portal, broke loose in the strong second half, riddling the nets for 18 points and leading Perry to victory, 47 to 42, in a hotly-contested game in which neither team substituted. Freshman Lee Martin tossed in 14 points, Pierce Staples and Frank Holland contributed 6 points apiece, and Francis Marshall made 3.

Region 2B Championship: Perry vs. Bradwell Institute

Coach Staples had to find a way to stop Bradwell Institute's balanced scoring attack—especially the tallest player in the tournament, 6' 5" John Salter, who had scored 45 points in the first two tournament games and was almost unstoppable around the basket. Staples' strategy was to limit the scoring of the other four players and to concede to Salter his points. His defensive tactics worked as planned: Salter dropped in 25 points while his other four teammates collectively could muster only five points. Although the first half was close with Perry leading, 19 to 18, at the intermission, the last half turned into a riot as the Panthers downed Coach Toby Fountains' Bradwell Institute by a runaway score of 51 to 30.

For the Panthers, Boot Hunt and Lee Martin each scored 18 points. Francis Marshall pitched in 7, Pierce Staples-6, and Frank Holland-2.

The Panthers were headed for the Class B state tournament in Macon.

Perry-51 **Bradwell Institute-30**
Hunt-18 Bagwell-2
Staples-6 Salter-25
Marshall-7 Gassoway-1
Holland-2 Crowley-2
Martin-18 Smiley-0
Subs: Perry: none; Bradwell Institute: Brown and Stafford
Score at half: Perry-19, Bradwell Institute-18

The Panthers, having played their best basketball of the season during the region tournament, were now headed for the state tournament in Macon. Perry's defense had been superb, limiting foes to 40.2 points per game. A defining moment was holding a powerful Bradwell Institute club to only 30 points. With high scoring juggernauts like Seminole County and Heard County coming to Macon, the Panthers would have to turn up their defensive intensity another notch. While scoring an average of only 54.4 points per game, the Panthers rarely turned the ball over and milked each possession for the high percentage shot. While taking nothing for granted, this senior-dominated team knew that the possibility of a Staples brothers' rematch, Eric of Perry versus Don of Heard County, loomed ahead. Such a semifinal match would offer Eric an opportunity to avenge an early loss to brother Don and earn a shot at his fifth state title.

Class B state tournament: March 5-7 at Macon's City Auditorium

Perry vs. Tucker

Perry brought a record of 24 wins and 4 losses into the tournament against its first opponent, Tucker, the region 4 runner-up, with a 9-16 won-loss record. The game turned out to be no contest for the Panthers as they shellacked the Tigers, 47 to 24.

Boot Hunt led Perry's offense with 21 points followed by Lee Martin with 16. Pierce Staples scored 4, Francis Marshall-3, and Frank Holland-1. Perry reserves getting into the fray and providing continuity in executing Coach Staples' game plan were Derry Watson, Derrell Davis, Charlie Etheridge, Wilson Martin, and Jerry Wilson-2 points.

This win bolstered Perry's hopes of competing for its fifth state championship in school history. Standing in its way, however, was the much heralded Heard County, coached by Don Staples, who had hammered the Panthers earlier in the year, 56 to 48. Heard County had humiliated a strong Folkston quintet, 54 to 42, to advance to the semifinals.

State Semifinals: Perry vs. Heard County

The game was a sportswriter's dream. It pitted brother against brother. Coach Eric Staples was Perry's mentor. His younger brother, Don, was head coach at Heard County. Eric had once coached Don years ago and Don had learned well—so well, in fact, that he could now turn the tables on his older brother in the biggest stakes game of his career.

The game would be a clash of the two top defenses in Georgia, possibly two of the best defenses ever to meet in a state Class B tournament. Brother Eric had to find a way to slow down Heard County's Roy Awbrey. Brother Don faced double jeopardy in trying to rig a defense to stop the Panthers' forward Boot Hunt, a consensus all-state player and leading scorer, and his explosive running mate, guard Lee Martin, a freshman sensation, who was facing a brilliant career and considered one of Central Georgia's most promising players.

The game started off as expected. Superior defenses were stifling offensive penetration and clear shots were not to be had. At the first quarter's end, the score stood at an unheard of low score: Heard County-5, Perry-2. The slow, deliberate style of play continued into the second quarter, but Perry ratcheted up its offense and scored 12 points while Heard County could garner only five. The halftime score was Perry-14, Heard County-10. At the end of the third stanza, Perry lurched ahead by three, 21 to 18. In the fourth and final period, the game became a see-saw battle with the lead changing four times.

"Macon Telegraph" sportswriter's type-sheet reflected Heard Co. as victors.

With slightly less than a minute remaining and Perry trailing, 28 to 30, based on the tempo of the game, it appeared that Heard County was in the driver's seat and would deny the Panthers another shot at the state title. Apparently "Macon Telegraph" Sports Editor Harley Bowers thought so. Horace Woodruff, 1930's era Perry player, was sitting right behind Bowers, who was at the official scorer's table typing his story for the morning paper. Woodruff said he could see over Bower's shoulder and that Bowers had already typed up a headline that showed Heard County defeating Perry and Eric Staples losing to brother Don. But Perry's Boot Hunt, a basketball warrior who had grown up competing over his head against older boys on dirt courts at Perry's Sand Hill community, had other plans. With 49 seconds left he drove for the basket, then pulled up, faking two defenders trying gallantly to stop him, and bagged a jump shot to tie the score 30 to 30. With a mere 13 seconds on the clock, the sensational Lee Martin released a gutsy jumper from the outside that hit nothing but nylon to put Perry ahead, 32 to 30. The Perry sidelines erupted in mass hysteria and the ever cool Martin never changed the serious expression on his face. Heard County immediately called time out. On Heard County's in-bound play, Frank Holland stole the ball and passed to Lee Martin who scored a driving lay-up as time ran out. Perry had defeated Heard County in one of the hardest fought and most sensational games ever played in the Macon City Auditorium's storied history. The final score: Perry-34, Heard County-30. "So effective was Perry's defense and blocking out on the boards, Heard County got only two offensive rebounds the whole ball game," wrote George Landry of "The Macon News," "and didn't even accomplish the first one until only 49 seconds remained in the first half." The difference in the game was Perry's superiority on the backboards led by Francis Marshall. Perry pulled down 30 rebounds to Heard County's 16.

As the final horn blew, Coach Staples rushed to his baby brother and frankly admitted to him, "We sure were lucky. You've got a fine ball club." Don Staples had lost a heart-breaker, but he took consolation in knowing that one Staples' family member still had a chance to win the coveted state crown.

State championship game: Perry vs. Seminole County

Coach Staples knew that the Seminole County Indians—22 wins and only three losses-- had the offensive firepower to bury almost any team in the Class B ranks. It was also a highly seasoned team with all starters being seniors. Staples considered Charles Spooner, Seminole

County's center, to be one of the greatest offensive threats he had faced in his long coaching career. He instinctively knew that a good defender might slow Spooner but that it would be impossible to stop him from getting his customary 30 points. Since Coach Staples' defensive tactics against Bradwell Institute and big John Salter had produced Perry's win in the region championship game, he employed the same approach against Seminole County. Coach Staples elected to concede to Spooner his points with only one man, Perry center Francis Marshall guarding him, but instructed his team to concentrate their defensive efforts on the other four Seminoles. It was the job of Boot Hunt, Lee Martin, Pierce Staples, and Frank Holland to contain the Indians' two guards and two forwards and to minimize their scoring.

Perry's Traffic Cop

Boot Hunt was the leader of Perry's defensive unit, much like a coach on the playing floor. Coach Jimmy Maffett, the outstanding basketball coach at Oglethorpe and Macon County, had nothing but high praise for Perry's defense. "Boot Hunt was a virtual traffic cop on defense," said Maffett. "He was constantly directing defensive traffic and shouting instructions to his teammates."

Perry freshman sets dome afire

Freshman guard sensation Lee Martin set the high-domed Macon City Auditorium ablaze with his 14-point barrage in the first two quarters. The Panthers moved out to a 12 to 8 first quarter lead and were leading, 26 to 14, at the half. At the end of the third quarter, Perry was still in the driver's seat, 33 to 22. During the torrid fourth quarter, Boot Hunt hit with uncanny accuracy as Perry out-scored Seminole County, 22 to 13. When the final seconds ticked off the clock, Perry had scalped Seminole County, 52 to 35, and won its fifth state championship.

Coach Staples' defensive scheme worked to precision, and Perry turned the ball over only once on superb ball-handling and smooth floor play. Charles Spooner ripped the nets for 31 points, but his other four teammates could find the basket for only 4 points among them. Boot Hunt and Lee Martin kept the nets swishing with 18 points each. Frank Holland had 7, Pierce Staples-5, and Francis Marshall-4. Staples' only substitution was Wilson Martin, who played an excellent floor game for the Panthers. Rebounding was even with both teams getting 25 rebounds. For Perry, Lee Martin pulled down eight rebounds and Boot Hunt six.

Perry-52	Seminole County-35
Hunt-18	Hornsby-1
Staples-5	G. Trawick-0
Marshall-4	Spooner-31
Martin-18	Simpson-0
Holland-7	M. Trawick-3

Subs: Perry: W. Martin; Seminole County: none
Score at half: Perry-26, Seminole County-14
Officials: Caswell and Brannon

The 1959 team held three tough opponents in the state tournament to only 89 points, an unbelievable 29.7 points per game—a defensive record in Perry state tournament history.

Peter Zack Geer presented trophies

Peter Zack Geer, Governor Ernest Vandiver's executive secretary, who later became Lieutenant Governor of Georgia, presented miniature basketballs to all the Perry players. Amid bursts of whoops and hollers from the big and enthusiastic Perry contingent, Geer remarked, "I have never seen a better coordinated, better working team in Georgia. After your fine demonstration here tonight, you ought to go up and play Kentucky. You have a great team."

Coach Zack T. Williams of Seminole County summed it up as to why his team fell short: "They (Perry) shot the ball well, and they are a sound, well-coached club fundamentally."

Comments by Perry Coaches

Coach Staples said, "They've got the greatest potential of any team I've ever had. There might have been some with more ability, but none with more heart." A coach who always stressed unity, Coach Staples added, "They play together like brothers." Assistant Coach Frank Holland, a great coach himself and possessor of the famous 'Little Black Book' of scouting reports, told a screaming crowd of Perry supporters, "Sometimes you do (win) and sometimes you don't." After stepping down as a head coach at Chauncey and Byron, Holland had forged an 8 year partnership with Staples that was producing championships for Perry. This was particularly a proud moment for the two coaches as their two sons, Pierce Staples and Frank Holland, were starters and major contributors on the Perry state championship team.

State Class B tournament all-state team
Boot Hunt-Perry*
Lee Martin-Perry
Frank Holland-Perry

* Selected to all-state team the previous year, 1958

Honorable mention:
Francis Marshall-Perry
Pierce Staples-Perry

Perry's season record

Date	Opponent	Opponent Score	Perry Score
2-Dec	Wilkinson County	36	61
5-Dec	Cochran	41	60
9-Dec	Montezuma	49	68
12-Dec	Hawkinsville	21	71
19-Dec	Heard Co.	56	48
20-Dec	Lanier	36	42

Christmas Invitational Tournament

29-Dec	Warner Robins	53	59
30-Dec	Vienna	65	78
2-Jan	Hawkinsville	24	58
6-Jan	Warner Robins	48	43

Date	Opponent	Opponent Score	Perry Score
9-Jan	Crawford County	48	57
13-Jan	Dudley Hughes	43	49
16-Jan	Lanier	36	41
17-Jan	Willingham	32	40
20-Jan	Montezuma	56	43
23-Jan	Butler	52	56
27-Jan	Crawford County	60	62
30-Jan	Wilkinson Co.	37	52
31-Jan	Cochran	49	45
3-Feb	Warner Robins	50	59
6-Feb	Willingham	27	53
10-Feb	Dudley Hughes	28	46
13-Feb	Butler	45	49

Area 1, Region 2-B Tournament

Date	Opponent	Opponent Score	Perry Score
16-Feb	East Laurens	48	65
17-Feb	Dudley Hughes	39	49

Region 2-B Tournament

Date	Opponent	Opponent Score	Perry Score
19-Feb	Vidalia	44	75
20-Feb	Portal	42	47
21-Feb	Bradwell Institute	30	51

State Class B Tournament

Date	Opponent	Opponent Score	Perry Score
5-Mar	Tucker	24	47
6-Mar	Heard County	30	34
7-Mar	Seminole County	35	52

They Never Tasted Defeat: 1962 team

Bottom row, L-R: Assistant Coach Paul Hartman, Bobby Goodman, Butch Skinner, Ronnie Sanders, Ronnie Davis. Second row, L-R: Lee Martin, Dwayne Powell, Ronnie Griffin, Paul Bozeman, Coach Eric Staples. Back row, L-F: Melton Cloud, Dennis Fike, George Nunn, Jimmy Dorsett, Sonny Wilson-manager.

What transpired since 1959 state championship year

1960: Following the 1959 season in which Perry won its fifth state championship, all starters graduated except freshman sensation Lee Martin and Pierce Staples. Martin sustained a football injury and underwent knee surgery. He was unable to play basketball during the following season. Consequently, the 1960 Panthers, without the services of its superstar, were relegated to a rebuilding season.

1961: With Martin returning to the hardwood in 1961 and the emergence of a sophomore sharpshooter named Dwayne Powell, Perry's basketball fortunes were looking up. The 1961 Panthers put together a commendable 24-6 won-loss record during the regular season, but lost in the region tournament to Telfair County, the defending state champs.

Telfair returned one of the strongest duos in Georgia basketball in center Everett Copeland and forward Bonnie Strom. Strom had been a promising young B-team player at Perry until his family moved to Telfair County in 1959. There he developed into one of the state's top players. Perry was a young team at this stage and lacked the maturity and the muscle to compete with the veteran Telfair squad.

1962: As the curtain rose on the 1962 season, all starters were returning. The Panthers had gained maturity and possessed strong reserves. They were ready to do battle with any team in Georgia.

Staples beginning 35th year

Coach Staples was beginning his 35th year as a head basketball coach, having coached one year at Rockelo in Heard County, three years at Bowden and two at Tallapoosa before coming to Perry in 1933. Even the University of Kentucky's legendary Coach Adolph Rupp would have a hard time matching Staples' 809 victories against only 187 losses. At this stage in his career, Staples' teams had won 19 region championships and five state titles. His Panthers also had captured the runner-up spot four times in both state and regional competition.

First 16 games a cakewalk

Perry's first 16 games were like a cakewalk as winning was easily accomplished. The Panthers averaged 64 points a game and limited their foes to only 36, an average victory margin of 28 points. In the Panthers' wake of destruction were such teams as Telfair County, Cochran, Hawkinsville, Crawford County, Macon County, Vienna, Willingham, Dublin, East Laurens, and Unadilla. The closest any team had played the Panthers was Lanier who came within 13 points at Perry's gym, ending up on the low end of a 66 to 53 score.

Game number 17 would provide some anxious moments...

Winchesters were misfiring

Although Perry had beaten Coach Martin Almand's Willingham Rams 59 to 27 in Perry, the return engagement at Willingham's gym was fraught with disaster. The usually deadly Perry riflemen found their

Winchesters were misfiring. The Panthers experienced their worst shooting night of the year, making only 16 field goals of 54 attempts for 29.6 percent. To make matters worse, Perry's star, Lee Martin, played with an injured back and wore a cumbersome back brace that impeded his movement. Unable to buy a bucket during the last three minutes of the final period, Coach Staples chose to freeze the ball to preserve the lead and won by five points, 45 to 40. It was one of those nights that Coach Staples said was bound to happen to any team, but the Panthers still found a way to win and record their 17th win of the season.

Dwayne Powell hit for 15 points to lead Perry while Lee Martin, tormented by a bad back, tossed in 13. Dennis Fike scored 10, George Nunn-5 and Ronnie Griffin-2.

Perry hits 73 percent of shots

In win number 19, the Perry Panthers unleashed a blitzkrieg against their Houston County neighbors, the Warner Robins Demons, with a 79-point assault holding the Demons to a mere 34 points.

By shooting an amazing 73 percent from the field, the Panthers set a school record and possibly a state mark in field goal accuracy. The Panthers hit their first 14 attempts from the floor and ended the first quarter with a blistering 31-point assault while Warner Robins could muster only five points. Lee Martin hit a phenomenal eight shots in a row. Leading 73 to 23 as the third period ended, Coach Staples sent in Perry's reserves to play the final period. Four players wound up in double figures: Dwayne Powell-19, Lee Martin-17, George Nunn-16, and Dennis Fike-14.

The thriller in Knoxville

Sporting 19 straight victories, the high-flying Panthers rolled into Knoxville, Georgia, the county seat of Crawford County, one cool January evening to take on the same team they had beaten earlier in the season by 25 points, 68 to 43. The Panthers never suspected that Crawford County's legendary coach J. B. Hawkins had planned a slumber party just for them, putting the Perry scoring machine to sleep with his ball control and game-delaying tactics. Hawkins reasoned that Perry's superior offensive team couldn't score when they didn't have the basketball. Coach Hawkins' charges would hold the ball for long nerve-wracking intervals to get the high percentage shot and score--their motive being to minimize the point spread throughout the game. The Crawford defense played the best they had played all year and clung to the Panthers like magnets. To make matters worse, the Panthers suffered an inability to execute their offensive patterns in the smaller confines of the old Crawford County gym and were shooting less than 30 percent, a rarity indeed for Perry's sharpshooters. At halftime, the score was Crawford County-15, Perry-14.

The second half was identical to the first. Crawford continued to play with one purpose in mind: to hold onto the ball and to keep the score close. Crawford held a 2-3 point lead throughout most of the third and fourth quarters.

During the final minute of play, behind 29 to 27, Coach Staples called time out. He moved Martin from his normal guard position and positioned him on the low post. Ronnie Sanders bounce-passed the ball to Martin who faked his defender, spun and scored. The score stood tied, 29 to 29. Thirty seconds remained. Crawford County came down the court looking for the final shot and the win. An Eagle broke open toward the basket, but George Nunn jumped high to intercept the intended pass. Nunn fired the ball down court to Dennis Fike who drove to the basket and scored. Perry had narrowly escaped defeat at Knoxville, 31 to 29. Lee Martin-11 points and Dwayne Powell-9 markers led Perry's offense. Crawford County was led by Mike McAfee, who was a thorn in the side of the Panthers all night with 15 points, over half of his team's points. This low scoring contest goes down in history as a testimonial to the coaching genius of Coach J. B. Hawkins, whose team almost beat the Panthers. Perry's last minute come-from-behind victory attested to Coach Eric Staples' brilliance to pull the rabbit out of the hat just in the nick of time, as he had done some many times in the past. At tournament time, this gutsy and determined Crawford County quintet went on to capture the runner-up trophy in the state Class C tournament.

Perry-31	**Crawford County-29**
Powell-9	McAfee-15
G. Nunn-3	Justice-8
Fike-6	O'Neal-3

Martin-11   Maddox
Sanders   Hollis-2
Griffin-2   Horne-1

Storm clouds brewing: Improved Lanier Poets loom ominiously over horizon

Perry, a Class B school, was scheduled to play the Class AAA Lanier Poets in Macon's City Auditorium on January 24, 1962. Macon sportswriters and Lanier fans alike considered Coach Henry Middlebrooks' Poets to be vastly improved since the earlier encounter in Perry and ready to break the Panthers' 21-game winning streak. Lanier was the tallest and most physical team in central Georgia with three players 6-foot, 5-inches and over. Featuring twin towers, 6' 7" Don Biggs and 6' 6" Al Gerhardt, plus the high scoring Woodrow Fincher and Ken Bonifay, Lanier entered the game with a 10-5 record, but had won its last seven games in a row, including recent wins over Class AAA powerhouses. Since the Poets were beginning to show promise as a state title contender, the game was foreseen as a tight, bitter struggle for the Panthers who were playing on the Poets' home court. With no player over 6'1", the Panthers were expected to face a serious disadvantage in competing for rebounds against their taller foes. The Panthers' only hope was to have a hot-shooting night.

The Panthers, undefeated through 21 games, had squashed their foes by an incredible average score of 26 points. Perry was averaging 62 points a game and limiting its opponents to a 36 point average.

Perry featured a talented starting five in Coach Eric Staples' unconventional alignment of two forwards, two post players, and one guard. The two forwards, Lee Martin and Dwayne Powell, played primarily on the flanks, and the two post players, George Nunn and Dennis Fike, positioned themselves outside the foul lanes and not down low. There was only one guard in this offense, a highly efficient and turnover-free point guard, Ronnie (Zorro) Sanders, who distributed the ball evenly to Martin and Powell to initiate Perry's devastating pick and roll plays. Ronnie Griffin was an outstanding sixth man coming off the bench, alternating with Sanders at point guard. Every team knew what formations and plays Perry would run, but none had succeeded in slowing down Eric Staples' scoring machine. After 21 games, Martin was averaging 20 points a game and Powell 18. George Nunn and Dennis Fike had demonstrated strong rebounding on the backboards. Guards Sanders and Griffin kept the Panthers rolling like a finely oiled machine. The Perry team was ranked as one of the top defensive squads in Georgia, thanks to the defensive mastermind of Coach Staples.

Clash of the titans

Possibly the largest crowd ever to attend a game at Macon's City Auditorium came to see the clash of the titans. When the game began, Lanier came out in an unusual defensive alignment. Since they feared the outside shooting of Dwayne Powell who could hit with uncanny accuracy from anywhere on the court, instead of playing their big man, Al Gerhardt, under the basket, Coach Henry Middlebrooks placed the 6' 6" Gerhardt guarding Powell out front. With his long hands stretched high into the air, Gerhardt tried to limit Powell from cutting down on the Poets at the top of the key. Coach Staples signaled to Powell to back up several feet closer to the center line and then shoot over Gerhardt. Staples believed in Powell and needed him to start hitting early on to free up Lee Martin, playing out of the corner, who was being double-teamed. Powell released his first missile in a high trajectory. Up through the dome of the basketball arena it went and as it came crashing down through the net with the classic snap, the Perry fans erupted into a thunderous roar. Then Powell did it again, and again, and again. When the horn blew ending the half, Powell had bucketed nine long range shots in a row and walked off the court with 19 points.

When Powell started hitting, the Poets were forced to back away from their double-teaming of Martin and to concentrate their efforts to stop Powell. Martin then went to work and also scored 19 points by halftime. As Poets' coach Henry Middlebrooks led his team off the court at intermission, behind a whopping 20 points, 44 to 24, he appeared stunned and bewildered by Perry's awesome shooting. Macon fans had never seen such a display of offensive fireworks, and were shaking their heads in disbelief.

Martin conducts basketball clinic

With 19 points already logged in the official scorer's book, Lee Martin came back for an even more sensational second half. Playing like a magician on the court, he could have passed for Harry Houdini dressed in a maroon and gold basketball uniform. In fluid motion, occasionally going into overdrive, he dribbled around, under, and through the Poets. He wooed the Perry crowd repeatedly as he sank unbelievable shots. Just before the horn blew ending the third quarter, Martin got off a quick shot behind center court that hit nothing but nylon. This brought the house down! He continued his wizardry into the final period. With 2:20 left in the game, Staples removed all of Perry's regulars except Martin, who stayed until he topped the 40-point mark with a driving lay-up with 1:40 to play. Martin's exhibition was one of the finest individual performances ever seen in Macon's City Auditorium, which over the years had hosted many great teams and great players. Martin added 22 points in the second half to his 19 first half tallies for a 41 point outburst that would have inspired Macon's famous poet, Sidney Lanier, after whom the school was named, to write a sonnet about basketball at its best.

The final score: Perry-78 and Lanier-47. Powell chipped in 23 points to add to Martin's game high of 41. This was Perry's 22nd consecutive win of the season.

Perry-78	Lanier-47
G. Nunn-2	Seward-4
Powell-23	Gerhardt-6
Fike-6	Biggs-7
Martin-41	Fincher-19
Sanders-2	Bonifay-11

Subs: Perry: Griffin-2, Goodman-2, Riner, Skinner, Dorsett, Davis, Ellis; Lanier: Anderson, Willingham.
Score at half: Perry-44, Lanier-24

Demons seething with revenge

The Warner Robins Demons, embarrassed by the 79 to 34 trashing at Perry's gym, were seething with revenge to upset the Panthers before an overflow crowd of 1700 fans who gathered in the Demon's den. They almost pulled it off, for a half anyway. The Demons led 12-8 toward the end of the second quarter, before field goals by Lee Martin and Dwayne Powell evened the score 12 to 12 as the first half ended.

Perry rolled out to a 31 to 22 margin at the third quarter mark and won the game, 41 to 33. This eight-point victory was the third closest game for the Panthers. The Demons had only one comforting note in defeat. They held Lee Martin to his lowest output for the season, a mere nine points, on a night when his shots weren't falling. His sidekick, Dwayne Powell, however, picked up the slack with a 17-point barrage, 16 of these points coming in the second half as he hit an incredible eight of nine attempts under heavy defense. The Demons did not have a single player in double figures. Bill Cecil, who fouled out with 4:17 remaining in the fourth quarter, was the Demon's high scorer with eight points. George Nunn, Lee Martin, and Dwayne Powell claimed five rebounds each. The Demons hit 39 percent from the field while the Panthers connected on 43 percent.

Perry's third undefeated regular season

The Perry Panthers achieved their third undefeated regular season during the Staples' era when they defeated Dublin's Irish in the Perry gym, 58 to 45. Dublin surprisingly led 33 to 27 at halftime on the fantastic shooting of Dublin's Billy Billue who scored 20 for the game. While Dublin concentrated defensively on Lee Martin and Dwayne Powell, Dennis Fike's 20 point outburst, most of these points coming in the second half, provided the margin of victory. The win over Dublin marked the 27th straight victory with no defeats for Coach Eric Staples' 1962 squad. Two other Perry teams posted perfect regular season marks: the 1935 and 1956 teams.

Coach Staples' 1935 team, his second at Perry, went undefeated during the regular season. In state tournament competition, the 1935 quintet defeated Dublin, LaGrange, and Canton but lost to Albany in the state finals. Players on this team were Allen Martin, Horace Grimsley, James (Preacher) Howard, Dick Edwards, Joe Davis, Aldene Lasseter, Harris Rape, Watt Rainey, G. T. Pierce, Marvin Griffin, Charles Andrew, Donald Clark, and Powers Lawson.

Staples' 1956 club also achieved a perfect regular season record of 26 wins and no loses. Although Perry had defeated Vienna twice during the year, the 1956 team suffered its lone defeat at the hands of Vienna in the 3rd district B and C championship game. It is significant to note that both Perry and Vienna went on to capture the respective Class B and Class C state crowns that year.

As Perry moved into tournament play, Coach Staples had four regulars with better than 42 percent on field goal accuracy. Forward Dwayne Powell led the Panthers with 53 percent, followed by Dennis Fike-46 percent and George Nunn-45 percent. The heralded Lee Martin, averaging 20 points per game, was hitting on 43 percent of his attempts. Powell, the only junior in the starting lineup, was averaging 18 points a game followed by Dennis Fike-9 points per game, George Nunn-7,

Perry's Dynamic Duo: Lee Martin (R) and Dwayne Powell (L) scoring in the state tournament. Other Perry player in right photo: Boot Hunt (#12). Other Perry players in left photo are Garold Spena (#31) and Bert Bozeman (#22).

Ronnie Sanders-2, and Ronnie Griffin-2. These statistics came from game records kept by Perry's longtime official scorer Wilson Martin, Sr. The scoring averages would have been higher had the starters played entire games and the 3-point shot been in effect. In lop-sided victories, which were frequent, Staples used Perry's reserves extensively during the final quarter of play.

The dynamic duo of Lee Martin and Dwayne Powell was the most feared twosome in the state. They were both deadly shooters and offensive superstars. If a team attempted to double-team one of them, the other one would prove to be the game wrecker. During the decade of the 1960s, Martin and Powell were the two best high school basketball players in Georgia ever to play on one team. That assessment may hold true for any era of Georgia basketball. Their one-two punch helped carry Perry to an undefeated season and its sixth state championship.

Perry also boasted of two outstanding point guards in Ronnie Sanders and Ronnie Griffin, both floor generals for Staples' fabled offense. Sanders was the starter, and Griffin logged considerable playing time as Perry's sixth man. Dennis Fike and George Nunn ranked among the premier rebounders in Perry history. The entire Perry team played textbook defense.

Region 2B, Area I tournament: February 19-20 at Perry

Perry vs. Wilkinson County

Perry whacked Wilkinson County, 87 to 23, in the opening round of play. At the halftime, Wilkinson, obviously outmanned, had scored only 9 points to Perry's 42. Dwayne Powell was the top Panther scorer with 23 points. He was followed by Lee Martin-13, Dennis Fike-9, George Nunn-5, and Ronnie Sanders-4. Reserves joining the scoring parade were Paul Bozeman-10, Jimmy Dorsett-10, Bobby Goodman-6, Ronnie Davis-4, Melton Cloud-2, Ronnie Griffin-1, and Butch Skinner.

Perry vs. Hawkinsville

The Perry Panthers left no doubt about being the top team in Region 2B, Area 1, as they buried the Hawkinsville Red Devils in an avalanche of baskets, 71 to 44, for the area title. Fabulous Lee Martin pumped in 31 points for the night. Other Perry scorers were Dennis Fike-11, Dwayne

Powell-10, George Nunn-9, Ronnie Sanders-4, Ronnie Griffin-4, and Paul Bozeman-2.

Region 2B tournament-February 22-24 at Vidalia

Perry vs. Telfair County

Perry rolled to its 30th straight victory of the year by clobbering the Telfair County Trojans, 68 to 39. Perry's victory avenged a loss suffered to the Trojans who, in the previous season, knocked the Panthers out of a trip to the state meet. Although he played only three quarters, Powell led all scorers with 18 points. He was followed by Lee Martin-13, George Nunn-11, Dennis Fike-10, Ronnie Griffin-8, Paul Bozeman-4, and Jimmy Dorsett-4.

Perry vs. Metter (region semifinal)

Perry's powerful Panthers rapped Metter, 51 to 32. This victory marked the Panthers 31st consecutive win of the season without a setback. Perry's Lee Martin ripped the nets for 23 points. Dwayne Powell was good for 10 points while Dennis Fike and George Nunn had eight and seven points respectively. Ronnie Sanders and Ronnie Griffin played excellent floor games.

Perry vs. Southeast Bulloch (region final)

"The Macon Telegraph" sportswriter stated that the Perry Panthers had less trouble disposing of Southeast Bulloch for the region title than they would have pulling off their jerseys. The Panthers humbled Southeast Bulloch, 73 to 38. Flashy Lee Martin scored 28 points on 13 field goals and two of three from the foul stripe. Dwayne Powell chipped in 10 points while Dennis Fike and George Nunn had 9 and 8 points respectively. Point guard Ronnie Sanders did an outstanding job of distributing the ball and keeping Perry's high-powered offense running on all cylinders.

Perry's win placed the Panthers in the same state tournament bracket with Fort Valley, which meant they would meet in the semifinals if both teams advanced past the opening round. Due to the fight in 1949, Perry and Fort Valley were still barred from regular season play and allowed to compete against each other only in tournament action.

State Tournament: March 7-10 at Macon City Auditorium

Perry vs. Mitchell County

Mitchell County was the first team to fall as the Perry Panthers made their march toward a sixth state title under veteran coach Eric P. Staples. The score was Perry-44, Mitchell County-26. Mitchell County was never in the game, and Perry used subs in the third and fourth quarters.

Lee Martin hit on 10 of 20 attempts from the floor and finished the game with 23 points. Dwayne Powell experienced a rare off-shooting night, connecting on 4 of 16 attempts for 9 tallies. Dennis Fike and Ronnie Sanders each had four points and George Nunn added two markers. Reserves receiving playing time were Wayne Riner, Ronnie Griffin, Jimmy Dorsett, Melton Cloud, Paul Bozeman-2, and Butch Skinner.

The game of all games: Perry vs. defending state champions-Fort Valley (state semifinals)

The Perry-Fort Valley game was Macon's first televised state tournament basketball game. The gates opened at 3:15 p.m. for the 8 p.m. game, and the crowds immediately began to pour into the arena. The Perry cheerleaders arrived an hour and a half before game time to organize the cheering and to whip the Panther faithful into a fever pitch before tip-off. When Coach Staples made his appearance early in the evening, the entire Perry sidelines stood up and cheered wildly. Fort Valley's fans came with high expectations of seeing their beloved Green Wave team upend the Perry Panthers, who were undefeated and sporting a 34-game winning streak

The first quarter started with both teams playing cautiously and looking for the clear shot. It ended in a 10 to 10 tie. With one minute left in the second quarter, Perry had moved out front 24 to 19, but Tee Faircloth, Coach Norman Faircloth's son, closed the gap with two long two pointers to make it 24 to 23 at halftime.

A wave of apprehension swept over Perry's fans. The Panthers were playing good basketball, yet the Green Waves were matching them basket-for-basket and rebound-for-rebound. This game had every indication of developing into a nail-bitter right down to the final buzzer. It would have been embarrassing for top rival Fort Valley to end the Panthers' perfect season and the dream of a sixth state championship. If Fort Valley won, the bragging would go on for decades.

With 5:01 remaining in the third stanza, Perry led by only four points, 31 to 27. At that point Fort Valley went cold, and Perry quickly opened up a 12-point margin. Perry continued to spread the gap and was ahead 19 points, 47 to 28, as the third quarter ended.

Perry's fans breathed a sigh of relief, but their respite was premature because the Green Wave would make one final run at the Panthers. Coach Staples decided to nurse the 19-point lead and play ball-control offense during the final period. However, this worked against the Panthers. Tee Faircloth got hot and bombarded the nets from long range, and the Green Wave fought their way back into the game. With two minutes remaining in the contest, the Green Wave moved within four points of the Panthers, but Coach Staples continued his daring strategy of holding onto the ball and limiting Fort Valley's scoring opportunities. Perry rode out Fort Valley's rally to prevail by eight points, 52 to 44. Lee Martin tallied 25 points for the Panther cause. Dwayne Powell added 13 points, his baskets coming at key times when they were badly needed, on occasion taking the starch out of the Green Wave's gallant comeback efforts. George Nunn played his best game of the year against Fort Valley, defending smartly and adding 9 points to the Perry victory. Dennis Fike, always a demon on defense, teamed with Nunn to put the clamps on any effort by the Green Wave to drive to the basket. Opponents never got a good shot over Fike all night as he pressured the shooter and deflected a number of balls. Ronnie Sanders and Ronnie Griffin, the two point guards, proved to be sharp ball-handlers and fast on defense.

In retrospect, Perry's ball control tactics definitely slowed down the Panther's offense as they scored only 5 points during the fourth quarter while Fort Valley was riddling the nets for 16 points. However, Staples' gamble worked as the 11-point differential in Fort Valley's fourth quarter scoring was offset by Perry's 19-point third quarter lead, thus the eight-point cushion of victory. Again, Coach Staples had demonstrated his innovative genius as well as his commitment to stay the course with a strategy he believed would keep the Panthers' title hopes alive. Had Staples turned his charges loose in the final period, Perry may well have won by a much larger margin, but a win is a win.

Perry-52	**Fort Valley-44**
Fike-5	Lawhorn-2
Powell-13	J.Hardeman-3
Nunn -9	Tharpe-4
Martin-25	D. Hardeman-2
Sanders	Tee Faircloth-30

Subs: Perry: Griffin; Fort Valley: McDaniel-3, Tucker, Harrelson
Score at half: Perry-24, Fort Valley-23

Would Fort Valley have beaten Perry with Ray Pearson in the line-up?

Fort Valley Coach Norman Faircloth in a published newspaper interview with "Macon Telegraph" sports editor Harley Bowers, stated he felt that his 1962 club "would have beaten Perry" if his star center Ray Pearson had not been sidelined with a knee injury. Coach Faircloth added that his 1961 state championship team was "20 points better" than his current team that lost to Perry in the state semifinals.

Perry's confident fans were quoted in the "Macon Telegraph" as saying that "Pearson and four professionals could not have beaten the Panthers." In comparison, Fort Valley with Pearson in the line-up lost to the same Lanier Poet team 48 to 46 that Perry routed 78 to 47. In Fort Valley's loss to the Poets on January 3, 1962, Tee Faircloth and Ray Pearson led Fort Valley's scoring with 16 and 15 points respectively, but the Green Wave effort fell two points shy of victory.

Perry vs. Clinch County (state championship)

Only one team stood in Perry's path for the school's first undefeated season and an unprecedented sixth state championship—Clinch County. Clinch County, where Homerville is the county seat, had defeated

Southeast Bullock and Oconee County to reach the finals and appeared to be a formidable opponent for the Panthers.

Clinch County put fear into the hearts of the Panther faithful during the first quarter, as practically every shot they fired seemed to find the bottom of the net. Perry gallantly fought back and moved to within two points, 11 to 13, at the end of the first period. Clinch County began to fade in the second quarter as Coach Eric Staples' crew assaulted the nets for 20 points while holding Clinch County to only nine. The score at intermission stood, Perry-31, Clinch-22.

With 3:22 remaining in the third quarter, Perry moved out to a commanding 20-point lead, 46 to 26. By the end of the third quarter, the margin had increased to 55 to 32 and Perry seemed to be in the driver's seat.

The third quarter was not without its theatrics. Only seconds before the buzzer sounded ending the period, Lee Martin brought the ball up the court and released a one-handed shot 55-feet from the basket in the backcourt that banked off the backboard and popped through the net. This awed the 3,000 fans packed into the City Auditorium and brought the Perry contingent to its feet. At this point Martin had 25 points.

During the final period, Martin continued his barrage, scoring 16 points on a combination of long and short range jumpers and driving, twisting lay-ups. He finished the night with 41 points, tying his previous high of 41 against Lanier, as the Panthers crushed Clinch County 77 to 45 for Perry's 35th consecutive victory, the school's first undefeated season, and its unprecedented sixth state championship. When Martin wasn't leading the scoring parade, Dwayne Powell was slowly but steadily collecting 19 points, eleven in the last half. Dennis Fike pitched in 10 points. Fike and George Nunn led the team in rebounding and kept the offense clicking by setting screens for Martin and Powell. Point guards Ronnie Sanders and Ronnie Griffin played outstanding floor games and kept the Panthers' offense purring.

Perry-77	**Clinch County-45**
Fike -10	Harrison-8

Powell-19	Tomlinson-8
Nunn-2	Barrett-11
Martin-41	Cason-5
Sanders	Dunn-6

Score at half: Perry-31, Clinch County-22
Subs: Perry: Griffin-5; Clinch County: Bateman-2, Oliff, Bennett-3, Allison-2

Greatest basketball player in Georgia

When Bob Bonifay, general manager of the Macon Peaches, presented the Perry captain, Lee Martin, the gold basketballs for the Perry team at the trophy ceremonies, he called Martin "the greatest high school basketball player in the state of Georgia." Martin's scintillating play all season left little doubt that he really was the very best. Evidence of this distinction was the number of college scouts who were camping out on Martin's doorsteps.

Panthers place six players on "All-State" teams:

Macon Telegraph "All-State" team
Lee Martin-Perry
Dwayne Powell-Perry
Dennis Fike-Perry
George Nunn-Perry
Tee Faircloth-Fort Valley
Nim Tharpe-Fort Valley
Herbert Tomlinson-Clinch County
Mira Barrett-Clinch County
Jimmy Dunn-Clinch County
Jimmy Crayton-Pike County

Honorable Mention:
Ronnie Sanders-Perry
Ronnie Griffin-Perry

Atlanta Constitution "all-state" team
Lee Martin-Perry
Dwayne Powell-Perry
Ronnie Griffin-Perry
Tee Faircloth-Fort Valley
Ron Harrison-Clinch County
Herbert Tomlinson-Clinch County
Scotty Anderson-Southeast Bulloch
Billy Bishop-Oconee County
Jim Crayton-Pike County
Benny Dukes-Pike County

Honorable mention:
Dennis Fike-Perry
George Nunn-Perry
Ronnie Sanders-Perry
Jody Hardeman-Fort Valley
Nim Tharpe-Fort Valley
Mira Bartlett-Clinch County
Larry Good-Mitchell County
Bill White-White County

Just how good was the 1961-62 Perry High School basketball team? Harley Bowers, Sports Editor of the "Macon Telegraph," addressed this question in his column after the basketball season ended. Below are excerpts:

- "There is no doubt in our mind that on the night they crushed the Lanier Poets, Perry was the best that ever walked on a court."

- "When both Lee Martin and Dwayne Powell are on target, there is little a defense can do."

- "Perry was undoubtedly the best defensive club we watched all season."

- "Perry would have walloped the AAA champion, Columbus, without much difficulty, and certainly they would have defeated the Class A (Central Gwinnett) and C champs (Marion County), whom we saw play here the last two weeks. As for the AA (Murray County) we cannot say, not having seen the tournament, but one must rank the Panthers ahead here, too."

- "The lone dissenter to the Perry ballyhoo was Fort Valley coach Norman Faircloth who insisted his 1961 champions were better (than Perry's 1962 team) and said his 1962 club would have beaten the Panthers had big center Ray Pearson not been sidelined with a football knee injury."

- "The conclusion we reached was that it will never be definitely settled as to whether Perry is the best ever. No one can argue that they're not among the greatest. A team doesn't win 35 games in this day and age by accident."

Perry Season Record

Opponent	Perry Score	Opponent Score
Christmas Tournament		
Crawford County	83	55
Macon County	53	37
Regular Season		
Unadilla	62	25
East Laurens	60	44
Cochran	63	22
East Laurens	68	45
Crawford County	68	43
Mc Rae	57	38

Opponent	Perry Score	Opponent Score
Willingham	59	27
Hawkinsville	60	30
Macon County	64	40
Vienna	68	32
Lanier	66	53
Cochran	80	37
Dublin	51	30
Unadilla	61	20
Willingham	45	40
Telfair	52	39
Warner Robins	79	34
Crawford County	31	29
Butler	69	31
Lanier	78	47
Vienna	73	41
Macon County	55	42
Hawkinsville	76	45
Warner Robins	41	33
Dublin	58	45

Region 2B, Area 1, Tournament: Feb 19-20 at Perry

Wilkinson County	87	23
Hawkinsville	71	44

Region 2B Tournament: Feb 22-24 at Vidalia

Telfair County	68	39
Metter	51	32
Southeast Bulloch	73	38

State Tournament: March 7-10 at Macon City Auditorium

Mitchell County	44	26
Fort Valley	52	44
Clinch County	77	45

The Miracle Team: 1963 team

1963 Perry team. Front, L-R: Bert Bozeman, Porter Staples, Paul Bozeman, Charles Harrison, Jimmy Suber. Back, L-R: Dwayne Powell, Alton Ellis, Jimmy Dorsett, Melton Cloud, Garold Spena.

Bad News-Good News

When the 1962-63 school year began, Perry High School boasted of six state championship awards in its trophy case, but there was little hope in town of the Panthers repeating in 1963. The bad news was that Perry had lost to graduation four of its "all-state" starters from the undefeated 1962 state championship team: Lee Martin, Ronnie Sanders, George Nunn, and Dennis Fike. Also lost to graduation was Ronnie Griffin, the sixth man, who was named to the "Atlanta Constitution's" all-state team. Capable reserves not returning were Butch Skinner, Ronnie Davis, and Bobby Goodman.

The good news was that the lone junior in the starting lineup, Dwayne Powell, was returning for his senior year. In 1962, the dynamic duo of Lee Martin and Dwayne Powell was considered by many to be the best guard-forward combination ever to play Georgia high school basketball. While Martin was averaging 20 points a game, Powell was complementing him with 18 per game. And they rarely played an entire game as Perry overpowered most opponents with its lethal offensive machine. When schools tried to double-team Martin, Powell would break the game wide open. When they shifted back on Powell to cool him down, then Martin would go on a rampage. So for opposing coaches it was a catch-22 situation of choosing which way they wanted to lose, by Martin or by Powell since the Panthers in 1962 never tasted defeat.

Varsity returnees from the 1962 team other than Powell were Jimmy Dorsett, Melton Cloud, and Paul Bozeman, all of whom had played sparingly as reserves during the past season. Former B-team players expected to compete for several starting positions were Bert Bozeman, Garold Spena, Porter Staples, Alton Ellis, Joe Martin, Charles Harrison, and William Suber.   In summary, if the Panthers were to make a run at a second straight state crown, several untested players would have to mature and blossom in a hurry.

Perry vs. perennial powerhouse Telfair County

Before playing Telfair County, always a contender in region 2 and a quintet to be reckoned with at tournament time, the Panthers had marched over Unadilla 86 to 40, Butler 75 to 38, and Crawford County 57 to 53. Telfair came out smoking and played Perry close during the first half, but Dwayne Powell began to tattoo the basket during the last half, scoring 33 points for the game, as the Panthers pulled away with a decisive 71 to 44 triumph. Jimmy Dorsett contributed 10 points, Paul Bozeman-8, Bert Bozeman-8, Melton Cloud-6, Alton Ellis-2, Charles Harrison-2, and Garold Spena-2.

Panthers and Rams Collide in Panther Lair

Willingham Ram Coach Martin Almand started a veteran team against the young and inexperienced Panthers: senior forwards Mark Bowen, 6'2", and Pete Gaines, 6'0"; junior center Ralph Pulliam, 6'4"; and senior guards Bobby Bryant, 6'1", and Thelston Goss, 5'10."

Perry took an 18 to 13 first quarter lead and moved to a

commanding 35 to 21 halftime lead. Dwayne Powell had 22 points at intermission. During the last half, the Rams outscored the Panthers 22 to 20, but their rally came too late and too short to overcome their first half deficit. Perry won the contest 55 to 43 as Dwayne Powell topped all scorers with 29 points. Bobby Bryant led Willingham with 12 markers.

Perry-55	Willingham-43
P. Bozeman-2	Bowen-7
Dorsett-8	Gaines-6
Cloud-8	Pulliam-4
B. Bozeman-8	Bryant-12
Powell-29	Goss-8

Subs: Perry: none; Willingham: Payne-2, Goodman, Clay-2, Colson, Hester-2
Score at half: Perry-35, Willingham-21

Battle Clouds across the Macon County line

Always formidable were the Macon County Rebels coached by Bill Martin, whose 1948 and 1950 teams captured the state Class C crown. Macon County and Perry were tied with less than a minute to play in the first half when Dwayne Powell hit two long range shots in a row that were well beyond the top of the key to send Perry into the dressing room with a four-point lead. The Panthers poured it on in the second half and won, going away, 66 to 49. Dwayne Powell, double-teamed all night long, pumped in 38 points, hitting an unbelievable repertoire of shots. Bert Bozeman added 15 tallies, Melton Cloud-9, Jimmy Dorsett-2, and Alton Ellis-2.

Poets poised to end Panthers' 45-game winning streak

The Panthers' win-streak stood at 45 games. This included the victory in the region consolation game in 1961, the 35 games during the undefeated 1962 season plus 9-straight wins during the current season.

During the first half, Lanier and Perry matched basket-for-basket, but the Panthers shot ahead 21 to 18 at halftime. Midway the third quarter, the Poets regained the lead 25 to 21, and later in the period led on two occasions, 29 to 25, and 31 to 27. Each time the Panthers dropped behind, Dwayne Powell hit a flurry of baskets. Powell scored all eleven of the Panther points during the third period and finished with a five-point outburst just before the quarter ended, putting the Panthers back out front, 32 to 31.

The fourth quarter was not conducive to the faint of heart, for the lead changed hands six times. With 4:42 to play, Perry moved from a one-point deficit to a 38 to 37 lead on a jumper by Jimmy Dorsett, which proved to be the winning basket. At this point Coach Staples decided to employ his famous stalling tactic designed to run the clock down and draw fouls. At the 1:30 mark, Lanier's Don Biggs muffed a lay-up. With 47 seconds left, the Panthers blew two free throws that would have iced the game. The Poets attempted to tie the game, but turned the ball over on a bad pass. Perry resumed its freeze until Bert Bozeman was fouled. Bozeman hit both foul shots, but the second was nullified because a Perry player prematurely stepped into the lane. Lanier didn't have time to get the ball down court, and Perry won a nail-bitter, 39 to 37.

Harley Bowers, "Macon Telegraph" Sports Editor, wrote: "Dwayne Powell, firing with the long-range accuracy of a Nike missile, rifled home 28 points here Wednesday night to lead the Perry Panthers to a narrow 39 to 37 victory over the Lanier Poets....The Maconites missed a chance to end a Perry winning streak that now stretches to 46 games ...(and) become the first team to beat last year's state Class B champions in two seasons.... The victory was the 854th for Perry coach Eric Staples in a coaching career that is now in its 36th year."

Perry-39	Lanier-37
P. Bozeman	Gerhardt-12
Dorsett-6	McLendon-13
Cloud	Biggs-6
B. Bozeman-5	Bonifay-4
Powell-28	Jordan-2

Subs: Perry: Ellis; Lanier: none
Score at half: Perry-21, Lanier-18

Perry Christmas Invitational Tournament: December 27-28 at Perry

Perry won the opening round against Crawford County 66 to 51 on the hot-shooting of Dwayne Powell who tallied 36-points. Jimmy Dorsett hit for 13, Bert Bozeman-9 and Alton Ellis-8.

In the championship game, Perry was pitted against an upset-minded Macon County team that on the previous night had knocked the Class AAA Warner Robins Demons from the ranks of the unbeaten.

Macon County's Rebels contrived an outstanding defensive plan aimed at stopping Dwayne Powell. It slowed him down for two quarters until he put on a dazzling display of offensive fireworks in the second half. The game was nip and tuck from the starting tip-off until the last second ticked off the clock.

During the closing minutes of the final quarter, Macon County forged ahead 43 to 41 on a pair of charity tosses by Billy Easterlin. Perry's center, Melton Cloud, tied it 45 to 45, and Alton Ellis and Dwayne Powell added four more to put Perry out front 49 to 45. Jerry Brown made a 25-footer to pull Macon County within two points, 49 to 47. With 18 seconds on the clock Steve Haugabook was awarded a two-shot foul, and a chance to tie the game. He made the first and missed the second. The Panthers prevailed in a thriller, 49 to 48, and recorded their 48th consecutive victory since the region consolation game in 1961.

Macon County's Jerry Brown, a 5' 6" defensive wizard, held Dwayne Powell to only 11 shots and 13 points in the first half, but committed four fouls in the process and saw limited action the rest of the game. Powell came back with a 21 point explosion in the second half for a 34-point performance. Other Panthers in the scoring column were: Bert Bozeman and Porter Staples with 4 each, Jimmy Dorsett-3, and Alton Ellis and Melton Cloud with two points apiece. This win established Perry's winning streak at 49 games.

Perry's 50th consecutive victory

The Perry Panthers blistered the Hawkinsville Red Devils, 63 to 45, and recorded their 50th consecutive win over a two year span. Dwayne Powell scored 40 points, Jimmy Dorsett-15, Bert Bozeman-7, and Alton Ellis-1.

Waterloo in Leprechaun Country

When the Perry Panthers invaded Dublin, home of the Irish and their leprechaun mascots, they were sporting a 50-game winning streak. Dublin coach Minton Williams devised a unique defensive scheme to slow down the Powell Express. He alternated two players on Dwayne Powell and played a zone against the remainder of the Panther squad. Coach Williams was quoted in the "Macon Telegraph" as saying his team might not beat Perry's, but "Powell's just not going to score 30 points."

Coach Williams' plan to limit Powell's scoring was sound, for in the 14 games in which Powell had played (didn't play in Unadilla game) he had scored 405 points that averaged a fraction less than 30 points a game. He had scored 405 of Perry's 836 points. This 6'1", dead-eyed sharpshooter, had hit on 173 field goals out of 323 attempts for 54 percent, a fantastic percentage when considering that most of his baskets were made from long range with one to two men attempting to guard him. He was also hitting 90 percent of his foul shots. The above statistics were reported by "Macon Telegraph" Sports Editor Harley Bowers in his column, dated January 6, 1963, and by Gordon Stem, "Macon News" Sports Editor, in his column published the same day.

Coach Williams alternated two men on Powell, Eddie Scott and Chuck Frost, giving each plenty of rest so they could go full speed at all times. These two quick speedsters literally followed Powell all over the court. There never was a time when either Scott or Frost could not touch Powell. When Perry called timeout, they followed him step-for-step to the sidelines. When the timeout ended, they walked back on the floor beside him. When Powell was at the free throw line, they stood just outside the foul circle either behind him or beside him. At halftime, one of them followed Powell off the court and nearly to the dressing room. They were doing exactly what their coach had instructed them—and it worked, since Powell was held to 15 points, far off his usual pace. To make matters worse, Williams' Dublin Irish crew played a slow down game, limiting Perry's possessions and Powell's chances to score.

If you were not a partisan Panther fan, this was a great spectator game, more like a chess match, as Coach Minton Williams methodically and meticulously pulled off the game of the year, snapping Perry's 50-game winning streak spanning two years, and winning by a one point margin in a low scoring contest, 44 to 43. Coach Minton Williams will be long remembered as the coach who dethroned the Perry Panthers and broke their winning streak. And he did it with a team that subsequently lost three times to the Panthers in 1963, once in regular season play and twice in tournament competition.

In the scoring department along with Powell's 15 points, Bert Bozeman contributed 14, Jimmy Dorsett-6, Alton Ellis-4, and Porter Staples-4. Tom Perry hit a game high of 21 for Dublin followed by Mike Belote-13, Chuck Frost-6, Dorminy-2, and Eddie Scott-2

State Record

Gordon Stem, "Macon News" Sports Editor, wrote in his column on January 6, 1963, that "Perry's 50-game winning streak is believed to be a state record. Charles Gates of the Georgia High School Association said Saturday that no basketball records are kept, but it was the longest streak he'd ever heard of."

In actuality, Perry's record is thought to be the second longest winning streak up to that point in the history of Georgia high school boys' basketball. The Irwinville Farmers, coached by Georgia Sports Hall of Fame coach, Wallace "Country" Childs, won 78-consecutive games, including two straight state Class B championships in 1950 and 1951.

16-1 Panthers vs. 13-2 Demons

In Perry's game with their Houston County neighbors, the Warner Robins Demons, a Class AAA team, the lead see-sawed back and forth for three quarters. After playing a fast-breaking game for the first three quarters, Perry slowed the game down and played ball control during the final period, looking for the high percentage shot. As Powell started hitting with regularity and the Demons began to foul, Perry began to pull away, scoring 23 points in the fourth quarter while the Demons hit for 15. The final score was Perry-64, Warner Robins-53.

Powell was top point-getter with 22 points. The Demons' Jimmy Tucker did a commendable job of guarding Powell and holding him below his 30 point average. Jimmy Dorsett added 14, Joe Martin and Melton Cloud-9 each, Garold Spena-6, and Bert Bozeman-4. The Demons' Mike Davis was the game's high scorer with 27. David Moore tallied 9, Alton

Knight and Clarence Channell had 7 each, and Jimmy Tucker added 3.

Warner Robins was coached by Don LaBlanc, one of Georgia's finest coaches during that era, who will be long remembered for the outstanding teams he consistently produced.

Season review as tournament play begins

Important milestone

The 1962-63 school year was Perry's first venture into the Class A ranks, having been a Class B school since basketball was started there in 1919. This move was an important milestone in Perry basketball history.

Season record

Perry's season record prior to tournament competition was 23 wins against only three losses. The losses were to the (1) Lanier Poets with whom they split during the season, the (2) Dublin Irish who broke the Panthers' 50-game streak but lost to Perry 58-41 in the last game of the regular season, and the (3) Warner Robins Demons whom they beat in Perry and lost to in Warner Robins. Don LaBlanc's Demons went on to capture the runner-up spot in the state Class AAA tournament.

Region 2A North Sub-Region tournament: February 12-13 at Cochran

Perry vs. Dudley Hughes

Perry completely dominated Dudley Hughes in the region 2A north opener, jumping out to a 15 to 0 first quarter lead. The Panthers were ahead 27 to 11 at halftime and 44 to 25 after three quarters. The final tally was Perry-57, Dudley Hughes -34. Powell tossed in 35 points, Jimmy Dorsett-10, Garold Spena-8, Bert Bozeman and Melton Cloud-2 each.

Perry vs. Dublin

The Dublin five, who earlier had ended Perry's 50-game winning streak, started out like they were going to pour salt in the Panthers' wounds by denying them a trip to the state tournament. Dublin's 15 to 11 first quarter lead was short-lived, however, as Perry found the range during the second stanza and built a 23 to 22 lead at intermission. With

Jimmy Dorsett and Melton Cloud controlling both boards and Powell getting hot, the Panthers widened the gap to 34 to 28 as the third quarter concluded.

Dublin outscored Perry 14 to 13 during the final period, but went down to defeat, 47 to 42, as Dwayne Powell bombarded the nets with regularity during the four quarters with 9, 8, 4, and 6-points respectively and scored 27 of his team's 47 points. Garold Spena contributed 11, Jimmy Dorsett-4, Bert Bozeman-3, and Melton Cloud-2.

Region 2 Tournament finals : February 15-16 at Swainsboro

Perry vs. Effingham County

Dwayne Powell crawled out of bed with the flu to lead the Panthers to a 53 to 27 verdict over Effingham County, although he played about half of the game and his 19 points were well below his season average. After the game, Powell was put back in bed as the Panthers stayed overnight in Swainboro for the region 2A championship against Dublin.

In the Effingham County game, Coach Staples used seven reserves during much of the final period: Porter Staples-2 points, Edgar Barfield-2, Paul Bozeman, Joe Martin, Charles Harrison, Jimmy Suber, and Alton Ellis. Other Perry starters scoring were Garold Spena-12, Bert Bozeman-9, Jimmy Dorsett-8, and Melton Cloud-1.

Region championship: Perry vs. Dublin

This game marked the fourth time Perry would play Dublin. They had split with Dublin during the regular season, losing the first game 44 to 43 (which ended the Panthers' 50-game winning streak), and winning the return encounter, 58 to 41. Only two days earlier in the region 2-A north, sub-region finals played at Cochran, Perry had downed Dublin 47 to 42.

Dublin began the game playing conservatively on offense and concentrating defensively on the Panthers' Dwayne Powell. It appeared the Irish were vying for another upset as they battled Perry to a 7 to 7 draw at the first quarter mark. Although Perry eased out front 19 to 16 at halftime, a nerve-wracking half lay ahead in which either team could prevail. Soon after the third quarter began, Dublin's fortunes quickly turned into a nightmare. The Panthers, clicking on all cylinders, turned the once close contest into a rout, racing to a 39 to 23 third quarter margin. The Panthers then coasted the remainder of the way for a 52 to 41 triumph.

Dwayne Powell, still recovering from a bout with the flu, led the Panther scoring with 22 points. Bert Bozeman and Garold Spena added 11 each; Melton Cloud and Jimmy Dorsett had four apiece. Tom Perry was Dublin's top gun with 18 markers.

This victory marked the third time Perry had defeated Dublin since its earlier loss to the Irish. Perry was headed to the state Class A tournament in Macon with a chance to capture its second straight state championship, having won the Class B title in 1962.

State Class A Tournament: February 28-March 2 at Macon City Auditorium

Perry vs. Toccoa

The Panthers led 15 to 10 at the end of first quarter and exited the hardwood for the halftime breather nursing a narrow 27 to 25 lead.

In the third period, Dwayne Powell connected on four consecutive shots from "down town" and the Panthers moved out to a 46 to 29 lead with just 30 seconds to play in the quarter. At that point, Toccoa, reeling from Powell's outburst, began a gallant comeback that pushed them to within seven points, 46 to 39, with 6:12 to play; and after another surge, pulled to within two points, 48 to 46, with 4:05 on the clock. Powell drilled another from the deep corner, but Toccoa's 6' 7" Carroll Ivester matched his basket with a bank shot off the glass. The score was 50 to 48. Powell added a free throw, making it 51 to 48. Al Westmoreland's jumper cut Perry's margin to only one point, 51 to 50. Jimmy Dorsett and Porter Staples each hit a foul shot, putting Perry in the lead, 53 to 50. Garold Darnell hit a driving lay-up moving Toccoa to within one point again, 53 to 52. During the final 22 seconds, Powell killed Toccoa's hopes with four clutch free throws. Bert Bozeman followed with two more and Perry prevailed, 59 to 52, to advance to the semifinal game against Americus, whom many considered the tournament favorite.

Powell, whose scorecard by quarter read 8-4-12-9, ended the game with 33 points. Bert Bozeman, a deadly southpaw, backed up Powell's outburst with 14 points, and Garold Spena collected 9. Spena, Jimmy Dorsett, and Porter Staples did a superb job on the boards against the taller Toccoa five featuring its 6' 7" center, Carroll Ivester. For Toccoa, Garold Darnell and Al Westmoreland scored 16 points each on strong outside shooting. Carroll Ivester chipped in 12 and was a demon on the boards.

Perry-59	**Toccoa-52**
Dorsett-1	Bagby-2
Spena-9	Holcombe-2
Powell-33	Ivester-12
B. Bozeman-14	Darnell-16
Staples-2	Westmoreland-16

Subs: Perry: J. Martin; Toccoa: Spearman-4, Taylor
Score at half: Perry-27, Toccoa-25

State semifinals: Panthers vs. Panthers

Four South Georgia teams advanced to the semifinals of the state Class A tournament: Perry and runner-up Dublin from region 2 and Americus and runner-up Blackshear from region 1. The Perry Panthers (27-3) coached by veteran Coach Eric Staples, and the Americus Panthers (25-3) coached by Jimmy Hightower were co-favorites to win the state title. Ironically, Perry, the region 2 champs, and Americus, the region 1 champions, drew the same bracket while the teams they beat in the region, Dublin and Blackshear respectively, were placed in a different bracket. Consequently, the Perry-Americus game was expected to determine the eventual state champion.

The Perry-Americus game was as much of a roller-coaster as it had been forecast to be. The lead changed hands 15 times and the contest was tied on four occasions. Americus was ahead 25 to 24 at the half. With two minutes remaining in the third quarter, Perry had moved ahead, 34 to 33. The real drama developed from this point. . .

Angels on the Hardwood

Powell hit a long range missile to put Perry ahead, 36 to 33. It was then that Garold Spena took a 20-foot jump shot in the coffin corner and a foot behind the line of the backboard that skimmed the backboard and went into the basket. This was an unbelievable bank shot from a technically impossible angle--the most miraculous shot in Perry basketball history. The only explanation is that angels were guiding the basketball in flight. Perry's miracles were not over. Americus' Steve Posey hit a bucket with a second left in third period to cut Perry's lead to 38 to 35 as the third quarter ended.

Early in the fourth stanza, Hugh Watts and Steve Posey each made field goals for Americus; John White added a free throw and Americus moved ahead 40 to 38. Perry's Spena responded with a single free throw, and then two more gratis tosses, moving Perry ahead, 41 to 40. First Johnnie Southwell and then Hugh Watts answered Spena with field goals as Americus pulled away, 44 to 41.

With less than two minutes on the scoreboard clock, Americus forward Hugh Watts added another foul shot, upping the score to 45 to 41 in favor of Americus. With 1:45 left to play Dwayne Powell missed the first of a one-if-one free throw. Eleven seconds later, at the 1:34 mark, Powell redeemed himself with a three point play—hitting a jumper at top of the key and drawing a foul as two defenders leaned into him. The Panthers had moved within one point, 45 to 44. The Perry crowd went wild. Perry still had hope. The city auditorium was rocking on its girders. The smell of victory was in the air...and Lady Luck seemed to be smiling! Twenty-two seconds later, Garold Spena was fouled and hit both shots from the foul line, putting Perry in the lead 46 to 45.

With 1:10 to play, Americus' Steve Posey missed the first of a one-if-one free throw opportunity. Perry regained possession with 55 seconds left. The cagy ol' fox, Eric Staples, signaled for the Panthers to freeze the ball. Americus fouled Jimmy Dorsett with six seconds on the clock; however, Dorsett missed both shots. With time running out, Americus didn't have time to cross center court. A desperation shot from the back court sailed over the backboard and Perry had won another squeaker, 46 to 45. Staples' Panthers had staged one of the most miraculous comebacks in Perry basketball history. Perry's championship hopes were still alive.

Would the angels return for the title game?

Garold Spena was Perry's man of the hour and the Panther's top scorer with 17 points, one more than Dwayne Powell who garnered 16 hard-to-get baskets. Powell was limited to 18 field goal attempts by a stingy Americus defense orchestrated by the defensive genius of Coach Jimmy Hightower. Bozeman hit for nine, Jimmy Dorsett-3, and Porter Staples-1. Perry had no substitutions. Hugh Watts of Americus led all scorers with 19 points followed by Steve Posey-9, Chambliss-6, John White-5, Ryals-1, and Johnnie Southwell-5.

Americus led in rebounds 32 to 19. Porter Staples, son of coach Staples, only 5'10", filled in for the injured Melton Cloud, Perry's center, and pulled down seven rebounds, having to compete on the backboards with Americus' 6' 8" center John White. Staples also played an excellent floor game and contributed heavily to the Panther victory.

Panthers had beaten Dublin twice in region; would they meet again for state title?

Blackshear disposed of Dublin 56 to 51 in the semifinal game, so Perry would not have to play the persistent Dublin crew for the fifth time during the 1962-63 season. The big question facing the Panthers was-could they defeat the strong Blackshear quintet?

State finals: Perry vs. Blackshear

A crowd of 2,350 fans watched the showdown between Perry and Blackshear. This large crowd for the finale pushed the tournament's total attendance mark to over 7,000 fans, eclipsing the old record of 6359 set in 1959. Perry, being in the Class A ranks for the first time with its large fan base, contributed significantly to this new attendance record.

Blackshear was never in the game. The Panthers led the Tigers 16 to 8 at the end of first quarter, 33 to 17 at the half, 48 to 29 as the third stanza ended, and won decisively by a 24 point margin, 67 to 43. The state crown was the second in a row for Perry—their first as a Class A team. The Perry team wound up the year with an impressive 30-3 record, one of the best in school history.

Powell led all scorers with 30 points. Powell would join his teammate of last season, Lee Martin, at UGA. There Martin was leading the Georgia freshman with 20 points per game. Powell saved his best for the last game. After scoring five points in the first quarter, eight in the second and three in the third, he closed out his high school career with a scintillating shooting exhibition of 14 points in the final eight minutes. Other players with outstanding performances were Garold Spena, who accounted for 15 markers, Porter Staples and Bert Bozeman who contributed 8 points each, and Jimmy Dorsett who collected 6. Perry's center Melton Cloud missed the tournament because of an ankle injury, but was indispensable to the Panthers' outstanding season record and their march through the regional tournament.

Perry-67	**Blackshear-43**
Dorsett-6	Brown-10
Spena-15	David-1
Staples-8	Moody-19
Powell-30	Jones-9
Bozeman-8	Griffis-4

Subs: Perry: Martin; Blackshear: Strickland, Taylor, Cochran

Most prolific scorer in Perry history

Dwayne Powell, who played sparingly as a freshman but was a starter during his sophomore, junior, and senior years, scored 2043 points during his career, the highest point total in Perry basketball history. He averaged 29.9 points a game during his senior year, which was also a school record, and hit over 50 percent of his field goal attempts. He was 90 percent at the foul line, hitting a phenomenal 50 straight free throws without a miss.

Powell is probably the only Panther to play in a freshman game, a B-team game, and a varsity game the same night. In the varsity game, during the fall of 1959, Coach Staples sent this gangling 5' 7" freshman into the game as the fourth quarter started. Powell scored 14 points on long range bombs against a strong Crawford County quintet.

Coach Eric Staples was quoted by "Atlanta Constitution" sportswriter, Charlie Roberts as stating, "Powell is the best shot I have ever seen in high school basketball. I said it last year. I still say it."

Class B All-State team:
Dwayne Powell: team captain-Perry
Bert Bozeman-Perry
Garold Spena-Perry
Porter Staples-Perry
Steve Moody-Blackshear
Jimmy Jones- Blackshear
Hugh Watts- Americus
Steve Posey-Americus
Tom Perry-Dublin
Mike Belote-Dublin

Prospects for coming season
    With three all-state players, Bert Bozeman, Jimmy Dorsett, and Garold Spena, plus two talented reserves, Alton Ellis and Joe Martin, returning for the 1963-64 season, Coach Staples' charges had an excellent opportunity of winning a third consecutive state title. The potential was definitely there, but winning state championships requires more than talent—it requires luck. One errant shot or an unintended bounce of the ball can alter a game.   Consequently, the Panthers' fortunes in the upcoming season depended upon Lady Luck and her visitation plans.

Perry's season record:

Date	Opponent	Perry Score	Opponent Score
19-Nov	Unadilla	86	40
20-Nov	Butler	75	38
27-Nov	Crawford County	57	53
30-Nov	Telfair County	71	44
4-Dec	Willingham	55	43
7-Dec	Hawkinsville	53	26
8-Dec	Unadilla	44	38
11-Dec	Macon County	66	49
14-Dec	Vienna	67	31
18-Dec	Lanier	39	37

Date	Opponent	Perry Score	Opponent Score
21-Dec	Cochran	60	43

Perry Invitational Tournament: Dec 27-28 at Perry

Date	Opponent	Perry Score	Opponent Score
27-Dec	Crawford County	66	51
28-Dec	Macon County	49	48
3-Jan	Hawkinsville	63	45
4-Jan	Dublin	43	44
8-Jan	Willingham	59	57
11-Jan	Cochran	78	43
15-Jan	Warner Robins	64	53
18-Jan	Crawford County	74	67
19-Jan	Butler	60	52
23-Jan	Lanier	56	60
23-Jan	Vienna	65	36
29-Jan	Macon County	68	53
1-Feb	Telfair County	76	62
5-Feb	Warner Robins	52	69
8-Feb	Dublin	58	41

Region 2 Sub-Region Tournament: Feb 12-13 at Cochran

Date	Opponent	Perry Score	Opponent Score
12-Feb	Dudley Hughes	57	34
13-Feb	Dublin	47	42

Region 2 Tournament finals: Feb 15-16 at Swainsboro

Date	Opponent	Perry Score	Opponent Score
15-Feb	Effingham County	53	27
16-Feb	Dublin	52	41

State Tournament: Feb 28-Mar 2 at Macon City Auditorium

Date	Opponent	Perry Score	Opponent Score
28-Feb	Toccoa	59	52
1-Mar	Americus	46	45
2-Mar	Blackshear	67	43

Come-From-Behind Gang: 1964 team

1964 Perry team. L-R: Paul Barrett, Joe Martin, Ricky Cotton, Alton Ellis, Jimmy Dorsett, Garold Spena, Edgar Barfield, Hugh Hill, Currey Gayle, Tommy White, and Bert Bozeman. Not pictured were David Hathaway and Alrie Adams. Front, L-R: Coaches Eric Staples and Paul Hartman.

Three Gunslingers Return

Lost through graduation was two-time all-state player, Dwayne Powell, who averaged 30 points a game and scored 2043 career points and whom Coach Staples called the greatest shooter in high school basketball. Also graduating were Melton Cloud, a great rebounder, Porter Staples, an all-state selectee, and two capable reserves: Paul Bozeman and Charles Harrison. Jimmy Suber's family moved from Perry.

The 1963-64 season would not be a rebuilding year because Perry already had five men who could start on most teams in central and south Georgia. Whereas the previous seven Perry state championship teams had one or two gunslingers, the 1963-64 edition of the Perry Panthers returned three gunslingers who could knock a gnat off the rim at 20 paces and literally bury a team with an offensive avalanche: Bert Bozeman, a 5' 8" southpaw guard, Garold Spena, a 6' 3" forward, and Jimmy Dorsett, a 6'2" center. Bozeman and Spena were all-state selections in 1963, and Dorsett was a multi-talented player poised for greatness. Rounding out the starting line-up would be Joe Martin, 5'10", a promising sophomore and brother of 1962 sensation Lee Martin, and either Alton Ellis, 6'1" and 210 pounds, a muscular and physical front line player, or Ricky Cotton, 6'1", an exceptional outside shooter. Top reserves would be Edgar Barfield, 6'2", and Tommy White, 6'0". Also competing for varsity playing time were a scrappy and determined bunch of former B-team players: Hugh Hill, 6'1", Currey Gayle, 6'0", Paul Barrett 5'7", David Hathaway, 5'9", and Alrie Adams, 5'9."

This squad had the opportunity to achieve something that no school in Georgia had accomplished since 1940--win three consecutive state championships. Lanier of Macon captured three straight Class A state championships from 1938 to1940. Perry won the Class B state title in 1962 and the Class A crown in 1963. For Perry to win a third straight state championship was a long shot, but the basketball world had learned long ago never to sell Coach Eric Staples' teams short.

The 1963-64 season had the potential to be a record-breaking year in another respect as Coach Staples was closing in on his 900th career victory. Before the season began he had amassed 882 victories and was expected to reach the lofty 900 perch midway the current season.

Panthers Off and Running: Ten Straight Wins

Perry had marched over ten consecutive foes: Butler (won by 10; exact score unavailable), Reynolds (51-45), Crawford County (50-49), Dudley Hughes (68-51), Willingham (73-50), Washington County (70-29), Northside (46-37), Macon County (72-45), Vienna (62-48), and Lanier (60-57). As expected, the trio of Bert Bozeman, Jimmy Dorsett, and Garold Spena had led the scoring. Any one of the three could be counted on for a 20-point outburst on any given night. Opposing teams were reluctant to double-team any one of the three in fear the other two would rip their defenses apart.

The closest win through the first ten games was a one-point victory against Crawford County. With Perry trailing 49 to 48 late in the fourth quarter and only a few seconds left on the clock, Garold Spena, with two defenders dangling all over him, drilled a 15-foot jumper to win the game in a heart-stopper, 50 to 49. This was the first appearance of Lady Luck since the state semifinal win against Americus during the 1963 season.

Trumped by a Royal Flush

At the end of regulation play, the Perry Panthers and Cochran Royals were tied 66 to 66. On the opening play of overtime, Cochran got the tip and Wayne Dykes drove for the score, putting the Royals ahead, 68 to 66. Perry's Jimmy Dorsett then connected on a jumper near the top of the key, tying the score again, 68 to 68. Cochran missed from the field and Perry switched to a ball control offense, looking for the high percentage shot. With 15 seconds remaining in the overtime period, the Panthers worked the ball in to Garold Spena near the foul lane. Spena took a spinning jump shot that rolled off the rim. Cochran's Terry Holder was fouled as he rebounded the ball. With six seconds remaining, Holder hit the first of a one-if-one foul shot attempt and then netted the second to give Cochran a 70 to 68 advantage. With scant seconds on the clock, Perry fired up a desperation shot from the backcourt that fell short. The Royals of Cochran, coached by Bill Denney, had inflicted upon Perry its first defeat of the season.

The Panthers' Jimmy Dorsett led all scorers with 29 points. Terry Holder tossed in 26 for the Royals.

(Overtime)

Perry-68	**Cochran-70**
Spena-17	J. Coley-11
Ellis-3	Padgett-6
Dorsett-29	Phillips
Bozeman-8	Holder-26
Martin-11	Abbott-15

Subs: Perry: Barfield, Cotton, White, Hathaway; Cochran: W. Coley, Maddox, Dykes-12

Coach Staples chalks up 900th career victory

Coach Eric Staples, Georgia's "Mr. Basketball," reached another milestone in his legendary career when his Perry Panthers won a decisive battle over the Hawkinsville Red Devils 67 to 52. The game was played on January 11, 1964, in Hawkinsville.

Coach Staples was in his 37th year of coaching, his 31st season as the

Panthers' head man. Staples, 58-years old and the supervising principal of
Perry schools, had lost only 186 games. His unbelievable 900-186 record
was one of the most significant accomplishments in Georgia high school
basketball history.

Up to this point in the 1964 season, Staples' Panthers had lost only
12 games in the last four years (1961-7, 1962-0, 1963-3, 1964 -2). His
Perry teams had won six Class B state titles (1947, 1949, 1953, 1956,
1959, and 1962) and one Class A crown in 1963. A state championship
by the current team would give Perry the unique distinction of winning
three consecutive state titles.

Perry's terrific trio of Jimmy Dorsett, Garold Spena, and Bert
Bozeman led Perry's offense with 26, 17, and 14 points respectively. The
Red Devils' Collins topped all scorers with 28.

Perry-67	Hawkinsville-52
Spena-17	Jennings-5
Ellis-6	Paulk-8
Dorsett-26	Barfield-11
Bozeman-14	Collins-28
White-2	English

Subs: Perry: Barfield-2, Hill, Cotton, Hathaway; Hawkinsville: Tripp

Another one-point thriller

The Panthers had beaten the Crawford County Eagles, 50 to 49, at
Perry's gym on November 26, on a last second basket by Garold Spena.
Perry's return engagement against the Eagles was played in Roberta on
January 17.

The game was a see-saw battle from start to finish. Perry was trailing,
56 to 55, with 20 seconds on the clock. In a do-or-die situation, Perry
brought the ball down court and began looking for either Spena or
Dorsett to get open on the low post for the winning basket. Both were
heavily guarded. As the scoreboard clock ticked down to eight seconds,
Bozeman was suddenly double-teamed. Bozeman jumped high over the
two defenders to lob the ball to Alton Ellis, standing near center court.
In one motion, Ellis caught the ball and heaved it toward the basket. The

horn blew with the ball in mid-flight. A dead silence spread over the gym as Ellis' high trajectory shot sailed goal-ward. Swish! The nylon chords snapped as the force of the shot swung the net backward. Pandemonium broke loose on the Perry sidelines. Perry had won another thriller against the Eagles, 57 to 56. Lady Luck had returned. Everyone hoped she was not just randomly visiting, but would stay around for a while, especially with tournament time a month away.

These two gut-wrenching games attested to the competitiveness the two coaches instilled in their players: Eric Staples of the Panthers and J. B. Hawkins, the Crawford County mentor. In Perry's 57 to 56 victory, Garold Spena hit for 19 points, Jimmy Dorsett bucketed 17 and Bert Bozeman made 13, all from long range. The Eagles' magnificent Bobby Rowland scored a game high 36 points and was virtually unstoppable around the basket.

Perry-57	Crawford County-56
Spena-19	Breedlove-7
Ellis-6	Hortman-1
Dorsett-17	Rowland-36
Bozeman-13	Andrews-4
Martin-2	Bird-6

Subs: Perry: Barfield; Crawford County: Harris-2

Poets Seek revenge following earlier defeat

The Lanier Poets lost to Perry on December 19 at Perry's gym and were gunning to upset the Panthers in Macon on January 22. Coach Henry Middlebrooks' squad had regrouped and appeared ready to tame the Panthers. The Poets seemed to be heading toward victory as they led 33 to 27 at halftime and 45 to 40 as the third quarter ended.

With 4:10 left in the final period, the Poets clung to a 47 to 42 lead. At this point, the Panthers rallied on buckets by Bert Bozeman, Joe Martin, and Alton Ellis, and two free-throws by Bozeman to surge ahead 50 to 47 with 1:32 left to play. With 38 seconds remaining, Perry held a 54 to 48 advantage. Al Gerhardt scored a field goal and two foul shots to close the gap to 54 to 52. With two seconds remaining, Perry's Jimmy

Dorsett was fouled and calmly dropped in both attempts from the foul line. The game ended with Perry winning both season games from the Class AAA Lanier Poets: 60 to 57 in Perry and 56 to 52 at Macon's City Auditorium.

Perry's indomitable trio of Bozeman, Spena, and Dorsett scored 16, 16, and 13 points respectfully. Lanier's scoring was balanced: Tom Cornelius-17, Al Gerhardt-13, Frank Kelly-11, and Ken Bonifay-9.

Perry-56	**Lanier-52**
Spena-16	Gerhardt-13
Ellis-7	Bonifay-9
Dorsett-13	Kelly-11
Bozeman-16	Cornelius-17
Martin-4	Corbitt-2

Score at Halftime: Lanier 33, Perry-27
Subs: Perry: none; Lanier: Coleman

Panthers seek to even score with Cochran

On January 25, 1964, the Perry Panthers could not wait to replay the Cochran Royals, who had defeated the Panthers 70 to 68 just before Christmas. Since nothing had gone right in their earlier defeat at the hands of the Royals, the Panthers wanted to redeem themselves before their home crowd. Cochran played Perry close during the first quarter, but faded during the second stanza and were never in the game from that point forward. Perry won by a run-away margin of 25 points, 70 to 45.

Jimmy Dorsett led Perry with 20 points followed by Alton Ellis-18, Bert Bozeman-16, Garold Spena-12, and Joe Martin-4. Tommy White played an excellent floor game. Cochran was led by Jimmy Padgett with 17 points. Perry's collapsing man-to-man defense held Terry Holder, who scored 26 in the earlier contest, to only 6 points.

Perry-70	**Cochran-45**
Spena-12	Coley-10
Ellis-18	Padgett-17
Dorsett-20	Phillips-3

Bozeman-16   Holder-6
Martin-4   Abbott-2

Subs: Perry: White; Cochran: Fair-2, Maddox, Dykes-5, Hobbs

Hocus-Pocus in Demon Country

On February 4, the Perry Panthers journeyed over to the Demon's Den in Warner Robins to prove that the two earlier defeats at the hands of the Class AAA Warner Robins team were a fluke.

Two Previous Games

On December 28, 1963, Perry suffered its first loss to the Demons in the finals of the Perry Christmas Invitational tournament, 47 to 36. In that game Perry played without its ace forward, Garold Spena, who was out with an injury.

On January 14, 1964, Don LaBlanc's undefeated Warner Robins quintet again fought off Perry 49 to 43 at Perry's gym before a capacity crowd of 2,700 fans. An estimated five thousand tickets could have been sold had the gym been larger. The difference in shooting percentages produced the Demons' winning margin. Perry hit on just 18 of 62 for 29 percent while Warner Robins took fewer shots but connected on 19 of 39 for 49 percent.

Third Game

On February 4, 1964, only two weeks before tournament time, the third and final season game was held with Warner Robins. At the end of the first quarter, the Demons led, 13 to 6. At intermission the score was still in the Demons' favor, 21 to 17. As the third period ended, Perry had moved to within one point, 33 to 32. With less than a minute remaining in the final quarter, Perry was leading 41 to 40 and had the basketball in its possession. Instead of holding onto the ball, as Coach Staples had instructed, to force fouling by the Demons, an anxious Panther took an ill-fated shot that barely missed. The anxious Panther apparently saw Lady Luck in the stands or felt confident he could nail the shot and put the game out of reach. As soon as the Demons' Mike Davis rebounded the errant shot, he was fouled. Davis sank the foul shot, tying the game 41 to

41. Perry's Bert Bozeman attempted a desperation shot out of range that fell short, and the game ended in a tie, forcing an overtime period.

Overtime

In the overtime period, Garold Spena drew first blood with 2:36 left and the score stood Perry-43, Warner Robins-41. The Demons' Jim Tucker iced the game with a three-point play and the Demons inched ahead, 44 to 43. Perry threw away three straight chances to score because of wild passes. On the Demons' next possession with 15 seconds left, Mike Davis fed the ball to Jimmy Dodson who hit a short jumper, and Warner Robins increased its margin to three points, 46 to 43. The Panthers weren't finished as Garold Spena sank a 10-footer with three seconds to play. Quickly time expired and Warner Robins had squeaked by Perry, 46 to 45.

Panthers threw it away; Demons lucky to win

The Panthers obviously had improved since the two earlier encounters. With little time remaining in regulation play, the Panthers were in the driver's seat and only needed to hold onto the ball to possibly win the game, but an ill-advised shot sealed their doom. "Atlanta Journal" Prep editor, Tom McCollister, wrote: "The Panthers threw it away. Warner Robins was lucky to win and this is something that even Demon coach Don LaBlanc admits." In summary, Don LaBlanc's Demons did not capitalize on their home court advantage and had to conjure up all the black magic they could muster to defeat a very determined Panther five.

Garold Spena led Perry with 13 points, and Mike Davis hit a game high of 15 for the victors.

(Overtime)

Perry-45	**Warner Robins-46**
Spena-13	Channell-10
Ellis-9	Clarke-6
Dorsett-6	Tucker-8
Bozeman-10	Dodson-4
Martin-7	Davis-15
	Calloway-3

Season recap; Perry braces for tournament

As the Panthers prepared for tournament competition, they could point with pride to their superb 25-4 record. They lost early in the season to Cochran by two points, but a month later redeemed themselves with an impressive 25-point blow-out of the Royals. The other three loses were to AAA powerhouse Warner Robins. In the third game with Warner Robins, Perry committed a critical offensive miscue in the waning moments that possibly cost them the game. Even in the loss, the Panthers demonstrated they were a vastly improved team and would be highly competitive in the upcoming region tournament.

Region 2A Sub-Region Tournament: Feb 18-19 at Perry

Perry vs. Dudley Hughes

The Dudley Hughes Wolverines were never in the contest and were completely overwhelmed by Perry's persistent offensive attack. The Panthers, leading 36 to 23 at the end of third quarter, exploded with 27 points in the final stanza to bury the Wolverines by a run-away score of 63 to 35. Bert Bozeman was top man for Perry with 20 points followed by Jimmy Dorsett with 17 and Joe Martin with 12. Gene Ratliff sparked Dudley Hughes with 19 markers.

Perry-63	Dudley Hughes-35
Spena-9	Mimbs-5
Ellis-3	Furney-2
Dorsett-17	Ratliff-19
Bozeman-20	Flowers-2
Martin-12	Fountain-5

Score at Half: Perry-23, Dudley Hughes-12
Subs: Perry: Gayle, Hill-2; Dudley Hughes: Benfield-2

Perry vs. Cochran (Finals)

The Cochran Royals, who broke the Panthers' 10-game winning streak earlier in the season, put the Panthers to the test for the first three quarters of the game. The score at first quarter's end was tied 10-all. The

Panthers pulled ahead, 26 to 24, at halftime. The Royals overtook the Panthers, 38 to 37, as the third stanza ended. During the final period, the Panthers finished strong, scoring 13 points to the Royals' 9, resulting in the five point victory margin, 51 to 46, and the sub region title.

Jimmy Dorsett burned the nets for 23 points. Bert Bozeman chipped in 17. Terry Holder was Cochran's high man with 17.

Perry-51	Cochran-46
Spena-7	Coley-10
Ellis-4	Padgett-4
Dorsett-23	Phillips
Bozeman-17	Holder-17
Martin	Abbott-7

Score at half: Perry: 26; Cochran: 24
Subs: Perry: none; Cochran: Dykes-8, Hobbs, Sair

Region 2A Region Tournament: 21-22 Feb at Dublin

Perry vs. Statesboro

The Panthers adjourned for intermission trailing Statesboro 20 to 19 and appeared to be struggling. A halftime pep talk by Coach Staples galvanized the Panthers into action as they pumped in 13 straight points during the third quarter, soaring to a 45 to 32 lead. In the final quarter, Perry poured it on with a 19 point outburst while Statesboro could manage only 10 tallies. The Panthers prevailed by a 24 point margin, 66 to 42, and advanced to the region finals.

Perry's leading scorers were: Jimmy Dorsett-20, Bert Bozeman-19, and Garold Spena-17. Pacing Statesboro's offense was Jackie Smith with 20 points.

Perry-66	Statesboro-42
Dorsett-20	Moore
Bozeman-19	Thompson-9
Spena-17	Evans-8

| Ellis-6 | Page-3 |
| Martin-4 | Smith-20 |

Score at half: Perry-19, Statesboro-20
Subs: Perry: none; Statesboro: McGregor, Story, Barnes-2

Region Finals: Would it be Cochran Again ?...

...Yes, the Cochran Royals were just like the Dublin Irish in 1963—they kept showing up. The previous season, Perry had to face Dublin in the sub-region and the region and narrowly missed having to play them for the state championship, as Dublin was finally eliminated in the state semifinals. During the current season, Perry had already beaten Cochran three times: twice during the regular season and once in the sub-region finals.

As it turned out, Perry had little trouble with the Cochran Royals and won the region 2A championship. The Panthers assaulted the nets for 21 points in the first quarter while Cochran could make only two free-throws. From that point on, the Panthers ran roughshod over the Royals, winning by a 16 point margin, 66 to 50. This was Perry's fourth win over Cochran.

Jimmy Dorsett was the Panther's man of the hour with 32 points. Bert Bozeman added 19. The Royals were paced by Terry Holder with 17 and Jimmy Padgett-13.

Perry-66	Cochran-50
Martin-2	Padgett-13
Dorsett-32	Holder-17
Spena-10	Abbott-4
Bozeman-19	Coley-8
Ellis	Phillips-1

Score at half: Perry-33; Cochran-19
Subs: Perry: Cotton, Hathaway-2, Barrett, Gayle-1, Hill, Barfield; Cochran: Pritchett, Thompson-5, Hobbs, Dykes-2, Horton.

State Tournament: Feb 27-29 at Macon City Auditorium

No one counting Panthers out

The Perry Panthers were defending state champions, having won the state tournament two consecutive years: the Class B crown in 1962 and the Class A title in 1963. Tom McCollister, Prep Editor of the "Atlanta Journal," wrote: "Perry is defending boys champs and although there's considerable doubt Coach Eric Staples' lads can do it again, no one is counting them out."

Perry's first opponent in the state tournament was a formidable force in northwest Georgia, the Berry High Falcons of Rome with a 25-7 record. Berry owned a 56-point scoring average and had held opponents to 40 points a game. Waiting in the wings was the powerful Cass High School boasting a 25-5 record and the victor over Berry in the region 3A tournament, 42 to 34. But neither school had faced the likes of Jimmy Dorsett, Bert Bozeman, Garold Spena, Alton Ellis, and Joe Martin.

Perry vs. Berry

Perry's awesome Panthers, intent on giving Coach Staples his eighth state title, began their title quest with a crushing defeat of Berry, 70 to 50. Perry led 33 to 22 at the end of first half. During the first 16 minutes of the second half, Perry connected on an amazing 54-percent of its field goal attempts, 15 of 28 shots. Leading 70 to 46 with 1:30 on the clock, the Panthers played reserves the rest of the way.

Four Panthers finished in double figures: Garold Spena-17, Jimmy Dorsett-16, Joe Martin-14, and Bert Bozeman-12. Alton Ellis pitched in 8 points. Jerry Chastain, a reserve, was Berry's top scorer with 11 points.

Perry-70	Berry-50
Dorsett-16	Smith-8
Ellis-8	Childre-10
Spena-17	Parrish
Bozeman-12	Butler-8
Martin-14	Logan-8

Score at half: Perry-33, Berry-22

Subs: Perry: Cotton-1, White-2, Hill, Barfield, Hathaway; Berry: Carlisle-5, Chastain-11.

Semifinals: Perry vs. Mitchell County

Mitchell County from Camilla, the Region 1 representative and a dark horse in the tournament, pushed the Panthers to the limit. A crowd of 2,468 spectators poured into Macon's high-domed City Auditorium to witness the battle.

Perry took the lead 16 to 11 at the first quarter mark and coasted to intermission, 35 to 23. The Panthers increased their lead to 40 to 26 early in the third period, but Mitchell County employed a full court press and began to narrow the gap. With 1:57 remaining in the third period and Perry leading, 53 to 37, Perry's sharpshooter Jimmy Dorsett, with 31 points to his credit, fouled out. Perry's reserve center, Edgar Barfield, replaced Dorsett. With an offensive weapon lost for the game, the Panthers had to regroup and brace for Mitchell County's surge. With 56 seconds left in the third, Mitchell took the lead 54 to 53. The tide had turned. Mitchell County's frenzied fans were cheering wildly and smelling victory, but Bert Bozeman quieted them down with a missile from "down town," pushing the Panthers ahead, 55 to 54, as the third quarter ended.

During a wild fourth quarter, Mitchell again forged ahead 59 to 55, but Perry tied the score on two free throws by Joe Martin and another outside bomb by Bert Bozeman. After that exchange, the lead changed five times and the score was tied on three occasions. With 1:21 remaining and the Panthers behind 70 to 69, Bert Bozeman scored again from long range, giving Perry the lead, 71 to 70. At this critical point, Perry lost its outstanding floor general, Joe Martin, to a sprained ankle. Reserve guard Currey Gayle replaced Martin. With two regulars on the bench and Alton Ellis one foul away from eviction, the Panthers were in deep trouble.

Mitchell County moved quickly down court and fired a field goal that barely missed. Perry claimed the rebound and with 1:12 left, Coach Staples signaled to his Panthers to freeze the ball. Forced to foul, Mitchell County hacked Alton Ellis with 49 seconds to go, again stopping the clock. Mitchell County's sidelines roared loudly to rattle Ellis, but he sank both shots, moving Perry ahead, 73 to 70. With 33 seconds left, Edgar Barfield was fouled. The cool and composed Barfield hit both clutch free-throws, increasing Perry's margin, 75 to 70. With 24 seconds on the clock, Alton Ellis fouled out. Reserve forward Tommy White, who had spelled Ellis earlier, entered the game. Mitchell County wasn't through. Its sensational forward, Larry Good, drove the length of the court and scored just before the final horn, reducing the margin to three points, 75 to 72.

The Panthers' ability to consistently hit from the foul line was the key to victory. They cashed in on 14 straight gratis tosses during the final period. Jimmy Dorsett led the Panthers with 31. Bert Bozeman, Perry's clutch shooter, connected on 16 points, most from long range. Garold Spena also collected 16. Perry reserves Edgar Barfield, Tommy White, and Currey Gayle played significant roles in Perry's victory. Barfield and White each hit two critical free-throws when the game was hanging in the balance. This game proved once again that capable reserves are indispensable to winning championships.

Mitchell County was led by Larry Good who scorched the nets for 35 points and was one of the top offensive threats in the tournament. Jimmy Melvin of Mitchell County, a 22-year old in his first year as head mentor, coached a magnificent game and went head-to-head with the old master, Eric Staples, almost bringing his boys back from a 14-point, third-quarter deficit.

Perry-75	Mitchell County-72
Dorsett-31	Good-35
Ellis-4	Temples-9
Spena-16	Bryant-6
Bozeman-16	Tyson-10
Martin-4	Stripling-10

Score at half: Perry-35, Mitchell County-23
Subs: Perry: White-2, Barfield-2, Gayle; Mitchell County: Smith, Mullis-2

Perry was one game away from claiming its third consecutive state crown. Lady luck had returned to the City Auditorium, but would she stay over for the championship game on Saturday night with Cass High of Cassville, Georgia?

State finals: Perry vs. Cass High

Panthers behind 13 points with 8 minutes to play

A packed house of 2,872 fans came to see the Panthers take on Coach J. B. Bearden's Cass High Colonels of Cassville. The spectator turn-out for the final game hiked the three-day attendance to 7,976, an all-time record for the state Class A tournament.

Cass High started the game with every intention of blowing the Panthers off the court. The uncanny shooting of C. H. Lee and Clyde Abernathy almost buried the Panthers in a hail of baskets during the first three quarters. Cass was leading 20 to 13 at the first quarter and 32 to 24 at intermission. The Panthers lost ground in the third period and were down 13-points as the quarter ended.

Lady Luck almost waited too late

Lady Luck was late for the championship game, and her absence was evident during the first three quarters. She didn't make her appearance until the final eight minutes.

Few spectators gave the Panthers a chance to win. Perry fans were praying that Coach Staples could work his magic once again and somehow win the game. Staples had a plan. He changed his defensive strategy completely, instructing his Panthers to aggressively press Cass full court and to do so with reckless abandon because there would be no tomorrow. Although team members may have harbored doubt that they could erase a 13-point deficit with only eight minutes remaining, Coach Staples assured them they could. His charges walked back on the court with an unfaltering determination to win and to leave no unexpended energy on the court.

As the fourth quarter began, Garold Spena drilled a 15-foot jumper and Bert Bozeman added two free-throws. Bozeman struck again from long range and bucketed a free throw. With 5:57 left, the Panthers had shaved seven points off the lead and were within striking distance, 46 to 40. Perry's press, engineered by Coach Staples, was already paying dividends as Joe Martin stole a Cass pass with 5:32 on the clock and further cut the Colonels' lead to 46 to 42. Cass' Clyde Abernathy hit a field goal but Perry's Jimmy Dorsett countered with two hard-earned goals around the basket to move Perry within two points, 48 to 46.

Game tied with three minutes left

Bert Bozeman, Perry's "Mr. Clutch," brought Perry's fans to their feet as he fired another bomb from long range that swished the net and tied the score, 48 to 48, with less than three minutes to play.

Perry moves ahead with 70 seconds on clock; Staples employs freeze

Now it was anybody's game; the team with the greatest desire would win. At the 1:10 mark, Perry moved into the lead, 52 to 51, and Coach Staples told his team to freeze the ball. Forced to foul, Cass picked on the wrong Panther, Jimmy Dorsett. With 31 seconds remaining, Dorsett made both foul shots. With 13 seconds in the game, Dorsett added another basket for good measure to increase the lead, 56 to 51. With two seconds left, Cass got the final basket on a goal by C. H. Lee, and the Panthers pulled off possibly the greatest come-from-behind victory in Perry basketball history. Thanks to Lady Luck, the Panthers had snatched victory from defeat two nights in a row. Perry's fans, basking in the glory of an unprecedented third state title, could hardly believe their eyes. The scoreboard read: Perry-56, Cass-53.

Jimmy Dorsett poured in 23 points, 12 in the first half and 11 in the second. Bert Bozeman was also over the twenty-point mark with 21, most from long range. Bozeman scored nine of his points during the torrid fourth quarter when they were really needed. Garold Spena added 10. C. H. Lee bagged 20 points to lead Cass High and was followed by Clyde Abernathy with 18. Neither team substituted. This was Coach Staples' eighth state championship (six in Class B and two in Class A), and his third in a row. The 1964 Perry Panthers had achieved the impossible.

Perry-56	Cass High-53
Dorsett-23	Lee-20
Ellis	Barnett-8
Spena-10	Abernathy-18
Bozeman-21	Moore-2
Martin-2	Mullinox-5

Score at half: Cass High-32, Perry-24

Subs: none

Class A All-State team:

Jimmy Dorsett-Perry

Bert Bozeman-Perry

Garold Spena-Perry

Clyde Abernathy-Cass High

C. H. Lee-Cass High

Tommy Mullinox-Cass High

Larry Good-Mitchell County

Clarence Bryant-Mitchell County

Sidney Smith-Bacon County

Donny Jackson-Bacon County

Perry finished year with an enviable 32-4 record.

Date	Opponent	Site	Perry Score	Opponent Score
19-Nov	Butler	Home	Perry by 10	*
22-Nov	Reynolds	Home	51	45
26-Nov	Crawford County	Home	50	49
27-Nov	Dudley Hughes	Away	68	51
3-Dec	Willingham	Home	73	50
6-Dec	Washington Co.	Home	70	29
7-Dec	Northside**	Away	46	37
10-Dec	Macon County	Home	72	45
13-Dec	Vienna	Away	62	48
19-Dec	Lanier	Home	60	57
20-Dec	Cochran	Away	68	70

Perry Invitational: December 27-28 at Perry

27-Dec	Macon County	Perry	64	43
28-Dec	Warner Robins	Perry	36	47
2-Jan	Hawkinsville	Home	67	41

Date	Opponent	Site	Perry Score	Opponent Score
3-Jan	Dublin	Away	59	49
7-Jan	Willingham	Away	69	51
10-Jan	Dudley Hughes	Home	61	44
11-Jan	Hawkinsville ***	Away	67	52
14-Jan	Warner Robins	Home	43	49
17-Jan	Crawford County	Away	57	56
18-Jan	Butler	Away	61	46
22-Jan	Lanier	Away	56	52
24-Jan	Vienna	Home	72	57
25-Jan	Cochran	Home	70	45
28-Jan	Macon County	Home	76	33
31-Jan	Dublin	Home	65	57
4-Feb	Warner Robins	Away	45	46
7-Feb	Washington Co.	Away	79	43
14-Feb	Northside	Home	68	35

Region 2A sub-region:18-19 Feb at Perry

18-Feb	Dudley Hughes		63	35
19-Feb	Cochran		51	46

Region 2A region finals: 21-22 Feb at Dublin

21-Feb	Statesboro		66	42
22-Feb	Cochran		66	50

State tournament: 27-29 Feb at Macon City Auditorium

27-Feb	Berry		70	50
28-Feb	Mitchell County		75	72
29-Feb	Cass High		56	53

* Perry won by 10 points according to "The Atlanta Journal"; score unavailable

** Perry B-team beat Northside varsity, 46 to 37

*** Coach Staples' 900th career victory

The Cardiac Kids: 1966 team

1966 Perry team. Kneeling, L-R: Marion Cloud, Joe Martin, Terry Todd, Ed Pierce,
Charles Ayer. Standing, L-R: Assist. Coach J. T. (Sonny) Brady, Lee St. John, Assist. Coach
Grover Hicks, Carlton Bessinger, Ed Harley, Eddie Watson, Rodney Lowe, Eugene Graham,
Donald Norris, Kenny Stefanini-manager, Coach Paul Hartman. Not pictured:
Charles Malone-manager.

What happened during 1964-65 season?

The 1964-65 season was a rebuilding year. The Panthers had lost
three all-state players from the 1964 state championship team: Jimmy
Dorsett, Bert Bozeman, and Garold Spena. Also graduating was starting
forward, Alton Ellis, an outstanding rebounder and defensive player. Of
the 1963-64 team starters, only guard Joe Martin returned for the 1964-
65 season.

The 1964-65 Perry team finished the regular season with a record of
15-12. In the sub-region, the Panthers beat Washington County, 52 to
44, in the opening round, but lost to Cochran, 64 to 46, in the sub-region
title game. Coach Jim Denning's Cochran Royals had one of its best teams
in school history and went on to win the Class A state championship in
1965. As sub-region runner-up, Perry advanced to the region tournament,

but lost on opening night to Statesboro, 49 to 45. The Panthers finished the year with an overall record of 16-14.

Staples retires; picks Hartman as successor

Coach Eric Staples, called by "Macon Telegraph" Sports Editor Harley Bowers "the finest high school basketball coach in Georgia history," retired at the end of the 1964-65 season, after his 32nd year as head coach at Perry High School. Coach Staples passed the mantle to 29-year-old Paul Hartman, his capable assistant for six years, who in 1960 had replaced Frank Holland as Perry's assistant coach. Hartman, a native of Cuthbert, had been an outstanding basketball player at Piedmont College (two years) and Troy State Teachers College (two years) and was a devoted student of the game.

In picking Paul Hartman as his successor, Coach Staples stated: "Hartman is a fine young coach....He has a good knowledge of basketball and he knows how to manage boys....He had a lot to do with our winning record in recent years, and I am confident he will continue to give Perry representative teams."

Pantherville's hopes dim for 1965-66 season

Lost to graduation were three starters from the 1964-65 team: Edgar Barfield, Tommy White, and Ricky Cotton.

Only one player on the 1965-66 roster stood over six feet tall. Heir apparent to the guard positions were returnees Joe Martin, 5'10", and Charles Ayer, 5'6". Other likely starters were two 5'11" forwards, Terry Todd and Ed Pierce, and a 6'1" center, Marion Cloud, the tallest man on the team. Lee St. John, an excellent floor general and the son of Herb St. John, Perry's legendary football coach, was projected as the sixth man. Other capable reserves competing for playing time were Carlton Bessinger, Ed Harley, Donald Norris, Rodney Lowe, Eugene Graham, and Eddie Watson. This squad simply didn't have the height to compete on the boards or defend around the basket against taller adversaries. Further, a rookie coach was replacing a legend. Basketball observers had essentially written off this team as a serious title contender. No one in Pantherville expected to add another loving cup to its bulging trophy case in 1966.

Panthers defy odds; win first 12 games

Before the Christmas tournament in late December 1965, Perry had won its first 12 games in succession: Vienna (56-54), Taylor County (58-56), Crawford County (64-41), Dudley Hughes (69-54), Vienna (59-50), Washington County (57-43), Northside (63-53), Macon County (71-47), Hawkinsville (68-38), Lanier (55-53), Cochran (63-54), and Dodge County (54-42).

Perry won three cliff hangers early in the season, each by two points: (1) a last second basket to down Vienna, 56 to 54, (2) a dramatic, come-from-behind 58 to 56 victory over Taylor County, on a 25-footer by Joe Martin with five seconds left, and (3) another come-from-behind 55 to 53 victory against the Lanier Poets, in which Charles Ayer sank two clutch free throws with 12 seconds on the clock.

The Panthers were averaging 62 points a game and holding their opponents to a 48-point average. Joe Martin was quickly blossoming into one of Georgia's most prolific scorers with an incredible 26 points-per-game average. This was especially noteworthy as most teams were expressly gearing their defenses to contain Martin. His sidekick at guard, Charles Ayer, only 5'6", was hitting 49 percent from the field, which prompted Coach Hartman to encourage Ayer to shoot more to take the pressure off Martin. Terry Todd was the Panthers' top rebounder with 8.5 per game, followed by Ed Pierce-6.8 and Marion Cloud-5.9. The entire team was a scrappy bunch with quick hands that played tenacious defense.

Hartman a carbon copy

Hartman was a carbon copy of Coach Staples in his approach to the game. He employed the same basic offensive patterns and utilized the same man-to-man collapsing defense that Staples had used so effectively, and it was paying dividends. Surprisingly, the vertically-challenged Panthers were beating their opponents on the backboards by a wide margin of 337 rebounds to 213. Obviously, Hartman had taught his shorter Panthers how to block-out their taller opponents to gain rebounding position. Taking another chapter from Staples' coaching philosophy, Hartman had improved his team's ball-handing skills and passing techniques to the extent the Panthers were committing fewer turnovers than their opponents which provided the victory margin in close games.

Perry Christmas Tournament: Dec. 30-31 at Perry

Perry vs. Crawford County

Perry buried Crawford County, 70 to 20, in the opening round of the Perry Christmas tournament. Perry led 11 to 2 at the first quarter mark, 30 to 6 at the half, and 48 to 15 at the third quarter mark. Perry's reserves played considerably during the game. Joe Martin was Perry's leading scorer with 19 points. Terry Todd bagged 12, Ed Pierce-12, Donald Norris-6, Marion Cloud-6, Charles Ayer-4, Carlton Bessinger-4, Rodney Lowe-4, and Lee St. John-3. No Crawford County player scored over 6 points.

Perry vs. Wilkinson County for tournament championship

The night before, the Wilkinson County Patriots had decisively trounced Macon County 71 to 53. The Patriots' coach, Bob Podskoc, was quoted as saying he wouldn't have any trouble with the Panthers. He was wrong. The Panthers humbled Wilkinson County, 70 to 48, to capture the tournament championship and its 14th straight victory.

Top scorers for Perry were Joe Martin-20 and Terry Todd-19. The Patriots' Roy Faircloth, who had scorched the nets for 30 points the previous night against Macon County, was held to 10-points. Donnie Bloodworth led the Patriots with 15 markers.

Perry-70	**Wilkinson County-48**
Todd-19	Faircloth-10
Pierce-10	Keene-1
Cloud-5	McCall-8
Martin-20	Moye-10
Ayer-10	Bloodworth-15

Score at half: Perry-42, Wilkinson County-20
Subs: Perry: St. John-6, Lowe, Norris, Bessinger; Wilkinson County: Shell, Tomberlin, Luther-1, L. Keene, Clack, McDonald-2, Crenshaw-2

Demons sharpen pitchforks

By early January 1966, the Perry Panthers had won 16 games in a row. Standing in their path were the perennially strong Warner Robins Demons, a Class AAA team endowed with considerable height and talent. High-spirited and vocally optimistic Perry fans packed the Panther lair hoping to see the home team derail their Houston County neighbors and claim victory number 17.

The Demons raced to a 15 to 7 first quarter advantage on red-hot shooting and capitalized on Perry's cold shooting streak during the second stanza to lead at intermission, 30 to 19.

Perry's hope diminishes as Martin fouls out

Joe Martin kept the Panthers close on the tails of the Demons until he fouled out with three minutes remaining in the third quarter. With their main offensive weapon sidelined, the Panthers found themselves behind 17 points, 44 to 27, as the third period ended. In desperation, Perry opened the fourth period with a pressing defense that resulted in fouls, allowing the Demons to cash in at the gratis line and maintain their lead.

Warner Robins not only broke Perry's winning streak, but embarrassed Perry 59 to 40 before their homefolks. Perry's Joe Martin, who played less than three quarters, made 18 points in a losing cause while the Warner Robins ace, Wayne McConnell, topped all scorers with 24 points.

Return engagement with the Demons

Three weeks later, Perry journeyed to the Demons' den and played a much improved game against Warner Robins. At the third quarter mark, it was anybody's game as Warner Robins led by only two points, 44 to 42. In the final period, however, superior rebounding by the taller Demons took its toll against the smaller and lower classification Panthers. Warner Robins scored four more points than Perry in the final stanza, 18 to 14, and won by a six-point margin, 62 to 56.

The Panthers gave a better account of themselves than the earlier game when they lost top scorer, Joe Martin, to fouls and lost by 19 points. Leading Perry were Joe Martin and Charles Ayer with 18 points each.

A trio of standouts led the scoring parade for Coach Lamar Deavers' Demons: Charley Bob West-15 points, David Davidson-13, and Wayne McConnell-12.

Although this was the Panthers' second loss, their won-loss record at this late stage in the season was a phenomenal 21-2.

Panther Nemesis: Lanier Poets seeking revenge

Perry, who beat Lanier by two points, 55 to 53, in Perry early in the season, was sporting a 23-2 record, but facing the daunting task of playing the Poets on their home court, Macon's City Auditorium. Lanier came out smoking to ease by Perry 20 to 16 in the first quarter and retained its momentum into the second period to hold the lead 33 to 28 at halftime.

As the third quarter ended, Perry took the lead 49 to 45 on the sensational shooting of Joe Martin. Martin, suffering with the flu and having to come out for short respites during the first half to catch his breath, must have found a fresh source of oxygen during the third quarter when he bombarded the nets for 16 points.

Both teams turned it up a notch in the torrid final quarter. With only 45 seconds left in the game, Perry was leading 67 to 66 when Lanier's Jimmy Corbitt was fouled. Corbitt hit both free throws, shifting the advantage to Lanier, 68 to 67. With 34 seconds on the clock, Perry brought the ball down the court. Charles Ayer saw Martin shake loose from his defender and quickly fired the ball to Martin. With precious seconds ticking away, Martin fired a Nike missile from the deep corner that ripped the chords and sent Perry ahead 69 to 68. Perry's fans erupted into a thunderous roar. Just before the horn blew, Lanier got off a desperation heave that fell short. Perry's fans sank back into their seats, physically wrung out and emotionally exhausted. The Cardiac Kids had done it again!

Martin led Perry with 28 points. Next was Terry Todd-15 and Charles Ayer-13. Jimmy Corbitt paced Lanier with 22 followed by Bonifay and Davis with 16 and 15 respectively. Marion Cloud and Ed Pierce played outstanding defense and were strong on the boards. Reserve Lee St. John played an excellent floor game.

Perry-69   **Lanier-68**
Todd-15   Hale-10
Pierce-6   Putnal-2
Cloud-5   Davis-15
Martin-28   Corbitt-22
Ayer-13   Gordy-2
St. John-2   Bonifay-16
                     Goldbaugh-1

Score at half: Lanier-33, Perry-28

Martin-less Panthers take on Northside

The last game of the regular season pitted the Panthers against Coach Olin Harp's Northside Eagles of Warner Robins. With the heralded Joe Martin fighting the flu and unable to play, Perry would be at a disadvantage. The Eagles, realizing Perry's vulnerability, made a serious run at the Martin-less Panthers and led 18 to 16 at halftime. During the third period, Perry began to penetrate the Eagles' defense and moved ahead by seven points, 36 to 29, as the quarter ended.

During the final eight minutes, Perry's sharp-shooting guard Charles Ayer caught fire and lit up the scoreboard for 14 markers to lead the Panthers to victory, 59 to 45—their 24th win of the season against only two losses.

Charles Ayer assaulted the nets for a season high of 28 points. Terry Todd collected 15 when they were most needed. Bruce Coburn knocked down 22 for the Eagles followed by Joe Montgomery with 10.

Perry-59   **Northside-45**
Todd-15   Coburn-22
Pierce-4   Hutto-1
Cloud-8   Forehand-1
Ayer-28   Montgomery-10
St. John-2   Jones-1

Score at half: Northside-18, Perry-16
Subs: Perry: Harley-2, Bessinger, Norris; Northside: Martin, Norman-4, Sauls-1, Perdue-4, Wood-1

Regular Season in Retrospect

When the season started and Coach Hartman had to build a team around two returning starters, Joe Martin and Charles Ayer, and few seasoned reserves, no one figured that Perry at season's end would be voted by the "Atlanta Constitution" as the top Class A team in the state. With tournament time drawing nigh, the Panthers could expect to face some of these top ten teams in Georgia in either regional or state competition. These teams and their relative state rankings were: number 2 team in the state-Mitchell County (Camilla), number 3-Bacon County (Alma), number 4-Rockmart, number 5-Thomson and Madison County (Danielsville) tied for 5th, number 7-Central Gwinnett (Lawrenceville), number 8-Cochran, number 9-Cartersville, and number 10-Statesboro.

The Panthers, in achieving a 24-2 won-loss record, had lost only to Class AAA Warner Robins. The Panthers were dubbed the "Cardiac Kids" for come-from-behind victories and prevailing in four close games by a total of seven points.

Coach Hartman hadn't changed a thing, including Perry's winning habits. While other teams were running sophisticated offenses such as the shuffle and the wheel, the Panthers were keeping it simple by sticking to fundamental screening, picking and rolling, a Staples' trademark. Hartman's team, with its tallest player only 6-1, had excelled on rebounding by blocking out and getting good position over taller opponents. Shooting was the Panthers' forte—they were hitting approximately 46 percent from the field and scoring an average of 62 points a game. Joe Martin was averaging 25 points a game, Terry Todd-11, Charles Ayer-10, Marion Cloud-8, and Ed Pierce-8. Hartman, a disciple of Staples, was a firm believer in man-to-man defense. "Good shooting teams will beat a zone, but not a strong man-to-man defense," observed Hartman.

The Panthers were now a marked team; everyone was gunning for them. For this small team to climb up the ladder in region and state competition, they would need fierce determination and a lot of luck in the close games that would surely come.

Sub-Region 2A Tournament: Feb 17-18 at Perry

Perry vs. Washington County

Washington County was never in the game as Perry shellacked the quintet from Sandersville by a run-away score of 82 to 38. Joe Martin pumped in 23 points for the Panthers as Walker led Washington County with 10. Also contributing to Perry's offensive explosion were Charles Ayer with 14, Terry Todd-10, Ed Pierce-10, and Ed Harley-10.

Sub-Region championship: Perry vs. Cochran

The Panthers handily defeated Coach Jim Denning's Cochran Royals, the defending state Class A champs, 66 to 53, for the sub-region crown.

However, the contest was closer than the final score indicated. At one stage during the fourth quarter, the Royals came within five points, but Perry's stalling tactics forced the Royals into fouling. The Royals desperately wanted to wrest the ball away, but the Panthers, determined not to let the same fate befall them as the previous year when the Royals defeated them in the sub-region finals, controlled the tempo of the game.

Four Panthers scored in double figures: Joe Martin-21, Ed Pierce-18, Terry Todd-13, and Charles Ayer-11. Marion Cloud was strong on the backboards and played excellent defense, and reserve Lee St. John played well in Perry's controlled offense. Parker and Howell with 18 and 14 markers respectively led the Royals.

Perry-66	**Cochran-53**
Todd-13	Parker-18
Pierce-18	Pipkin-4
Cloud-3	Horton-9
Martin-21	Fair-8
Ayer-11	Howell-14

Score at half: Perry-33; Cochran-24
Subs: Perry: St. John; Cochran: Sawyer

Region 2A Tournament: February 25-26 at Statesboro

Perry vs. Statesboro

Perry sent Statesboro back home, 65 to 59, on the offensive heroics of Joe Martin who scored 36 of Perry's 65 points. Perry maintained a 6 to 8 point cushion throughout the game on the strength of Martin's phenomenal shooting as he was smoking hot from the opening tip to the end of the game. Charles Ayer was Perry's next high scorer with 12. Perry center Marion Cloud contributed 9, Ed Pierce-5, and Terry Todd-3. Perry made no substitutions. Story, Blizzard, and McGregor hit in double figures for Statesboro with 13, 12, and 10 points respectively.

Region championship: Perry vs. Thomson

If there ever was a game to shut down a ticking heart, the Perry-Thompson battle was a strong candidate. The Thomson team, coached by Robert Stephens, was a tall and physical crew sporting a 19-3 record and ranked fifth in Class A. With neither team shooting well, the score stalled in the teens throughout the first half.

Midway the third quarter, Perry moved out to a 10 point advantage and tried to sit down on the lead. At this point Thomson went into a zone press. Thomson not only chopped away Perry's lead but pulled ahead 35 to 33 in the waning moments of the final quarter.

Perry had lost the game until...

With 20 seconds left in the game and Thomson's victory all but assured, Thomson's guards brought the ball down court. Charles Ayer had a plan and Joe Martin saw it developing. Ayer pressured Thomson's guard toward the sidelines where he killed his dribble. Fearing Ayer would tie him up, he did exactly what Ayer was hoping for--he made an across-the-court pass to his backcourt teammate. Joe Martin picked off the pass and drove the length of the court to score. Not only did Martin tie the game 35 to 35 on his lay-up, but he was fouled in the process. With two seconds on the clock, Martin drilled the free throw and the Panthers won the region championship, 36 to 35, definitely a thriller. This was possibly the single greatest defensive play in the history of Perry basketball.

Martin was the hero of the game, but it was the quick thinking, aggressive play, and undeniable spirit of Charles Ayer that made the winning basket possible. No one saw her, but Lady Luck had returned to tournament play in what had to be her finest hour. She had breathed life into a dead corpse. This was indeed a miracle finish that brought the Panthers from the precipice of defeat to the pinnacle of victory. Would Lady Luck honor he Panthers with her presence at the state tournament starting the following week?

Perry-36	**Thomson-35**
Martin-15	Chalker-12
Ayer-10	Joesbury-3
Pierce-5	Russell-9
Todd-2	Knox-2
Cloud-4	Cranford-8

Subs: Perry-none; Thomson: Norris-1, Blackburn

State Tournament: March 3-5 at Macon City Auditorium

Perry vs. Madison

The Panthers' first opponent in the opening round of play was Madison County of Danielsville coached by Jim Perkins. Madison County was the fifth ranked team in Class A with a 24-6 record.

The Panthers, although leading 12 to 9 at first quarter, 26 to 20 at the half, and 35 to 31 as the third period mark, had to fight right down to the wire to turn back a taller and relentless Madison County quintet.

At the 1:57 mark in the final period, Joe Martin lifted the Panthers to a 42 to 36 margin, but two consecutive floor mistakes by the Panthers, which Madison County converted into field goals, tightened the score to 42 to 40. The game hung in the balance until Joe Martin dropped in two free throws with only 31 seconds remaining to increase Perry's lead to 44 to 40. With 16 seconds on the clock, Martin added another pair from the gratis line to put the game safely out of reach, 46 to 40. Madison's Pat Graham drove swiftly down court for a basket with only four seconds left to narrow the score, 46 to 42.

Joe Martin and Charles Ayer each scored 16 points for Perry. Madison's County's chief weapon was 6'5" Cauthen Westbrook who had averaged 25 points a game during the season. The 5'11" Ed Pierce held Westbrook to only 14 points despite the height disparity. Tyner added 12 for Madison County.

Perry-46	**Madison County-42**
Todd-5	Westbrook-14
Pierce-8	Jones-6
Cloud-1	Graham-5
Martin-16	Tyner-12
Ayer-16	Lord-5

Score at half: Perry-26, Madison County-20
Subs: Perry-none; Madison: Thomason, Freeman

State semifinal: Perry vs. Mitchell County-David vs. Goliath

Mitchell County from Camilla, the second ranked Class A team with a 22-6 record, towered over the smaller Panthers. With only one Panther standing over 6 feet, and he only 6' 1", the Mitchell County crew lined up at tip-off with a 6'6" center, two 6'4" forwards, and a couple of outstanding guards. It was the classic David versus Goliath match-up.

Mitchell Coach Predicts Victory

Mike Perry, the impulsive and flamboyant coach of the boys from Camilla, stated to the press before the game, "No doubt about it. We're going all the way," implying the Perry Panthers would fall. His comments evidently were buoyed by his team's performance the previous night. His second-ranked Mitchell County five had buried Cartersville, number nine in the polls with a 22-5 record, 77 to 57, in an awesome display of offensive firepower and backboard strength.

Mitchell County takes 16-point lead

Coach Mike Perry's words seemed prophetic as Mitchell County rushed out to a 20 to 12 advantage at the first quarter's end and rapidly built its lead to 28 to 12 at the 2:26 mark in the second period. The gritty Panthers, digging deep for that intangible attribute called Panther pride, began holding their own against the taller Mitchell Countians on the boards and came roaring back to trail only six points, 34 to 28, at intermission.

Slingshots slay the giant

Joe Martin and Terry Todd cut the lead to 34 to 32 within the first 34 seconds of the third period. Perry tied the score twice at 36 to 36 and 38 to 38 but couldn't take the lead until Charles Ayer drilled one from the outside with 11 seconds left in the third quarter. That moved Perry out front, 41 to 40 as the final stanza began.

During a torrid fourth quarter battle that ensued, the score was tied five times and the lead changed hands on four occasions. With 1:13 left, Martin hit a jumper and Perry went out front to stay, 55 to 54. With 1:13 remaining, Martin scored again, making it 57 to 54. Mitchell missed a shot and, after the Panthers gained possession, Coach Hartman called for the freeze, forcing Mitchell County to foul. Marion Cloud and Terry Todd hit two free throws each, and Perry widened its margin to 61 to 54, which was the final score.

Joe Martin ripped the chords for 28 tallies and Charles Ayer added 15. Marion Cloud, Ed Pierce, and Terry Todd scored 6 points apiece. Guard Mike Morrell, who fouled out with 2:34 left in the game, led Mitchell County with 18. The other Mitchell guard, Lee Burnett, chipped in 12. Greg Lee, Mitchell's big center, and forward Glenn Dixon hit for 9 each; the other forward, Steve Jones, garnered 6.

Perry-61	Mitchell County-54
Todd-6	Jones-6
Pierce-6	Dixon-9
Cloud-6	Lee-9
Martin-28	Morrell-18
Ayer-15	Burnett-12

Score at half: Perry-28; Mitchell County-34
Subs: Perry-none; Mitchell County: Bennett, White

State championship: Perry vs. Commerce

The Commerce Tigers, the region 4 champs and unranked in the state's top ten due to its 17-10 record, were considered by many to be the tournament dark horse. In advancing to the title game, Commerce had turned back a strong Thomson squad (58-53) that lost to Perry in the region finals by one point, and had routed Rockmart (57-38), the state's 4th ranked team, in the semifinals. The Tigers were a better team than their record indicated, as they had lost seven one-point decisions before Christmas and were peaking just at the right time. Coach Bob Skelton's Tigers had demonstrated a devastating fast break and a full-court press that would cause Coach Paul Hartman to adjust his game plan.

Shoot-out at O. K. Corral

Commerce, on the incredible shooting of guard Steve Gary, led for the first three quarters of the game: 16-13, 35-34, and 52 to 50. Commerce built an eight-point cushion on four occasions in the second quarter and held a six-point advantage twice in the third. On several occasions it appeared the Panthers were ready to fold under Gary's steady assault, but they would not be denied and kept charging back. While the Tigers' Gary was bombarding the nets, Perry's ace Joe Martin was matching him basket-for-basket. It was more like the shootout at O. K. Corral with no shortage of bullets by either side.

Down by two, 52 to 50, as the third stanza ended, Perry caught up at 52 to 52 and again 54 to 54 early in the final period. With 5:23 to go, Perry finally went ahead 58 to 57 on the dazzling shooting of Joe Martin. In the next two minutes, Charles Ayer added a field goal, Marion Cloud hit two clutch free throws, and Martin rifled another from long range as the Panthers increased their margin 64 to 57 with 3:05 showing on the clock. At this point, Coach Hartman signaled for the freeze, forcing Commerce to foul repeatedly to halt the timeclock countdown. During the last three minutes, Perry scored 5 points on foul shots and Commerce answered with 6 tallies. When the final horn blew, the Panthers had defeated a gallant Commerce quintet, 69 to 63. This victory marked the fourth time in five years that Perry had won the state championship (1962, 1963, 1964, and 1966), an unprecedented feat in the annals of Georgia high school basketball.

Although Commerce's Steve Gary scored a game high 35 points, Perry's Joe Martin blistered the nets for 31, many of his shots coming at crucial times to prevent Commerce from taking an insurmountable lead. Terry Todd and Marion Cloud hit for 10 points each, Ed Pierce tallied 9, Charles Ayer contributed 8, and top reserve Lee St. John hit a free throw in the critical final period. Johnny Nix and Tony Davis added 12 and 9 points respectively for Commerce.

Perry-69	**Commerce-63**
Cloud-10	Davis-9
Pierce-9	C. Hood-2
Todd-10	W. Hood-4
Martin-31	Nix-12
Ayer-8	Gary-35
St. John-1	Smith
Norris	Touchtone-1

All-State Team
Joe Martin-Perry
Terry Todd-Perry
Charles Ayer-Perry
Ed Pierce-Perry
Marion Cloud-Perry
Mike Morrell-Mitchell County
Steve Jones-Mitchell County
Lee Burnett-Mitchell County
Steve Gary-Commerce
Johnny Nix-Commerce

The team that never quit

The 1965-66 Panthers will go down in Perry history as a team that never quit. Although one of Perry's shortest teams, it left behind a legacy of unflinching determination in the face of adversity and an unbridled passion to win. This Perry team proved that gauging a player's heart is more important than measuring his height, for heart is the ingredient the 65-66 team members possessed in abundance that elevated them to greatness. You would have never known that Coach Staples wasn't still coaching as Coach Paul Hartman didn't change a thing and kept Staples' offensive and defensive patterns intact. Hartman, handpicked by Eric Staples, had been steeped in the Staples' basketball philosophy and kept the dynasty alive in 1966 with an unbelievable record of 31 wins against only two loses. When Staples said Hartman was the man to take over the dynasty he had built over 32 years, the sly old fox knew what he was talking about.

Hartman retires from coaching

After winning the state championship in 1966, Coach Hartman coached another three years, compiling an impressive overall record of 76 wins and 34 losses. He retired from coaching after the 1968-69 season and took a job in private industry. Since Coach Hartman was an extension of Coach Staples, his departure from Pantherville essentially ended the Perry basketball dynasty that began in 1933 when a young coach named Eric Staples arrived in town to change Perry's basketball fortunes forever. In 1977, Hartman returned to the Perry school system as assistant junior high principal. He retired in 1997 as the beloved principal of Tucker Elementary School, a position he held for 12 years.

Season record

Date	Opponent	Site	Perry Score	Opponent Score
16-Nov	Vienna	Away	56	54
19-Nov	Taylor County	Home	58	56
23-Nov	Crawford County	Away	64	41
24-Nov	Dudley Hughes	Home	69	54
30-Nov	Vienna	Home	59	50
3-Dec	Washington County	Home	57	43
7-Dec	Northside	Away	63	53
10-Dec	Macon County	Home	71	47
11-Dec	Hawkinsville	Away	68	38
14-Dec	Lanier	Home	55	53

Date	Opponent	Site	Perry Score	Opponent Score
17-Dec	Cochran	Away	63	54
20-Dec	Dodge County	Home	54	42

Perry Christmas tournament: 30-31 December

Date	Opponent	Site	Perry Score	Opponent Score
30-Dec	Crawford County	Home	70	20
31-Dec	Wilkinson County	Home	70	48

Date	Opponent	Site	Perry Score	Opponent Score
4-Jan	Willingham	Home	82	52
7-Jan	Dudley Hughes	Away	66	45
11-Jan	Warner Robins	Home	40	59
14-Jan	Crawford County	Home	74	43
18-Jan	Hawkinsville	Home	71	50
21-Jan	Cochran	Home	47	35
25-Jan	Dodge County	Away	48	39
28-Jan	Telfair County	Home	69	54
1-Feb	Warner Robins	Away	56	62
4-Feb	Washington County	Away	67	43
9-Feb	Lanier	Away	69	68
11-Feb	Northside	Home	59	45

Region 2A Sub-Region: Feb 17-18 at Perry

Date	Opponent		Perry Score	Opponent Score
17-Feb	Washington County		82	38
18-Feb	Cochran		66	53

Region 2A Region finals: Feb 25-26 at Statesboro

Date	Opponent		Perry Score	Opponent Score
25-Feb	Statesboro		65	59
26-Feb	Thomson		36	35

State Tournament: March 3-5 at Macon City Auditorium

Date	Opponent		Perry Score	Opponent Score
3-Mar	Madison		46	42
4-Mar	Mitchell County		61	54
5-Mar	Commerce		69	63

10 End of the Dynasty

After the 1964-65 basketball season, Coach Staples retired from coaching, but remained as principal of Perry High School for four more years, until the end of the 1968-69 school term. In tendering his letter of resignation from coaching to the county board of education, dated June 16, 1965, Staples wrote: "I want to thank the board for the rewarding and rich experience as coach for the last 32 years. The growth of Perry High School and the increasing duties of my office make it imperative for me to give up coaching." Coach Staples was only 59 years old at the time. His retirement was a surprise to many who thought he would coach at least five to ten more years before hanging it up.

There may have been reasons other than increased administrative responsibilities that prompted his resignation. I remember him once telling me that he could ride through town and see his teams of the future developing in the backyards of Perry. He could easily spot his future players in the fifth, sixth, and seventh grades. When one great team graduated, he always had another standing in the wings to take its place. But during the mid-to-late 1960s, that was not the case. I think Staples looked down the line and didn't see any reinforcements coming.

During the latter years of Coach Staples' coaching career, high school students had more distractions competing for their time. For example, during the 1940s and early 1950s, I had only a bicycle and a basketball. In the 1960s, many kids had automobiles. There was no TV in my day. In the 1960s era, everyone, including the high school set, was addicted to television. Staples did not allow football to be played at Perry until 1954. Prior to then, basketball was king in Perry; however, during the

1960s, football was quickly becoming the predominant sport at Perry. Prior to the institution of football at Perry, the basketball season started in early October. After Perry started playing football, the basketball season didn't kick-off until early December. Also, some players sustained football injuries that kept them out of the early games; some injuries were season-ending as was the case in 1960 when Perry's title hopes were shattered by knee injuries to two key players. Also, integration loomed ahead in the school system, which caused a flight of teachers from public to private schools. I realize that Coach Staples had gone through 38 years of coaching (32 at Perry and 6 in northwest Georgia), the rigors of which had taken their toll on him; however, I firmly believe that, if he had seen the basketballs still bouncing in the backyards and been able to spot burgeoning talent in the lower grades, he would have stayed on longer as coach.

Further, had Staples been able to gauge the determination and heart of the players comprising Perry's next team, the 1965-66 squad, he may not have bowed out in June of 1965. The 1966 team won 31 games, lost only two, and capped off the season with a state championship, Perry's ninth. No one figured this team of Panthers would get very far— including Staples—but they came from behind so many times to win key games, that they became known as the "Cardiac Kids." Watching their games was not good for the faint of heart. How Coach Paul Hartman survived that nail-biting season is a mystery to me.

Staples retired as Perry High School principal concurrently with the departure of the 1969 graduating class. In recognition of his remarkable contributions as principal and coach, the board of education and the community, in May 1969, held "Eric Staples Day" to honor their beloved coach and educator. Dr. Pierce Harris, a retired Methodist minister and long-time Staples' friend, was guest speaker at the camp-meeting style barbeque dinner. A number of Staples' former players, students, and friends took the rostrum to cite Staples' accomplishments and sing his praises. When it was over, Coach Staples thanked everyone for coming and stated that he and his wife, Chloe, would continue to live in Perry at the same 1101 Washington Street address, where they had resided for the past 30 years.

As a matter of information, from the time Staples came to Perry in

1933 until 1938, he lived as a boarder in Mrs. George Riley's house at 1117 Main Street, across the street from the Perry school. Perry's noted historian, Charles Shelton, and his parents also lived in the Riley house. On June 22, 1937, little Charles Shelton, a second grader at the time, his father, and Coach Staples listened to a radio broadcast of the heavyweight championship match between Joe Louis and James Braddock. Charles and his dad picked Joe Louis to win, and Coach Staples favored Braddock. To sweeten the bet, Coach Staples bet Charles a nickel that Braddock would beat Lewis. Staples paid little Charles a nickel the next day. Staples married Chloe Traylor on June 14, 1938, at the Perry Baptist Church. Staples and his young bride boarded at Mrs. Riley's house until they purchased their permanent home on Washington Street in August, 1939.

After Staples left the school system, he worked part-time as manager of a cable TV company, whose office was located in downtown Perry. He continued his strong civic and church involvement. For 38-years he taught the Adult Men's Sunday School Class at Perry's Methodist Church where his lessons were broadcast every Sunday over the radio. He was a church steward and a mason. He was a Silver Beaver Award recipient for his work with Boy Scouts and Cub Scouts. He was a charter member of the Perry Kiwanis Club and Perry's first citizen to receive the D.A.R. Award of Merit. He chaired drives for the Red Cross, March of Dimes, Easter Seals, and tuberculosis. He also coached American Legion Baseball. For his civic contributions, he was named Perry Civitan Citizen of the Year and Kiwanis Man of the Year.

Staples was selected Region Coach of the Year eight times and Georgia State Coach of the Year three times; was presented the Athens Coliseum Club's "Mr. Basketball" citation; and coached the South squad in the Georgia North-South "All-Star" Game on three occasions. Staples, an avid golfer, also excelled as Perry High School's golf coach. His golf teams captured nine state titles.

After a two-year fight with cancer, God called Coach Staples home on May 25, 1984, at the age of 78. His wife, Chloe, preceded him in death, passing in March 1982. Both were buried in Woodlawn Cemetery in Perry, Georgia.

After his death in 1984, awards kept coming in. In addition to Staples' induction into the Georgia Sports Hall of Fame during his

lifetime in 1957, the Georgia Athletic Coaches Association Hall of Fame
also enshrined him in 2002. The Atlanta Tip-off Club, at its annual
Naismith Awards Dinner in 1992, posthumously honored Coach Staples
by selecting him for the prestigious Steve Schmidt Award. United
States Senator Sam Nunn, an all- state player on the 1956 Perry state
championship team, accepted the award on behalf of Coach Staples and
his family. Senator Nunn's remarks captured the accomplishments and
genius of Coach Staples:

"Eric Staples is the man we called 'Fessor.' That was short for
professor; we didn't know how to pronounce professor so we called him
'Fessor.'

"How can I describe a coach, a man, a friend, a Christian role-model
in four minutes? How do I explain a teacher, a principal, a Sunday school
teacher, a community leader, a loving husband and father to those who
never knew him? How does a coach who never had a starter over 6' 3" tall
win 8 state championships, 25 regional championships, 924 games—83
percent of all the games he played with the highest percentage and the
greatest number of victories in American history for that many years?

"Well, let me try a few words from some of his players on
championship teams. Deryle Whipple (1947 state championship team):
'I was short and he convinced me to play tall.' Virgil Peavy (1956 state
champs): 'He taught me to pursue excellence in the classroom and on the
basketball court.' Lee Martin (1962 state champs): 'Next to my Dad,
he had more influence on my life than any other man.' Dwayne Powell
(1962-63 state champs): 'He taught us the three D's—determination,
desire, and dedication.' David Gray (1953 state champs): 'He taught us
that our objective is to perform to the limit of our abilities. Success is
having done that. Winning is the result of having done so at the right
time and the right place.' Billy Powell (1953 state champs): 'It was the
personal dimension that caused him to live on in the hearts of his players,
students, and friends. His Christian example served as a role model for all
of us to emulate.'

"How can I describe a man who never uttered a profanity, but
could frighten a referee with a stare that said it all? How do I convey
the impression—to this audience tonight—that Fessor Staples made on
his players when we did something stupid and he threw down his unlit,

soaking wet cigar that he chewed on. He stomped it like he was putting out a fire and finally picked it up and stuck it in his mouth. A coach with these communication skills did not need to curse.

"How can I describe Mrs. Chloe Staples, Professor Staples' wife and partner, except to tell you the truth—that she cooked and served a meal at her home, a pre-game meal, for the entire team for every out-of-town game and every tournament game for 32 years so we could eat at the right time and the right food.

"My time is running out, except for one personal experience which I believe should go down in the annals of coaching history. It was the state championship in 1956. Perry High School versus undefeated Valley Point, a team that had won 33 straight games that year. First half—hard fought, well played, both teams virtually deadlocked. We were exhausted and we believed we had played to the absolute limit of our abilities. Only 'Fessor' Staples, master strategist and psychologist, would use this strategy—and he probably only used it one time in 32 years with just this one team, and I don't advise it for any coach tonight, but it worked—he knew us, he psychoanalyzed us, he pulled it off. He did two things in that dressing room at half time. He first showed us the hole in their zone defense. He told us to move into the hole after the second pass, but then he said something I'll never forget, he said, 'Boys, you've had a great year. We're going to lose this game. They're too big, they're too strong, and they're too quick. You cannot beat them, but I'm proud of you anyway,' and he walked out. 'Fessor' enraged us. We played beyond our ability in the second half and we blew them away—we won by 25 points. We taught old 'Fessor' Staples a lesson. He couldn't insult our ability and get away with it. It wasn't until much later that I realized that the old fox knew what made us tick and like so many of his other teams, he taught us a lesson and meanwhile he won a state championship. As Georgia House Leader Larry Walker (1960 team) said not long ago about Staples, 'He got more out of the boys than they were capable of giving—he was a master psychologist.'

"So I ask Sherry Staples Hubbard, Pierce Staples, and Porter Staples to come forward for presentation of the Steve Schmidt award to my coach and my teacher and their father, Professor Eric Staples."

During 1993, Thomas (Boot) Hunt, an all-state player and captain

L-R: Valley Point captain, Billy Pelfrey, Valley Point Coach M. Acree, Perry Coach Eric Staples, Sam Nunn with 1956 state championship trophy, and Perry's Virgil Peavy.

of Perry's 1959 state championship team, contacted Pete Henderson, a free lance artist who specialized in color paintings of sports figures, about doing an acrylic painting of Coach Staples surrounded by his players. The painting would be called "Fessor's Boys." Hunt, putting down a sizeable deposit of his own money to enlist the services of Henderson, was able to line up 100 commissioners to financially underwrite the painting, mostly former basketball players. The painting, a 32" by 36" montage, featured Coach and Mrs. Staples, the old basketball gym, the Staples' home (where the teams were fed before games), the scoreboard, the Panther mascot, the school letter and class ring, assistant coaches and teachers who worked with the teams (Assistant Coach Frank Holland, Girl's Coach and Boys 'B' team coach Earl Marshall, Assistant Coach Bob Shuler, Football Coach Herb St. John, and grammar school and junior high principal Jim Worrall, who assisted with basketball), and over 100 players from 1933-1965 captured in various action poses.

Once the painting was completed and lithographs produced, a tribute for Coach Staples, organized by Hunt, was held at the Holiday Inn in Perry, Georgia, on November 25, 1994. Prior to unveiling the painting by the artist Pete Henderson, a program was held with Boot Hunt serving as emcee. Hunt began with a moving introduction to the memory of Coach Staples. He was followed by Billy Powell who presented "Reflections" and U. S. Senator Sam Nunn who delivered the keynote address.

Boot Hunt's introductory remarks included a litany of attributes that distinguished Eric Staples as an outstanding coach, educator, and community leader. Hunt observed, "All whose lives were touched by Fessor, I believe, realize even more as they grow older and wiser just how much an influence he had on them. That's certainly the case with me. We're better people because of him; the world's a better place because of him." Hunt added, "Too often we don't recognize people and the contributions they make—until it's too late—or they're gone. But the spirit of Fessor, of Perry High, of the Panthers, of 'His Boys' have been captured on canvas and will remain with us forever in a painting by well-known sports artist Pete Henderson."

Selected passages from U. S. Senator Sam Nunn's keynote address, which contained insightful comments about Coach Staples, are reflected below:

"Thank you very much, Boot, for what you and Pete have done today. This is really a great homecoming. Wouldn't it have been wonderful if we could have gotten all of Fessor's teams together and spent some time with him before he passed away? That would have been absolutely terrific. I took my son, Brian, to visit Fessor in the nursing home six months before he died. I was determined that Brian was going to get to know him, because he was going to hear about him all of his life, and I wouldn't take anything for that. So Boot, you and Pete have blessed me. You have done a masterful work. This painting will live forever in the hearts and minds of thousands of people who came under Fessor's fabled guidance.

"I have many stories that I could tell about Fessor Staples. I probably spent more time with him than any other adult, other than my mother and father. I remember the first venture I had with him--he had a worm bed in the back of his yard. My first job was to pick the worms from the manure pile and count them. I would then package them in little boxes, and he sold them. That was before he got me into the peach business. Of course, I worked in peaches every summer like many of you.

"I spent a lot of time with him on the golf course. He really
started me playing golf. The first time I played golf with him was at a
Montezuma course before they built the first nine-hole course in Perry.
After that, I played with him probably a thousand times. In addition to
his basketball accomplishments, Fessor's Perry golf teams captured nine
state championships.

"When I think about basketball coaches, I reflect on the story I
heard directly from coach K.C. Jones, Boston Celtics' coach for a number
of years. I was playing with him at a charity golf tournament. His story
brought to mind how great coaches deal with individuals. K.C. Jones
said he called time out in a game when the Boston Celtics were behind by
one point and only ten seconds remained in the game. While Jones was
sketching a play for the team to execute, Larry Bird looked at him and
said, 'Coach, forget all that stuff and just tell everybody to give me the ball
and get the heck out of the way.' Jones said he looked at him, and said,
'Bird, I'm the coach; you're not the coach; if you ever say anything like
that again and interrupt me when I am designing a play, I'm going to put
you on the bench, and you are going to stay there for the next two weeks!'
And then Jones said, 'Now here's what we are going to do. We're going to
give Bird the ball and get the heck out of the way!'

"What was unique about Mr. Staples is that he knew every
individual; he did not have a mass psychology; he had an individual
psychology. He treated different people in different ways, but never
unfairly. He knew what would motivate individuals, and he knew how to
motivate a whole team. But he didn't do it by simply treating the team, he
treated each individual. If one person responded to more discipline, he
gave more discipline. If one person responded to praise, he heaped more
praise. He had that innate ability that very, very few coaches have--to be
able to psychoanalyze and understand the nature of each individual.

"I particularly like the way Miss Chloe has been placed in a
prominent place on the painting. Mrs. Staples' smile, her beauty, her
sincerity, her absolute dedication have been captured in a magnificent way.
I will never forget her, because she played not only such an important role
in his life and in the lives of Sherry and Pierce and Porter, but in the lives
of everybody on the team. We used to go to her home for meals before

important ballgames – out of town ball games or district tournament or state tournament games. She would prepare dinner for us. There were a couple of reasons for that. One is that Fessor wanted us to eat three or four hours before the ball game. He did not want anyone coming to the ball game on a full stomach, so he made sure we ate at the right time.

"I also remember Miss Chloe sending me a letter after I was elected to the United State Senate. On a given day, I received 500 to 2000 letters and between 500 to 2000 phone calls. Everybody was advising me what to do on issues facing the country. That is the nature of the process, and that is good.

"Miss Chloe wrote me a letter one time about an important issue. It was a handwritten note, which stated: 'Sam, we watched you grow up. We know you came through the right kind of background; we know your parents... I'm not giving you any kind of instruction as long as you are in the Senate. All I ask you is that you do what you think in your own heart is right for this Country and this State.' I read that letter, and I kept

Mrs. Chloe Traylor Staples in front of a portrait of Coach Eric Staples.

it. I have read it many times since, because that was the toughest mandate anyone has ever given me--to do what is right. But that's the way she thought, and that is the kind of inspiration she imparted.

"There is a thin line between teaching someone to be a good loser and teaching someone to really get in the frame of mind of being a loser. And Fessor was able to draw that line. He didn't want anybody to enjoy losing, but he taught us to lose with dignity and to lose with grace and to lose by complimenting the other team, but he never wanted us to enjoy losing. To him that defeated the purpose of the competition.

"Fessor played golf a lot with Dr. Pierce Harris, a wonderful Methodist minister. I remember Mr. Staples sharing with me a story about Dr. Harris' golf experiences with another preacher. The preacher was the worst golfer Dr. Harris had ever seen. After every bad shot, his preacher friend would smile and pat everyone on the back, as if he were having a wonderful time. If his pastor friend hit ten balls in a row in the water, he would walk off smiling. Dr. Harris told the preacher one day that he ought to give up golf and never play again. The preacher responded, 'No, I enjoy it.' Dr. Harris countered, 'Anybody who plays as badly as you do and enjoys it; something is wrong with him.' Dr. Harris' comment to the preacher really captured Fessor's attitude: be a dignified loser, but never a joyful loser.

"I remember when my son Brian was a basketball player at Walt Whitman High School in Montgomery County, Maryland. Walt Whitman sometimes played Springbrook High, one of the state's top high school basketball teams. The principal at Springbrook was Tommy Marshall. Tommy and his brother, Earl, grew up here in Perry and played basketball for Coach Staples. I sat with Tommy at several games when Whitman was playing Springbrook. During the course of the game, Tommy would point out floor mistakes being tolerated by the coaches for which Fessor would promptly bench a player. Tommy has really learned the lessons of Fessor Staples.

"Fessor was a basketball coach. He was a Sunday School teacher. He was a wonderful educator. He was a wonder father. I considered him much more than a mentor. I considered him a friend. But he was not just a basketball coach, or educator, or Christian leader--he was all of those things, but he was also a character coach. There is no one here who played for Coach Staples that wouldn't tell you when he quit dribbling, when he quit shooting, and when he quit running that he was not still greatly affected everyday of his life by the character that Coach Staples implanted. He built character and character built the team. And the team won, usually, because of that character. That's the Fessor that we know and love and that's the Fessor that's been captured on the painting so magnificently."

Coach Staples is gone, but a testimonial to his life lives on—the old Perry schoolhouse built on Main Street in 1925. This building was

the heart and soul of Coach Staples. It is the only remaining edifice in
Perry that symbolizes the glory days of Perry basketball and the wonderful
memories of attending school there. Thirty years after the high school
moved to North Avenue, the old school had been relegated to a repository
for school books and a meeting place for the school board. It had reached
a serious state of disrepair and was moving closer to demolition. When
a school board member remarked one day that the space occupied by
the old school could be better used as a grammar school playground, he
cranked up metaphorical bulldozers in the minds of many who feared for
the worst...

11 Saving the Old Perry School

Perry School in 1925

Perry Mayor Jim Worrall was in a meeting with the Houston County School Board in 1989 when a board member suggested removal of the old school building to free-up space for a grammar school playground. To Worrall, it was more than idle chatter; the board didn't have the money to restore the building, much less maintain the 60-year old structure, which served no useful purpose except to store school books. The suggestion by the school board member conjured up visions of bulldozers and wrecking balls in the mind of Mayor Worrall, a former Perry grammar school and junior high principal, and served to fuel his resolve to protect the Perry school from demolition.

The PHS class of 1956 was the last to graduate from the old Perry school before the student body was moved to the new high school on

North Avenue in 1957. Because the building held special memories
for former PHS graduates and local citizens, mayoral candidate Jim
Worrall made a campaign promise in November 1988 to save the school
building. After his election in December 1988, Mayor Jim Worrall was
true to his word and began an aggressive crusade in early 1989 to save
the old building. In a letter writing campaign and through newspaper
interviews, Mayor Worrall pointed out the building was deteriorating and
urged the school board to stabilize the structure until a restoration plan
could be developed. So great was local concern to save the old building
that a public meeting was held in its auditorium to discuss the future
of the building. Adding impetus to Mayor Worrall's quest to save the
building was the full support given his initiative by the Houston County
Commission.

In May 1993, the Houston County Board of Education (HCBE)
proposed to sell the school building to the City of Perry for $1.2 million.
At that time, the city complex was seriously overcrowded. There was
insufficient space to house the police and fire departments as well as the
city administrative offices. Since Perry's city government had already
planned to construct a new $900,000 administrative building to alleviate
the overcrowding, it made a counteroffer to the HCBE for $900,000 to
use for school renovation with the stipulation that, after renovation, the
HCBE would move from its location next door on Washington Street
and relocate at the old Perry school building. In turn, the city would
move its overcrowded administrative offices (mayor, city manager, public
works, planning and zoning, utilities, purchasing, and tax administration)
into the vacated HCBE building next door. Further, the police and fire
departments would remain co-located in the public safety building. In
effect, the city would acquire the former HCBE office, and the school
board would use the $900,000 to renovate the old school. There was one
catch, however. The city's offer was $300,000 less than what the school
board had requested.

To work out a compromise regarding the $300,000 shortfall, a
meeting was held with Houston County School Superintendent Tony
Hinnant and school board members, the Mayor and City Council, and
members of the state legislative delegation in attendance. At this meeting,
State Representative Larry Walker of Perry brokered a deal between the

city and the school board. He suggested that the board accept the city's $900,000 offer and that the city and the board work together to raise the additional $300,000. The $900,000 paid the HCBE came not from ad valorem taxes, but from a funding reserve the city had accumulated through the sale of natural gas. To reduce construction costs, Rep. Walker obtained free prison labor from the state to help with the school renovation. This resulted in a cost avoidance of over $100,000. Prison labor was provided by the local correctional facility and included gutting the interior of the building and replacing its roof.

Architectural plans were drawn to completely rework the 28,000 square foot building inside and out. The renovation effort was begun in the fall of 1993 and was supervised by Bill Loudermilk, Houston County HCBE facilities department director. Loudermilk did a truly outstanding job in transforming the old school to new specifications, yet preserving the

Perry Mayor Jim Worrall standing in front of the renovated Perry School, which now houses offices of the Houston County Board of Education.

building's facade, retaining its prized auditorium, and installing hardwood that simulated the old flooring. He also allocated space for the Sam Nunn

Museum and the 1927 vintage classroom. Bobbe Nelson, a 1952 PHS graduate, spearheaded the design and placement of exhibits in the vintage classroom.

Work was completed in 1996, and the HCBE moved into the renovated building during the summer of 1996. The building and the Sam Nunn Museum were officially dedicated on September 8, 1996.

Jim Worrall, a confidant of legendary basketball coach Eric Staples and one steeped in Perry Panther tradition, was the catalyst who brought this project to fruition. The saving of this historic landmark was a dream come true for all Perry High graduates and local citizens.

In August 2005, this writer kicked off a campaign in the Houston Home Journal to have a street, school, or other significant landmark named after Coach Staples. After I had written emails to over 500 Perry High School alumni, dialogued the matter extensively on the PHS Alumni Website, and talked to local citizens, the overwhelming consensus reached was that the old Perry school be named after Coach Staples. There was one catch, however, the school board had a policy, enacted in March 1999, which stipulated that a school could not be named after an individual. A facility within a school such as an athletic facility, library, media center, etc. could be named after an individual, but not the school itself. Since the old Perry school housed the Houston County Board of Education, the building technically was no longer a school and had not been so since 1960. During mid-September 2005, I met with School Superintendent Danny Carpenter, who happened to be a strong advocate of Coach Staples and was very receptive to the idea of naming the building after him. Danny agreed that the school policy did not specifically prohibit the old Perry school building being named after someone. Danny promised to meet with the board members to feel them out on the issue and to recommend they name the building after Coach Staples. Since the PHS alumni had designated me as their spokesman to make the formal proposal to the school board, I immediately scheduled a meeting with the Houston County School Board at its next monthly meeting on October 11, 2005.

During the interim, Danny discussed the matter with all seven school board members and called me on October 3rd to advise that all board members would approve the proposal--stating it was a "done deal." Danny scheduled a preliminary meeting with me on October 5th. I asked Thomas (Boot) Hunt, Perry Mayor Jim Worrall, former state representative Larry Walker, and William Harrison to attend the meeting and to serve on a steering committee to plan the official dedication of the building. At the 5 October meeting, we discussed the agenda for the upcoming board meeting and the purchase of a bronze plaque, officially naming the building the "Eric P. Staples Memorial Building." The plaque would be 30 by 42 inches, incorporate a sculptured bust of Coach Staples and include in the inscription his academic achievements, coaching record, and service to his church and community. William Harrison accepted the task of designing the plaque and obtaining bids from prospective engraving companies.

State Representative Larry Walker

Subsequently, Larry Walker, former PHS basketball player and Georgia House Majority Leader for 16 years, made a sizeable contribution to underwrite the procurement of the plaque. Representative Walker was also responsible for securing over $2 million dollars in state funding from the fall of 1993 until the summer of 1996 to help renovate the old Perry school building. Superintendent Danny Carpenter is most deserving for his support of this PHS alumni effort, which was so important to all PHS alumni and local citizens.

At the October 11th meeting, my appearance before the school board turned into an acceptance speech rather than the presentation of a proposal. Board member Skip Dawkins, after presenting a biographical sketch and summary of academic and athletic accomplishments of Eric P. Staples, made the official motion to name the building after Staples. The vote was unanimous. All seven members voted affirmatively with a show

Houston County School Superintendent Danny Carpenter with Perry Panther jacket.

of uplifted hands: Pamela Greenway-Chairperson, Griff Clements-Vice
Chairperson, Jim Boswell, Skip Dawkins, Dr. Toby Hill, Tom Warner,
and Fred Wilson. God was surely in this initiative from day one, because
everything fell magically into place.

The formal dedication of the building was held on February 19,
2006. An impressive 30" by 42" bronze plaque weighting 160 pounds
and featuring a bust of Coach Staples—designed by William Harrison-
- was unveiled at the ceremony. The plaque's inscription summarized
Coach Staples' accomplishments as a coach and school principal and
his contributions to his church and community. The plaque will hang
prominently in the front hallway of the Eric P. Staples Memorial Building
among the other Staples' memorabilia. Coach Staples' heart and soul was
in that old Perry school. Since Coach Staples belongs to all PHS alumni
and we all belong to him, by naming the old schoolhouse the Eric P.

Staples Memorial Building, in effect, a part of the building is named after each of us.

"Name it and they will come," was the mantra that kept reverberating through my mind, as the project unfolded to name the old Perry school after Coach Staples. Similar to Kevin Costner's "Field of Dreams," where Shoeless Joe Jackson and the 1919 Chicago White Sox returned to play baseball, the old school is a "Building of Precious Memories," where unforgettable remembrances abound and the presence of Coach Staples is strongly felt. This building is now the Eric P. Staples Memorial Building. Although the Houston County Board of Education is housed there, the Perry High alumni claim unique and undeniable affiliation with their former home. With Coach Staples' plaque hanging majestically in the front entrance amid impressively showcased school memorabilia, the Panther nation will be flocking to the old school for years to come to soak up the nostalgia of this storied place and to relive the glory days of old Perry High.

A block east of the old Perry school sat the old wooden gym that was built in 1926 and opened for play in 1927. It burned to the ground in May, 1969, the cause of the fire unknown. Only a vacant lot stands in mute testimony of that once famous citadel of basketball. When the air is still at this site and I am perfectly quiet, I can still hear the balls bouncing...

12 I Can Still Hear the Balls Bouncing

Perry High's magnificent old gym burned in 1969.

An old backyard basketball buddy, Bobby Mayo, once wrote me, saying, "I have it on good authority that the old Perry gym is located 100 yards from the Pearly Gates." Yes, I hope the old gym is there when I get to Heaven. It mysteriously burned down during the wee morning hours of May 3, 1969, only hours after the "Coach Staples' Appreciation Day" observance on the evening of May 2, when the entire community gathered to honor Coach Staples, who was retiring. Strong speculation exists that an arsonist wanted to send Coach Staples off in a final blaze of glory.

I grew up in that gym. It was a big part of my life. Recently, I drove down to Perry and walked about the hallowed ground where the old gym once stood. When there was no noise, and I became completely still and closed my eyes, I could still hear the balls bouncing. It sounded just like a Perry team practicing and running drills. Maybe it's because I have heard those familiar sounds so many times that they still echo through the receptors of my mind. Or maybe the ghosts of teams past still inhabit the imaginary confines of the old gym. As I listened to the sounds of basketballs bouncing on the hardwood floor, I could envision Coach Staples sitting on the front row of bleachers, chewing his never-lit cigar and watching his offense run plays over and over, shouting reprimands for every turnover and every missed assignment.

That magnificent old gym served Perry basketball for thirty two years, seven under Coach Jim Gooden (1927-1933) and twenty five under Coach Eric Staples (1933-1958). On Tuesday and Friday nights, it was the favorite gathering place for the Perry fans, who came to see their Panthers play. Every Perry High alumni and every Perry fan remembers the old gym with great affection. The atmosphere of those games—the crowds, the cheering, and the winning tradition—are cherished memories that will last forever. Yes, those were the days of Camelot in Perry U.S.A., a magical time in history that has passed into the ages, never to be retrieved, yet never to be forgotten.

Life in the Perry community revolved around its basketball teams. Perry was an enchanting little town and its winning basketball teams created a community pride that was unsurpassed in this region and in our state. This pride still lives—it glows brightly in the hearts and souls of every Perry Panther and binds us together in a common appreciation of our glorious past. It is called "Pride of the Panthers."

Appendix I – Perry High School's Other Outstanding Teams: 1933-1969

1934 Perry team

Members:
Artemus Braddock
Hugh Braddock
Marion Brown
Curtis Clark
Joe Davis
Dick Edwards
Marvin Griffin
Lorie Gunter
Allen Martin
J. M. (Pepper) Martin
Bob Massee
Watt Rainey
Harris Rape
Hugh Lawson-manager

Regular season highlights

    The five starters on the 1934 team were Hugh Braddock, Artemus Braddock, Marion Brown, J. M. (Pepper) Martin, and Bob Massee. This was Coach Staples' first basketball team at Perry. His Panthers finished the regular season with 25 wins and only 3 losses. Against arch-rival Fort Valley, Perry won two games, lost one and tied one. The tie was a 19 to 19 deadlock played in Fort Valley on January 13, 1934. Fort Valley Coach Charles Rogers refused to play an overtime period to determine the winner. This left Coach Staples' boys disappointed, after they had fought so hard to win the game, and dissatisfied to walk away with a tie.

    One of Perry's greatest accomplishments was the defeat of Macon's Lanier Poets, 35 to 30, on the scintillating shooting of Perry's great forward combination, Hugh Braddock pouring in 19 points and J. M. Martin garnering 12. The Poets went on to win the GIAA state championship in 1934, an elite classification for Georgia's largest schools.

Third District Tournament:

Northern Division tournament at Perry

The northern division was one of four divisional tournaments held in the third district, which included both Class B and Class C schools. There were 12 teams in the northern division alone and some 50 teams in the entire third district, all competing equally for the district title.

Perry defeated Byromville on opening night, 36 to 15; downed Vienna in semifinals, 36 to 6; and lost to Fort Valley, 22 to 21, in the championship game. In the title game, with less than ten seconds on the clock and Perry leading Fort Valley, 21 to 20, Fort Valley forward Lowell Parks released a long desperation attempt near center court that ripped through the net as the game ended. Both division champs, Fort Valley, and runner-up Perry, advanced to the district tournament.

District championship at Cordele

Smarting from defeat in the northern division title game, Perry, in the district opener, pounced on Fort Valley with vengeance and won by a wide margin, 33 to 21. Brothers Artemus Braddock and Hugh Braddock of Perry led the scoring with 16 and 10 points respectively. In the semifinal game, Perry slipped by Cordele, 26 to 24. Perry had trailed until the very last minute of the game when reserve Allen Martin scored the winning basket. Martin tallied 14 points. Team captain Bob Massee and J. M. Martin were stalwarts on defense and center Marion Brown was outstanding on the backboards. Perry humbled Rebecca, 59 to 29, for the district title on the red-hot shooting of Hugh Braddock who scored an amazing 31 points, a rarity in the era of low-scoring games.

State Tournament at Woodruff Hall (UGA) in Athens

Perry advanced to the state Class B finals with a 42 to 27 victory over Hazelhurst behind the 21-point effort of Hugh Braddock. Perry lost to Canton, 42 to 23, in the championship game and captured second place in the state Class B tournament. Perry had defeated Canton 29 to 18 earlier in the season when Bob Massee held its high-scoring center, Jones, to only four points, but experienced a poor shooting night in the state final. This loss was a big let down for the Panthers. Nevertheless, Coach Staples, in his first year as Panther mentor, had sent shock waves throughout the state that his future Perry teams would be a force to be reckoned with for many years to come.

1935 Perry team

Members:
Charles Andrew
Donald Clark
Joe Davis
Dick Edwards
Marvin Griffin
Horace Grimsley
James (Preacher) Howard
Aldene Lasseter
Powers Lawson
Allen Martin
G. T. Pierce
Watt Rainey
Harris Rape

Regular season highlights

The Panthers ended the regular season undefeated: 29 wins and no losses. The starting five comprised Allen Martin, Horace Grimsley, James Howard, Joe Davis, and Dick Edwards.

Third District Tournament at Fort Valley

Perry blasted Buena Vista, 32 to 13, in the opener, and advanced to the semifinals to beat Chauncey, 27 to 26, on a last second field goal by Perry ace Horace Grimsley. In the title game, Perry thrashed Americus, 34 to 16, as Horace Grimsley tossed in 14 points followed by Joe Davis with 10.

All five Perry starters were named to the tournament all-star team: forwards Allen Martin and Horace Grimsley, center James Howard, and guards Dick Edwards and Joe Davis.

This was the ninth district title during the last ten years for Perry: 1927, 1928, 1929, 1930, 1931, 1932, and 1933 under Coach Gooden, and 1934 and 1935 under Coach Staples, who was in his second year of coaching at Perry. The tournaments from 1927 through 1932 were played in the old 12th District. The wins in 1933, 1934, and 1935 were in the newly formed 3rd District.

Third District Class B and C tournament at Fort Valley

The Panthers lost to Sycamore, its first defeat of the season.

State tournament at Woodruff Hall at UGA in Athens

First round: Perry-40, Dublin-24. Allen Martin scored 23 points

Quarterfinals: Perry-37, LaGrange-23. Allen Martin and Horace Grimsley shared scoring honors with 12 points apiece. James Howard, Perry's center, added 9 markers.

Semifinals: Perry-34, Canton-32. The game ended tied 31 to 31. In the first extra period, neither team scored. In the second overtime period, Allen Martin made a long one–handed shot near center court to put Perry in the lead 33 to 31. Hilton of Canton scored a free throw to pull his team within one point, 33 to 32. With time running out, Martin was fouled and nailed the free throw, making the final score, Perry-34, Canton-32. This win was sweet revenge for Perry who had lost to Canton in the state finals the previous year. Martin led all scorers with 20 points.

Title game: Perry was required to play two games the same day: Canton in the afternoon semifinals and Albany that night for the championship. Having played a hard- fought, double-overtime victory against Canton only hours earlier, Perry's players were exhausted and less than sharp for their championship battle with Albany. Albany prevailed 34 to 20, and Perry claimed the state Class B runner-up spot for the second year in a row.

All-state:
Allen Martin
Dick Edwards

1936 Perry team

Members:
John Arnold
James Chandler
Marvin Griffin
Horace Grimsley
John Houser
James (Preacher) Howard
Aldene Lasseter
Lenwood (Red) McInvale
Norman Parker
Lee Paul
Harris Rape
Eugene Smith
William Barfield-manager

Regular season highlights

Perry's starting line-up consisted of Horace Grimsley, Norman Parker, James Howard, Aldene Lasseter, and Marvin Griffin. Grimsley and Howard were returning starters from the 1935 state runner-up team. With all-state players Allen Martin and Dick Edwards graduated, the Panthers in 1936 faced a rebuilding year. Horace Grimsley was a long range sharpshooter and Perry's leading scorer. Illustrative of Grimsley's marksmanship was a 44 to 17 win over Chauncey in which Grimsley drilled 28 points with his patented one-hand push shot. A top reserve, Eugene Smith, shot himself in the foot in a hunting accident in January 1936 and was unable to play for the remainder of the season. His absence was a great loss to the team.

Third District tournament at Perry

With the star of the team, Horace Grimsley, in bed stricken with pneumonia, Perry entered the tournament at a decided disadvantage. In the opening tilt, Perry humbled Cuthbert, 24 to 7, but lost to Cordele in the semifinals, 23 to 20. Had Grimsley, who was averaging 20 points a game, been able to play against Cordele, the outcome of the game could have been different. Being eliminated in the semifinals, Perry met Vienna in the consolation game. The Panthers easily rolled over Vienna, 25 to 15, for third place in district competition.

Vienna was coached by J. B. Davis who succeeded Colonel Joe Jenkins, the revered and renowned coach who led the "Vienna Wonder Five" to three consecutive state titles in 1927, 1928, and 1929. Jenkins' Wonder Five teams were runner-up in the national championship game in Chicago in 1927, advanced to the national semifinals in 1928, and made it to the national quarterfinals in 1929.

Perry's top scorers in the district tournament, as recorded in Mr. Jim Gooden's "Little Black Book," were: Norman Parker-25, Aldene Lasseter-21, Harris Rape-12, Marvin Griffin-5, and James Chandler-4.

1937 Perry team

Members:
John Arnold
C. A. Boswell
James Chandler
Ernest Davis
Fred Griggs
Horace Grimsley
Willis Harrison
Virgil Hay
John Houser
Aldene Lasseter
Lenwood (Red) McInvale
Norman Parker
Lee Paul

Harris Rape
Eugene Smith
William Barfield-manager

Regular season highlights

Perry's regular season record was 28 wins and 2 losses. The starting five were Harris Rape, Norman Parker, Horace Grimsley, Aldene Lasseter, and Eugene Smith.

The 1937 team was still playing under the 'center jump' rule. After each score, the teams returned to center court for a tip-off. This provided an undue advantage to the team with the taller center. It also resulted in roughhouse tactics and flagrant fouling to gain possession of the ball after the center court tip. Coaches throughout the state were clamoring to eliminate this rule and to allow the team scored upon to bring the ball in under its own basket with a 10-second time limit to get the ball across center court. This rule change would remove height as the primary determinant in winning and give more emphasis to speed, quickness, and finesse. Coach Staples and Fort Valley coach, Grant Vennes, were in favor of this rule change. The 'center-jump' rule was rescinded, effective with the beginning of the 1938-39 basketball season.

Third District tournament at Pitts

On opening night, Perry blistered Sycamore, 34 to 18, and conquered Hawkinsville, 25 to 20, in the quarterfinals. In semifinal action, Perry outlasted Chauncey, 25 to 20, behind a balanced offensive attack. Norman Parker tallied 7 points, Horace Grimsley and Harris Rape-6 each, Aldene Lasseter-4, Eugene Smith-1, and Red McInvale-1.

Perry played Pitts for the district championship. Pitts was led by Norman Faircloth, who later became basketball coach at Fort Valley in 1950. Pitts nosed by the Panthers, 23 to 21, on last minute heroics by an unlikely player. With Perry leading by seven points late in the game, Norman Faircloth made a driving lay-up to reduce the margin to 5 points. Haynie of Pitts scored a free throw to move Pitts within 4. Then Jackson, an infrequent scorer during the season, sank an amazing three consecutive field goals to place Pitts in the lead by 2 points. This proved to be the winning margin. Perry had defeated Pitts twice during the regular season.

Jim Gooden, former Perry coach, 1919-1933, and Perry's present school superintendent, presented the championship trophy to Norman Faircloth, captain of the Pitts cagers. Gooden presented the game basketball to Captain Horace Grimsley as Perry's award for second place. Grimsley was high point man for Perry with 10 points. Jackson hit for 10 points, and Faircloth contributed 9 in Pitts' winning effort.

1938 Perry team

Front, L-R: Wilson Moody, Buford Chapman-manager, Lenwood "Red" McInvale, C. A. Boswell, Dot Roughton, John Houser, and Horace Woodruff. Standing, L-R: Willis Harrison, Lee Paul, Norton Buff, and Coach Eric Staples. Not pictured: Gene Boyd.

Regular season highlights

Perry's starting line-up was shuffled several times during the year with Willis Harrison, Lee Paul, Red McInvale, Horace Woodruff, Norman Parker, Dot Roughton, and John Houser alternating.

In the last home game, the Perry High Panthers downed the Fort Valley Green Wave, 27 to 22, before the largest crowd ever to witness a game at the Perry gym. Spectators overflowed into the aisles and doorways. Leading the offensive attack for Perry was Norman Parker with a game high 10 points. Willis Harrison pitched in 8 markers, Lee Paul-4, Dot Roughton-2, C. A. Boswell-2, Red McInvale-1, and Horace Woodruff-1. Perry center Willis Harrison was the Green Waves' nemesis on the backboards. Dot Roughton and Horace Woodruff played outstanding floor games and kept the offense clicking while Lee Paul, C. A. Boswell, and Red McInvale were tenacious on defense. Fort Valley was led by Hunnicutt, Thames, and Summers, who tallied 7 points each. Other Green Wave players were B. Mathews-1, Vaughn, and L. Mathews.

Third District tournament in Chauncey

Perry defeated Americus, 22 to 14, in the opener, and lost to Chauncey, coached by Frank Holland, by a score of 29 to 23 in the semifinals. In the consolation game, Perry claimed third place by blasting Hawkinsville 42 to 17. Norman Parker led Perry's scoring with 14 points. The other four starters for Perry were Lee Paul-6 points, Dot Roughton-4, Willis Harrison-4, and Red McInvale-2. Reserves seeing extensive action were John Houser-4, C. A. Boswell-4, Horace Woodruff-4, Norton Buff, and Wilson Moody.

Coach Frank Holland's Chauncey squad downed Pitts 41 to 26 for the Third District Class B title. Chauncey advanced to the state tournament and won the runner-up trophy in the state Class B ranks, losing to Hartwell in the title game, 29 to 20.

In that day, tournament ticket prices were 20 cents for children and 25 cents for adults.

Houston-Peach tournament

This tournament was played in early March 1938 after the district tournament. Perry again triumphed over Fort Valley, 29 to 18, and the next night prevailed over Byron, 13 to 11, in two overtime periods to capture the tournament championship. The regulation game ended in a tie, 11 to 11. Neither team scored in the first overtime. In the second overtime period, with the score still knotted, 11 to 11, Red McInvale sank a shot from mid-court with less than a minute remaining to give the Perry Panthers a hard-fought victory and bragging rights as the champions of both Houston and Peach Counties.

1939 Perry team

Members:
C. A. Boswell
Leroy Boswell
Julian Cawthon
Willis Harrison
Bobby Holtzclaw
William (Bill) Hunt
Dot Roughton
Ralph Tabor
Buddy Tolleson
Lee Warren-manager

Regular season highlights

Starters on Perry's varsity were C. A. Boswell, Leroy Boswell, Willis Harrison, Bobby Holtzclaw, and Dot Roughton.

Perry's 1939 edition of the Panthers, at times, was a very physical and aggressive team. In a heated and close contest between Perry and Chauncey played at the Chauncey gym, the game started out very rough and got even rougher as it progressed. With less than a minute to play, Pruett of Chauncey and C. A. Boswell of Perry got into a fistfight. The fight was stopped after several punches were thrown. Both players were ejected from the game. In the end, Chauncey came out on top, 27 to 23.

Possibly, Perry's most notable win during the regular season was its 29 to 27 triumph over Eatonton High, a game played at the Eatonton gym. Earlier, Eatonton had routed the Panthers 40 to 14 at Perry. Perry's ability to turn the tables on one of Georgia's strongest teams was attributed to the intense pre-game preparations and matchless strategy of Coach Staples. Leroy Boswell led all scorers with 16 points. A month later, the powerful Eatonton quintet won the state Class B championship by defeating the heralded Brunswick team, 22 to 20.

The 1938-39 season marked the end of the center jump rule. After each score, rather than jump center, the team scored upon brought the ball in under the basket with a 10-second time limit to advance the ball across center court.

Third District tournament at Americus

Opening game: Perry-35, Fort Valley-20. Dot Roughton led Perry with 11 points followed by Leroy Boswell-8 and Willis Harrison-7.

Semifinals: Perry-33, Pitts-18. High scorers for Perry were Dot Roughton-12 and Leroy Boswell-10.

District championship: Chauncey-25, Perry-18. Chauncey led 13 to 8 at halftime and scored 12 second-half points to Perry's 10. C. A. Boswell was top scorer for the Panthers with 6 points in a low-scoring, defensive game. Other Perry players in the scoring column were Leroy Boswell and Dot Roughton with 4 points each, Bobby Holtzclaw-2, and Willis Harrison -2. Perry used only one reserve, Ralph Tabor.

Chauncey's victory marked the second consecutive year the Comets, under Coach Frank Holland's tutelage, had won the Third District Class B championship.

1940 Perry team

Front row, L-R: Coach Staples, Leroy Boswell, Julian Cawthon, Dot Roughton, and
Norlis (Skeet) Chapman. Second row, L-R: Nathan Gilbert-manager, William (Bill)
Hunt, Carl Clark, Bobby Holtzclaw, and Fred Johnson. Back row, L-R: Walter Gray,
Courtney Mason, Ed Pierce, and Buddy Tolleson.

Regular season highlights

After a number of rebuilding seasons since the two state runner-up titles in 1934
and 1935, the 1940 Perry team appeared to be a legitimate contender for the state Class
B crown. In its starting line-up of forwards Leroy Boswell and Buddy Tolleson, center
Julian Cawthon, and guards Dot Roughton and Bobby Holtzclaw, Perry had a well-
balanced offensive attack, excellent rebounding, and a strong defensive unit. Bill Hunt
was a very capable sixth man.

As evidence of their strength in central Georgia, the Panthers trounced arch-rival
Fort Valley 48 to 16 with Leroy Boswell and Dot Roughton leading the way with 20 and
13 points respectively. The Panthers had the potential to go all the way, if everyone stayed
healthy.

"Macon Evening News"/Mercer University Invitational tournament, 25-27 Jan 1940

This tournament, held at Mercer University's Porter gym, comprised 36 teams
throughout Georgia, and was tantamount to a state play-off. Perry defeated four good

teams to reach the tournament finals:

Perry-37, Rhine-17: Leroy Boswell-13 points, Dot Roughton-8, and Bobby Holtzclaw-7 led Perry.

Perry-30, Fort Valley-14: Leading the attack were Leroy Boswell-9 and Buddy Tolleson-7.

Perry-33, Bonaire-15: Three players scored 9 points each: Leroy Boswell, Buddy Tolleson, and Dot Roughton.

Perry-24, Montezuma-7: Perry guard, Dot Roughton, sparked the Panthers with 14 points.

In the championship game, Perry met Albany, a tall and physical team that was the consensus pick to win the tournament. Coach Eric Staples' charges, known for their strong defensive play, held the favored Albany High Indians scoreless in the final quarter and coasted to a 28 to 23 victory.

Perry forward, Buddy Tolleson, connected on five set shots and one free throw for a game high 11 points. Center Leroy Boswell added 8 points. Julian Cawthon and Bobby Holtzclaw played outstanding defense and gave the Panthers the edge in rebounding. Dot Roughton and Bill Hunt played excellent floor games. Mercer President, Dr. Spright Dowell, presented a large championship trophy to a proud and deserving Perry team. Perry's star rebounder and defensive player, Bobby Holtzclaw, was named the tournament's "Most Valuable Player" and also was presented a trophy.

Total points scored during the five-game tournament by each of Perry's players: Leroy Boswell-43, Dot Roughton-38, Buddy Tolleson-34, Bobby Holtzclaw-19, Julian Cawthon-6, Fred Johnson-6, Bill Hunt-4, and Walter Gray-2. Skeet Chapman, Carl Clark, Ed Pierce, and Courtney Mason did not score, but played excellent basketball in reserve roles.

Third District tournament at Perry

Perry eliminated Hawkinsville, 30 to 17, in the opener; defeated Rochele 39 to 22 in the semifinals on the strength of Leroy Boswell's 25 point explosion; and ripped Chauncey, 31 to 7, for the Third District Class B championship. This was the first time in three years that Chauncey had been beaten in the district tournament.

In the title game, Leroy Boswell and Dot Roughton each scored 13 points to spark Perry's offense. Buddy Tolleson added 5 points. Perry's workhorses on rebounding and defense were Julian Cawthon and Bobby Holtzclaw.

Rhine won the third district Class C title, but Rhine failed to reach an agreement with Perry for an all-district playoff.

State Tournament in Athens at UGA's Woodruff Hall

Quarterfinals: Perry-21, Hazelhurst-16.

Leroy Boswell-8 points, Buddy Tolleson-8, and Dot Roughton-4 were Perry's offensive stars. Bobby Holtzclaw, an outstanding rebounder and defensive star, sprained his ankle in the game and could not play the next night in the semifinal game against Clarkston. Holtzclaw's departure dealt a serious blow to Perry's title hopes.

Semifinals: Clarkston-29, Perry-23.
The game had to be stopped due to a fight that occurred during the final minute of play. With nine seconds remaining in the fourth period, Spivey of Clarkston and Dot Roughton of Perry collided at center court. When both players started throwing punches, a melee erupted between the teams. Supporters of both teams spilled onto the court to join the fracas. Security guards were summoned to stop the fight. The referees, fearing someone might get hurt and reasoning that Perry could not overcome a 6 point deficit in the time remaining, declared Clarkston the winner without finishing the game. When the two teams headed toward the dressing rooms, a fight broke out again.

Leroy Boswell tallied 12 to lead Perry's offense. Bill Hunt, Perry's sixth man, filled in at the guard position for the injured Bobby Holtzclaw. The outcome of the game may have been different had Holtzclaw been able to play.

All-state:
Leroy Boswell

1941 Perry team

Members:
Cecil Armstrong
Leroy Boswell
Julian Cawthon
Carl Clark
Dever (Skip) Chapman
Norlis (Skeet) Chapman
Walter Gray
Courtney Mason
Ed Pierce
Ralph Tabor
Nathan Gilbert-manager

Regular season highlights
Prior to tournament play, Perry's Panthers won 27 games and lost only three. Perry defeated arch-rival Fort Valley four times during the regular season. Perry's starting line-up comprised Leroy Boswell, Ed Pierce, Julian Cawthon, Courtney Mason, and Walter Gray. Skeet Chapman, Ralph Tabor, and Carl Clark were top reserves.

Perry compiled a 19-game winning streak before losing a one-point heartbreaker to Lanier in a game played at Macon. The Panthers bounced back by snapping Leslie's 13-game winning streak. Leslie was coached by Don Staples, the younger brother of Eric Staples.

The Panthers continued their winning ways with a one point victory over their Houston County rival, Bonaire, led by center Dave Purdue. In the 24-23 thriller, Perry's Leroy Boswell connected for 12 tallies and Bonaire's Dave Purdue countered with 16.

Perry also squeaked by the powerful Americus quintet, 24 to 22. Leroy Boswell scored 16 of Perry's 24 points. "Chicken" Gatewood led Americus with 7.

Third District tournament at Cordele

Opening game:
Perry won by forfeit from Butler

Quarterfinals: Perry-39, Hawkinsville-14.
High scorer for Perry was Leroy Boswell with 19 points. Others Panthers in the scorebook were Courtney Mason and Walter Gray-4 points each, Ralph Tabor-4, and four players scoring 2 points each: Ed Pierce, Skeet Chapman, Carl Clark, and Cecil Armstrong. Julian Cawthon and Skip Chapman played exceedingly well but did not score.

Semifinals: Fort Valley-31, Perry-29.
Perry held a 27 to 26 lead late in the final period. Fort Valley's ace forward, Rudolph Cannon, hit a free throw to tie the count, 27 to 27. Moments later, Bufford Cannon sank a field goal to put Fort Valley ahead, 29 to 27. Each team scored a basket before the game ended, 31 to 29, in favor of Fort Valley.

Leading Perry were Leroy Boswell-12, Ralph Tabor-7, Julian Cawthon-6, and Walter Gray-4. Also playing for Perry were Ed Pierce and Courtney Mason.

Rudolph Cannon was top gun for the Fort Valley Green Wave with 14 markers closely followed by captain Linton Mathews with 12. Other Green Wave players were Bufford Cannon-4 points, Frank Flowers-1, and center Allen Young who did not score, but played an excellent game on the backboards.

Fort Valley was coached by G. O. Arvin, the new Green Wave coach and a new face in third district circles. His watchword all year long was "Beat Perry." Although Perry had beaten Fort Valley four times during the regular season by scores of 25-14, 17-15, 24-17, and 22-14, the Green Wave won when it counted the most.

Americus slipped past Fort Valley in a thriller, 29 to 26, to capture the district championship. Perry thrashed Chauncey, 39 to 19, in the consolation game. Leroy Boswell scored 26 points to lead the Panthers.

In the district playoff game between Americus, the Class B winner, and Bonaire, the Class C district champ, Bonaire rallied during the waning minutes of the nip and tuck battle and went ahead on Captain James Stafford's field goal to edge Americus, 31 to 30. Dave Purdue poured in 16 points to lead Bonaire. Smith was top scorer for Americus with 11.

1942 Perry team

Members:
Jack Arnold
Leroy Boswell
Dever (Skip) Chapman
Norlis (Skeet) Chapman
Lawton Daniel
Walter Gray
Roy Johnson
James McKinley
Dick Roughton
Albert Skellie
Neal Stembridge
Durwood Wilson
Bill Bostick-manager

Regular season highlights

On December 7, 1941, two months after the 1941-42 basketball season began, 360 Japanese warplanes bombed Pearl Harbor in a sneak attack. On December 8, war was declared on Japan. On December 9, President Franklin Delano Roosevelt addressed the nation, telling Americans to prepare for a long war "which we are going to win." On December 11, the U. S. declared war on Japan's axis partners, Italy and Germany. So high school basketball was played in Georgia and throughout the nation against the backdrop of a nation at war.

Starters on the Panther team were Leroy Boswell, Walter Gray, Lawton Daniel, Skeet Chapman, and Roy Johnson. Perry defeated Cochran four times during the regular season, annihilated a perennially strong Americus quintet, 30 to 12, and thrashed its chief South Georgia rival, Chauncey, 24 to 9.

Lanier, a higher classification GIAA school, eked out a 29 to 27 victory over Perry. In the return match, Lanier again emerged victorious in a 29 to 17 bitterly contested game. The game started out in a rough and fast manner, characteristic of Perry-Lanier games with the lead see-sawing back and forth. The contest was close until a fistfight broke out late in the game. In a mad rush to recover a loose ball, tiny Quincey Crawford of the Poets and giant Leroy Boswell of Perry came out of the scramble with fists flailing. Players, students and supporters of the two schools poured onto the playing floor to join the altercation. The fight could have gotten out of hand, but quick and cool-headed intervention by Coach Staples of Perry, Coach Tom Porter of Lanier, and several Perry faculty members stopped the skirmish and prevented serious consequences.

Earlier in the game, a Perry player had taken a swing at Lanier's Buddy Nolan who ducked the punch. A foul was called and Nolan was awarded a free throw.

Buddy Nolan, playing his best game of the year, led the Poet offense with 14 points. The Perry box score read: Leroy Boswell-8, Walter Gray-8, Skeet Chapman-1, Lawton Daniel-0, Durwood Wilson-0, and Roy Johnson-0.

Third District tournament at Perry

Opening game: Perry-43, Buena Vista-18
Walter Gray led Perry with 14 points. Leroy Boswell added 10, Roy Johnson-5, Skeet Chapman-4, James McKinley-4, Lawton Daniel-2, Neal Stembridge-2, Jack Arnold-2, Durwood Wilson-0, and Albert Skellie-0

Quarterfinals: Perry-33, Eastman-17
Top gunner for Perry was Leroy Boswell with 17 markers. Walter Gray chipped in 11.

Semifinals: Perry-17, Americus-16
In a game wherein the lead changed frequently, the Panthers nosed out Americus by a narrow one point margin on a field goal in the last minute of play. Top gunner for Perry was Leroy Boswell with 10 markers. Perry guard Roy Johnson picked up 5 key points in the last half.

Championship game: Perry-32, Chauncey-15
Perry led by only 2 points at halftime, but the Panthers' offense started clicking during the last half and pulled away for a 17 point decision. Leroy Boswell-16, Roy Johnson-9, Walter Gray-6, and Skeet Chapman with 1 point led Perry.

The top two scorers in the district tournament were "Chicken" Gatewood of Americus-55 and Leroy Boswell of Perry-53.

After the third district tournament concluded on February 27, 1942, Leroy Boswell reached his 20th birthday the next day, on February 28, and was ineligible to play in the Third District B and C tournament as well as the state tournament.

Perry, the Class B champs, defeated Preston, the Class C winner, by a score of 27 to 19 for the combined B and C district championship.

State tournament at Mercer's Porter gym in Macon

In 1942, the state tournament was moved from Woodruff Hall at UGA in Athens to Porter gym at Mercer University in Macon.

The Perry Panthers, badly crippled by the loss of its offensive leader, Leroy Boswell, faced Cochran in the opening round of the state tournament. Although Perry had defeated Cochran four times during the regular season, the prospects of beating Cochran became a daunting task without the point production of Boswell. Durwood Wilson, a steady player who was not flashy on offense, played forward in place of the ineligible Boswell. Perry came close to scoring an upset, but a last minute rally by Cochran overcame Perry. The final score was Cochran-19, Perry-15. Perry's center, Walter Gray, scored 8 points in a losing cause. Had Leroy Boswell been eligible to play, Perry's fortunes in the state meet most assuredly would have been vastly improved.

1943 Perry team

Members:
Emmett Cater
Lawton Daniel
Billy Etheridge
Walter Gray
Glenn Johnson
Walter Johnson
Eugene Lashley
James McKinley
Dick Roughton
Clarence Shurling
Albert Skellie
Walter Skellie
Charlie Watts
Otis Whitten

Regular season highlights

During the regular season, Perry won 25 games and lost only five: Cochran-twice, Lanier-twice and Fort Valley-once. Perry did not have a starting five per se, but used six men almost interchangeably. These six players were brothers Albert and Walter Skellie, Lawton Daniel, Walter Gray, Dick Roughton, and James McKinley. This Perry team showed great promise and had the potential to capture the coveted state crown.

Third District tournament at Fort Valley

Due to gas and tire shortages caused by the war effort, the traditional Third District Class B tournament featuring all 14 teams was not held. Instead, the top two teams, Perry and Fort Valley, participated in a championship playoff, the best two of three games.

Perry made a clean sweep of the series, winning the first game, 34 to 12, and the second, 60 to 24. In the first game, Walter Gray led Perry with 11 points. Walter Skellie added 9. In the second game, Walter Skellie hit for 21 and Walter Gray garnered 14. Robert Rouse was the top scorer for Fort Valley with 4 points in the first game and 16 in the second.

State tournament at Mercer University's Porter gym in Macon

Opening game: Perry-19, Reidsville-18

With Reidsville leading 18 to 15 and only 55 seconds remaining, Dick Roughton scored a quick basket, moving Perry to within one point, 18 to 17. Perry went into a full court press. Roughton intercepted an inbound Reidsville pass and drove for another score, putting the Panthers ahead, 19 to 18. Then Phillips of Reidsville was fouled and had a chance to tie the score, but his free throw bounced off the rim. That was the ball game. Perry had won a thriller. Walter Gray led Perry's offense with 8 points.

Semifinal game: Perry-26, Athens-24

The Athens squad had a perfect record except for a loss to the Athens Pre-Flight team of former high school stars, and was picked by sportswriters, coaches, and fans alike to capture the state diadem. Sympathy was extended to Coach Staples for the dubious distinction of having to play Athens High in the semifinals, but Coach Staples installed a strategic game plan that worked as planned. His Panthers took the fight to their talented adversaries and emerged as the tournament giant killer, toppling the mighty Athenians, 26 to 24. Lawton Daniel made 8 points, Walter Skellie-7, James McKinley-5, Dick Roughton-4, and Walter Gray-2. Albert Skellie did not score, but played one of the greatest defensive games in Perry basketball history.

Championship game: Cochran-27, Perry-17

Cochran, a team Perry had beaten twice during the season, refused to be intimidated by Perry's impressive win over Athens the previous night, and soundly defeated the Panthers, who experienced a cold shooting night, 27 to 17. Lawton Daniel, Walter Gray, and Walter Skellie paced Perry's offense with 6, 5, and 4 points respectively. Thompson-10 points and L. Coley-8 led Cochran to the winner's circle.

This was Staples' third 'state runner-up' team since he became Perry's coach in 1933.

All-State:
Walter Gray
Albert Skellie
Lawton Daniel

1944 team

Members:
Calvin Andel
Jackie Beavers
Lewis Bledsoe
Owen Burdette
Billy Etheridge
Gene Etheridge
Earl Marshall
Tommy Marshall
Charles Reeves
Frank Satterfield
Walter Skellie
Charlie Watts
Wendell Whipple
Otis Whitten
Jack Wilson
Dallas Ryals
Billy Lee-manager

Regular season highlights

Perry had a strong nucleus of seven players who were dividing time in starting roles: Charlie Watts, Jack Wilson, Walter Skellie, Billy Etheridge, Earl Marshall, Otis Whitten and Frank Satterfield. Although Walter Skellie was the only returning starter from the 1943 state runner-up team, the 1944 Panthers fielded a competitive team with the potential to win the district title and advance far in state competition. Perry got off to a good start with an upset victory over the Lanier Poets, of the elite GIAA, the highest classification in Georgia reserved for the largest schools. The Panthers' Charlie Watts chalked up a sensational 10 points in Perry's 29 to 23 victory over the Poets. Jack Wilson and Otis Whitten teamed up for 7 apiece and Walter Skellie bucketed 5. Perry defenders held the Poets' giant, 6' 8" center, and prolific scorer, Jim Nolan, to only 9 points. Forward Hall Roddenberry led Lanier with 10 markers.

Third District tournament at Perry

With World War II still underway and gas rationing curtailing team travel, the four best teams in the district were selected for a play-off instead of all teams in the district participating. In one bracket, Perry and Cordele competed in a three game series-best two of three. Likewise, in the other bracket, Fort Valley engaged Cuthbert. The respective winners met in a three game series for the Third District Class B championship.

Semifinals (best two of three games): Perry defeated Cordele, 40 to 20, in the first game, and 41 to 20 in the second game to capture the series. In the second game, Perry's scoring was balanced: Walter Skellie-8, Billy Etheridge-8, Charlie Watts-8, Otis Whitten-7, Jack Wilson-6, and Frank Satterfield-4. Also performing well were Lewis Bledsoe, Calvin Andel, Earl Marshall, Owen Burdette, Wendell Whipple, Gene Etheridge, and Dallas Ryals.

Since Fort Valley beat Cuthbert in the other bracket, the Green Wave and Panthers would play for the district championship. Perry had beaten Fort Valley, 37 to 34, during the regular season. Leading Perry's scoring were Walter Skellie-19, Otis Whitten-8, Jack Wilson and Billy Etheridge-4 each, and Frank Satterfield-2. Fort Valley's scoring was generated by Robert Rouse-15 points, Marshall Young-10, Virgil Young-4, Johnson-3, and Freeman Leverett-2.

Championship (best two of three games):

In the first game, Perry eked out a slim 1-point margin, 29 to 28, over archrival Fort Valley. In the second game, Perry plastered the Green Wave, 26 to 15. Perry's ace forward, Walter Skellie, riddled the nets for 10 points before a capacity crowd of over 1,000 spectators at the Perry gym. The Panthers played superb defense to hold the Fort Valley crew to only 15 points; in fact, Perry held Fort Valley to only one field goal in the first half.

Third District Class B and C tournament at Perry

Union High of Leslie coached by Don Staples (Eric's younger brother) had defeated Perry earlier during the season; however, Perry avenged the loss and emerged victorious in a hard-fought, nip and tuck battle for the combined Class B and C Third District crown.

State tournament at Mercer's Porter gym in Macon

Opening game:

In the Panthers' opening game against the favored Gainesville Red Elephants, the score was deadlocked 10-10 at halftime. The game remained close throughout the second half. During the final moments of play, Perry forged ahead by 1-point and held grimly to the lead to defeat Gainesville in a thriller, 21 to 20. Spearheading Perry's offense was the indomitable Walter Skellie with a game high 10 points. Charlie Watts and Jack Wilson tossed in 4 each, and Billy Etheridge rounded out the scoring with 3. The scoring for Gainsville was balanced: Strong-6, Henson-5, Mitchell-4, Jarrard-3, and Powell-2.

Semifinals:

The Perry Panthers lost in the semifinals to the Rossville Bulldogs by the narrow margin of 2 points, 25 to 23. Perry led at the half, 15 to 14, and in the third quarter, the score was tied 17 to 17. Late in the fourth period, Perry took the lead, 23 to 22.

Rossville's sharp-shooting forward, Wells, drilled one from mid-court to put Rossville out front 24 to 23. Rossville added a free throw to make it 25 to 23. With one minute remaining, Rossville gamely hung onto the ball to squeak out a victory over the scrappy Panthers. Walter Skellie sparked Perry with 15 tallies.

The next night, Rossville scalped Decatur, 38 to 23, to win the state crown.

All-state:
Walter Skellie

1945 Perry team

Members:
Jackie Beavers
Billy Bledsoe
Lewis Bledsoe
Clint Cooper
Gene Etheridge
Tommy Marshall
Carlton (Bubber) Pierce
Frank Satterfield
Walter Skellie
Wendell Whipple
Jack Wilson
Harry Dubois-manager

Regular season highlights

Perry won its first 18 games without a loss. Through the first 18 games, the Panthers scored 642 points to 371 for their opponents. Walter Skellie, center and team captain, had been selected to the All-State team the previous season when Perry advanced to the state semifinals. Skellie scored 189 points during the first 18 games of the 1945 season. Second in scoring during this same span was guard Lewis Bledsoe, a great all-around player, with 155 points. Third was forward, Jack Wilson, an excellent floor man and an expert shot with 140 points to his credit. Carlton (Bubber) Pierce, a junior forward demonstrating tremendous potential, scored 98 points. Guard Tommy Marshall, the outstanding defensive specialist on the team, scored 60 points, mostly from the outside. Reserves who contributed significantly to the 18-game winning streak were Frank Satterfield, Clint Cooper, Billy Bledsoe, Wendell Whipple, Jackie Beavers, and Gene Etheridge.

During the regular season, Perry's record was 29 wins and 3 losses. The Panthers lost once to Cochran and twice to the Lanier Poets, who won the GIAA state championship in 1945.

The Panthers shellacked arch-rival Fort Valley four times during the year. On January 27, 1945, Perry walloped Fort Valley 36 to 19. Leading Perry were Walter Skellie with 11 points, and Bubber Pierce and Lewis Bledsoe with eight each. Marshall Young sank 8 points for Fort Valley. In the preliminary game, Perry's second team downed Fort Valley's second team, 16 to 8.

Third District tournament

Opening round at Perry: Perry-50, Hawkinsville-15

Semifinals (best 2 of 3 games) at Perry:

Game 1: Perry-48, Cordele-16
Bubber Pierce led all scorers with 10 points followed closely by Lewis Bledsoe and Walter Skellie with 8 each.

Game 2: Perry-41, Cordele-25
Bubber Pierce again sparked the Panthers' attack, this time with 12 points. Walter Skellie was close behind in the scoring column with 11. On the Cordele side of the ledger, Harris tallied 8 markers and Waldrif shot 5 in a losing cause.

Championship series (best 2 of 3 games)

Game 1: Americus-24, Perry-20 (at Americus)

Game 2: Perry-37, Americus-19 (at Perry)
Lewis Bledsoe led Perry with 12 points

Game 3: Americus-26, Perry-25 (at Americus)
Americus led 16 to 12 at halftime. Perry committed 13 fouls to only 4 for Americus, as the referees' whistles seemed to catch few infractions by the Americus squad. Neither could Perry's offense get untracked. After almost doubling the score and blowing the Americus Panthers off the court in the second game, the Perry Panthers couldn't buy a basket in the third and final game. Perry suffered an unbelievably poor shooting night from the floor and, to make matter worse, scored a meager 2 points during the entire game from the gratis line.

Team captain, Walter Skellie, had several shots whip around the cylinder and pop out. Clint Cooper missed two close-in shots that rolled off the rim.

Perry finished second in the Third District tournament.

1946 Perry team

Kneeling, L-R: Ed Thompson, Richard Ogletree, Carlton (Bubber) Pierce, Billy Bledsoe, and Clint Cooper. Standing, L-R: Coach Eric Staples, Jack Watts, Earl Whipple, John Blue Calhoun, Sam Norwood, Deryle Whipple, Howard Peyton, and Bobby Ivey-manager

Regular season highlights

Coach Staples built his 1946 squad around Bubber Pierce, center and team captain, who was the only returning starter from the 1945 team, which finished second in the Third District tournament. The other four starters for the 1946 team were Ed Thompson, Clint Cooper, Billy Bledsoe, and Richard Ogletree. Perry had strong reserves featuring Deryle Whipple, Howard Peyton, Jack Watts, John Blue Calhoun, Earl Whipple, and Sam Norwood. The Panthers' regular season record was 19 wins and 10 losses.

This Perry team was gifted with considerable talent, but the inexperienced players assuming starting roles for the first time, as well as the reserves, had to mature quickly for the Panthers to be a championship contender.

Of the ten games Perry had lost, three were to archrival Fort Valley. Mr. Ernest Anderson, Fort Valley school superintendent, who had coached the Green Wave basketball team during the previous 1944-45 season, stepped down in middle of the 1945-46 season, and hired a new coach in January 1946. The new coach was Ned L.

Warren, a graduate of Georgia Teachers College, who had coached previously at Alma, Adrian, and Soperton and had just finished a three-year stint in the U. S. Navy.

Before turning over the coaching reins to Ned Warren in January 1946, Ernest Anderson's Green Wave team had racked up a record of 15 wins and one loss (to Cochran-later avenged). The Fort Valley team comprised Marshall Young, center and team captain who in 17 games had scored an amazing 241 points, forwards Emory Wilson and Bruce Haddock, and guards Morris McDaniel and Joe Jones. The height of the starting five averaged better than six feet per man. Other capable members of the team were Billy Cannon, Charles Bartlett, Jimmy Robinson, Carl Hill, Horace Bellflower, Gordon McDaniel, and Phelan Lowe.

In the fall of 1945, Fort Valley High School organized its first girls' basketball team of which the community was very proud. By mid-January 1946, the team had won six while losing three, and was hoping to peak at tournament time. Coached by Miss Beth Duncan, Fort Valley's first girls' squad comprised Jeanette Parks-captain and forward, Jewell Walton-forward, Elaine Wilson-forward, Haviland Houston-guard, Florence Kemp-guard, Ruby Joyner-guard, Marilyn Sanders-forward, Jerry Edwards-guard, and Jean Dawson-guard.

The Perry Panthers introduced Fort Valley's new basketball mentor, Ned Warren, to the fierce rivalry between the two towns with a 32 to 26 licking at the Perry gym on January 19, 1946. Perry led throughout the game. Bubber Pierce put on a scintillating show in all facets of the game, and led Perry's offense with 14 big points. Clint Cooper pitched in 12. Marshall Young was the Green Waves' big gun with 17 markers. Young and Cooper fouled out in the final minutes of the contest.

Third District tournament at Americus

Opening round:
Perry-47, Cordele-32

Semifinals:
Perry-38, Americus-32
Bubber Pierce racked up 16 points to pace Perry. Clint Cooper tossed in 7. Billy Bledsoe staged a brilliant shooting exhibition, hitting two high arching shots from long range in quick succession, plus two free throws for a total of 6 points.

Championship:
Perry-30, Fort Valley-27

Fort Valley had beaten Perry three times during the regular season; however, Coach Staples was known for having his boys ready for tournament play.

Bubber Pierce put on an offensive show with a game high 17 points. Ed Thompson played one of the greatest defensive games in Panther history, holding Marshall Young, Fort Valley's captain and leading scorer, to only 7 points. Fort Valley was led by forward Emory Wilson who tallied 8.

Third District Class B and C tournament

Perry-38, Montezuma-31

State tournament at Mercer's Porter gym in Macon

The Canton Greenies, the tournament favorite with a height advantage, defeated the Perry Panthers, 41 to 28, in the state quarterfinals.

Bubber Pierce played his last game as a Panther, scoring 16 points and showing why he was one of the best players in Georgia and worthy of All-State recognition.

Canton-41	Perry-28
Edwards-13	Ed Thompson-3
Beavers	Clint Cooper-5
Huey-17	Bubber Pierce-16
Tippens-4	Billy Bledsoe-1
McClure-4	Richard Ogletree-3

Score at half: Canton-27, Perry-12

Subs: Canton: Johnson-1, Cagle-2, Lawton, Hicks, White; Perry: Deryle Whipple-3, John Blue Calhoun, Jack Watts, and Sam Norwood.

All-state:
Carlton (Bubber) Pierce, captain of the Perry team

1948 Perry team

Members:
Ed Chapman
Billy Gray
Seabie Hickson
James Matthews
Howard Peyton
Mack Peyton
Bubber Riley
Bobby Satterfield
Martin Silcox
Bobby Sutton

Billy Whipple
Charles Whitworth
Pete Carlisle-manager
Charles Carter-manager

Regular season highlights

The Panthers began the season as the defending Class B state champs. All five starters on the 1947 team were lost to graduation; consequently, 1948 was a rebuilding year. Coach Staples had the daunting task of molding an inexperienced unit into a highly competitive team. The starting five were forwards Mack Peyton and Ed Chapman, center Billy Gray, and guards Seabie Hickson, and Bobby Satterfield.

Hickson came down with undulant fever in January 1948, and missed the remainder of the season. Bubber Riley, a sharpshooter; Howard Peyton, a great defensive star; and Charles Whitworth, an excellent floor general, alternated at the vacated guard position.

The Panthers pushed the Lanier Poets, the eventual 1948 state GIAA champions, down to the wire in a hard-fought contest on January 7, 1948, at Macon's City Auditorium. The game was tied six times and the lead changed hands eight times. Lanier won a thriller, 40 to 38, as the Poets' superior height under the basket took control in the waning minutes. Also, Perry ace, Ed Chapman, fouled out with six minutes remaining.

Billy Gray was the top scorer in the contest with 19 points. Mack Peyton chipped in 9, Ed Chapman-6, Bobby Satterfield-2, and Seabie Hickson-2. Howard Peyton played an outstanding defensive game, and Charles Whitworth performed well in the backcourt.

Big 6' 4" Claude Greene dominated the inside for the Poets and contributed 14 points. Bobby Schwartz hit for 9, Jimmy Holton-8, Eric Sauerbrey-3, Bill Fickling-2, Wyre-2, Ouzts-2, James (Tank) Lawrence-0, Lasseter-0, Stellies-0, and Newton-0.

Perry made a statement in scaring the daylights out of a Lanier team that won the GIAA crown in 1948. With all starters returning in 1949, the Panthers established themselves as a team to be reckoned with in the future.

Third District tournament at Perry

Sixteen boys' Class B teams assembled for the third district playoffs at Perry's gym. The top favorite was the Fort Valley Green Wave coached by Ned Warren. Also considered a strong contender was the Warner Robins five which boasted of the top scorer in the state in its 7-foot center, Bill Spivey. Spivey scored 40 points in Warner Robins' rout of Buena Vista in the quarterfinals, but was held to 13 by the victorious Fort Valley quintet in the semifinals.

The Perry gym seated 900 spectators; however, on big game nights, some 1200 tickets would be sold. The extra 300 people would be crowded in the aisles, standing in the entrances, doorways, positioned along the walls behind the basket, and sitting around the boundary lines, making it difficult for teams to inbound the ball.

Opening game: Perry-32, Dawson-26

Ed Chapman led Perry with 13 markers followed by Billy Gray-8 and Mack Peyton-7. Cook and Dick Dozier tallied 10 and 7 points respectively for Dawson.

Quarterfinals: Perry-32, Hawkinsville-16
Mack Peyton-10, Billy Gray-9, and Bubber Riley-9 paced Perry.

Hawkinsville's scoring was balanced: Woodard-4, Borum-3, McKinley-2, Browning-2, Ward-2, Davis-2, Evans-1, Southerland-0, Kirkus-0, and Fowler-0.

Semifinals: Perry-24, Ashburn-20
Top scorers for Perry were Billy Gray-10 and Bobby Satterfield-7. Spivey and Peacock led Ashburn with 6 each.

Championship game: Fort Valley-37, Perry-17

Fort Valley-37	**Perry-17**
Bartlett-13	Mack Peyton-2
Mullis-8	Billy Gray-7
Hutto-5	Ed Chapman-2
Swan-1	Bobby Satterfield
Cannon-10	Charles Whitworth-4

Subs: Fort Valley: Wilder; Perry: Bubber Riley-2

Fort Valley was eliminated in the first round of the state Class B tournament.

1950 Perry team

Members:
Buddy Batchelor
Bobby Brooks
Billy Gray
David Gray
Jack Hardy
Seabie Hickson
Herschel Lawhorn
Mack Peyton
Bobby Satterfield
Herschel Thompson
Pete Carlisle-manager

Regular season highlights

Perry won the state championship in 1949 and returned all starters in 1950 except All-State player, Ed Chapman. Returning were two All-State players, center Billy Gray and forward Mack Peyton. Also retaining starting roles were two veteran players: Bobby Satterfield and Seabie Hickson, who was ill with undulant fever during the last half of the 1949 season. Replacing the departing Ed Chapman was Jack Hardy.

In early January 1950, Perry won the prestigious 16-team Atlanta High School Invitational Tournament. The Panthers defeated Brown High of Atlanta, 44 to 39, in the quarterfinals; Murray County High of Chatsworth, 47 to 37, in the semifinals; and Rossville, 48 to 31, in the championship game. For the three games, Billy Gray was Perry's leading scorer with 62 points, followed by Mack Peyton-48, Jack Hardy-14, Seabie Hickson-8, and Bobby Satterfield-5.

The Perry Panthers downed the Lanier Poets, the eventual 1950 state Class AA champions, 41 to 39, at Macon's City Auditorium. Perry's offense was led by Mack Peyton with 18 points and Billy Gray connecting on 16. Lanier's scoring was more balanced: Tommy Mixon-9, Inman Veal-8, Bill Fickling-7, Richard Reid-6, Ed Defore-5, Bert Schwartz-4, and Jack Skinner-0.

During the regular season, Perry won 27 games, lost only 7, and had an excellent chance of repeating as state champions. Perry's losses were to Canton, Cochran, Lanier, and four times to Irwinville, the latter considered the top team in Georgia regardless of classification.

Third District tournament at Fort Valley

Opener and semifinals:
Perry easily smashed Buena Vista, 56 to 42, in the opening game, and blew by Cordele in the semifinals.

Championship game:
Perry drubbed the Fort Valley Green Wave, 51-30, in the district finals. Perry's Billy Gray and Mack Peyton buried the Green Wave in an avalanche of baskets, scoring 21 and 20 points respectively. Nick Strickland paced Fort Valley with 7.

Third District Class B and C tournament

Perry overwhelmed Montezuma, 44 to 28, for the Third District Class B and C title. Billy Gray was top man for Perry with 15 points followed by Seabie Hickson-11 and Mack Peyton-8.

Also playing in the game and contributing to the victory were Herschel Thompson-6, Jack Hardy-2, Herschel Lawhorn-2, Bobby Satterfield, Buddy Batchelor, James Mauldin, Jimmy Hammock, David Gray, Harris Satterfield, Mell Tolleson, Bo Wilson, Bobby Brooks, and Billy King.

With Montezuma's top gun, Carl Peaster, out with the flu, Joe DeVaughn and Linton DeVaughn stepped up to fill the offensive void with 9 tallies each.

State tournament at Macon City Auditorium

Opening game:
Perry unleashed a 45-point barrage by Mack Peyton-23 points, and Billy Gray-22, to slip by Cumming, 48 to 40. Cumming was paced by Hardin-14 and Bennett-11.

Quarterfinals:
Perry advanced to the state semifinals by defeating Quitman 39 to 25. Billy Gray pumped in a game high 23 points.
Also contributing to Perry's offense were Mack Peyton-7, Seabie Hickson-5, Jack Hardy-4, and Bobby Satterfield. Quitman was led by Murphy-10, Griffis-6, and C. Barker-4.

Semifinals:
Perry held a 24 to 18 halftime lead over Ludowici. As the third quarter ended, the Panthers were still out front, 34 to 29.
Perry's championship aspirations were dealt a heavy blow when Bobby Satterfield left the game with five fouls at the 5:35 mark in the final period. From this point, Ludowici rallied to close the gap. With 45 seconds on the clock and the score tied 41 to 41, Ludowici's Robbie Gordon scored to put his team in the lead, 43 to 41. Ludowici scored again in the closing moments, and upset the defending state champions, 45 to 41, in a thriller.
Mack Peyton led the Panthers with 24 points. Billy Gray had 10, Seabie Hickson-4, Jack Hardy-2, and Bobby Satterfield-1.
Ludowici's center, Jimmy Parker, who missed his first six field goals, and then hit nine baskets in succession, kept his team in the game with 24 points. P. W. Gordon was a bulwark on defense, and Dean Dunham, Carroll Combs, and Robbie Gordon all played key roles in the biggest upset of the tournament.
Irwinville High coached by Wallace "Country" Childs won the state Class B title by blistering Ludowici, 65 to 44. The victory was Irwinville's 35th in a row. Irwinville would extend its winning streak to 78 games over the next season, and win the Class B title again in 1951. Coach Wallace Childs was inducted in the Georgia Sports Hall of Fame in 2003.

1951 Perry team

Members:
David Gray

Jack Hardy
Billy King
Jimmy Hammock
James Mauldin
Billy Powell
Harris Satterfield
Mack Satterfield
Herschel Thompson
Mell Tolleson
Bo Wilson

Regular season highlights

Only guard Jack Hardy was a holdover from the 1950 team that reached the semifinals of the state tournament and won the 16-team Atlanta Invitational tournament. Gone were All–State players, Billy Gray and Mack Peyton, and two outstanding veteran players, Bobby Satterfield and Seabie Hickson.

Aside from Hardy, there were five players vying for significant playing time: James Mauldin and Joe Leverette at center, David Gray and Herschel Thompson at forwards and Harris Satterfield at guard. No player in the starting lineup stood over 6 feet tall. The 1951 season was a rebuilding year with a group of untested players whose primary experience had been playing B-team basketball.

Perry's most significant regular season win was a revenge victory over the Lanier Poets, the eventual Class AA state champions in 1951, who, earlier in the year, had overwhelmed the Panthers 44 to 32 at the Macon City Auditorium. In the return game at the Perry gym, Perry prevailed over Lanier, 44 to 42, in a close encounter. The Poets rallied from a 15-point deficit early in the fourth quarter to pull within two points of the Panthers, but ran out of steam as the game ended.

James Mauldin led all scorers with 15 points. Other Panthers scoring were Joe Leverette-8, Harris Satterfield-8, Jack Hardy-7, Herschel Thompson-4, and David Gray-2. Pacing the Poets were Tommy Mixon with 9 points followed by Joe Simmons with 7 and Joe Silas with 6.

The Panthers also split with the powerful Canton team and defeated two Class AA Atlanta teams twice: Murphy (35-29 and 42-33) and Bass (52-32 and 45-27).

Third District tournament at Cordele

Opening round: Perry-63, Warner Robins-28
Perry was led by James Mauldin with 17 tallies followed by Joe Leverette and Harris Satterfield with 13 apiece. Other Panthers entering the game were Herschel Thompson-6, Mell Tolleson-4, Billy Powell-4, Jack Hardy-2, David Gray-2, and Bo Wilson-2.

J. Swain and Peacock flipped in 7 and 5 points respectively for Warner Robins.

Semifinals: Perry-41, Cuthbert-40 (overtime)

The regulation game ended deadlocked, 38 to 38. In the overtime period, Perry scored 3 points, a field goal plus an extra point, while holding Cuthbert to a single 2-pointer.

James Mauldin was high man for Perry with 16 markers. Harris Satterfield garnered 11. Also contributing to the offense were Jack Hardy-7, Joe Leverette-3, Mack Satterfield-2, David Gray-2, Mell Tolleson, and Herschel Thompson.

For the Cuthbert squad, Lawson bucketed-13, Bell-10, Lowe-8, Fowler-5, and Childress-4.

Championship game: Fort Valley-41, Perry-37

The Fort Valley Green Wave, sparked by Jimmy Thompson with 11 points and Nick Strickland with 9, took the lead from the opening tip-off and stayed out front during the entire game. Pat Swann added 10 markers for the victors.

Perry ace James Mauldin, Perry's leading scorer all season, pumped in 14 points for the Panthers. Jack Hardy had 8, Harris Satterfield-6, Joe Leverette-4, David Gray-4, and Herschel Thompson-1.

1952 Perry team

Members:
Billy Beckham
Martin Beeland
David Gray
Thomas Grimes
Dick Hardy
Joe Leverette
James Logue
Olin Logue
James Mauldin
Tommy Mobley
Billy Powell
Harris Satterfield
Mell Tolleson
Billy Parker-manager

Regular season highlights

The Panthers returned all starters from the 1951 team, the Third District runner-up, except veteran guard Jack Hardy and forward Herschel Thompson. Coach Staples shifted his lineup many times during the season trying to find the right combination, but before tournament time had settled on James Mauldin and Billy Powell at forwards, Billy Beckham at center, and Harris Satterfield and Dick Hardy, Jack's younger brother, at guards. Also receiving much playing time were David Gray, Joe Leverette, Mell Tolleson, James Logue, and Olin Logue. During the regular season, the team won 18 games and lost 12.

The team, which regressed at times during the season, looked as if it had peaked in its last game of the regular season when it shellacked a respectable Spalding High team of Griffin, 74 to 51 on the 36-point outburst of ace guard, Harris Satterfield. James Mauldin pitched in 19, followed by Billy Powell with 16.

With the undefeated Fort Valley Green Wave fielding possibly its best team in school history, Perry's chances of winning the Third District tournament depended upon the Panthers playing at the top of their potential. Another archrival with a strong quintet was the Montezuma Aztecs, coached by Bill Martin, who was gunning for his third state Class C championship behind a strong supporting caste of Carl Peaster, John Albert Williams, Ben DeVaughn, Tommy Hurdle, Jimmy Taylor, team captain Calvin Porch, Bobby Ellison, Buddy Liggin, Jack Clark, and William Joiner.

Third District tournament at Fort Valley

Opening round: Perry-50, Butler-45

Billy Powell and Billy Beckham dropped in 16 points each to lead Perry. Milton Edmonson was high scorer for Butler with 17.

Semifinals: Perry-45, Dodge County-35

Billy Beckham took top scoring honors, garnering 11 tallies. Perry's scoring was balanced, however, as James Maudlin tossed in 10, Billy Powell-9, Joe Leverette-8, and Harris Satterfield-7.

Championship game: Fort Valley-44, Perry-42

A news report disclosed that the undefeated Fort Valley Green Wave team had pledged to beat the smaller Perry Panthers by 40 points. Over 2700 fans came to witness the game. Hundreds more were turned away because of lack of space. The scrappy and unrelenting Perry Panthers played the first half with authority and appeared ready to upset the mighty Green Wave team. At halftime, Perry was ahead 22 to 21. The lead swapped back and forth during the third and fourth quarters. During the final minute of play, with the score tied, 42 to 42, Green Wave guard Richard Aultman snuck by Perry's defense on an inbound screen play to score the winning basket with only scant seconds remaining.

Perry's sensational guard, Harris Satterfield, played an unforgettable game, leading all scorers with 18 points. Forward Billy Powell hit 12 from long range, and James Mauldin tallied 6. Fort Valley's twin skyscrapers, Ed Beck and Pat Swan, scored 14 and 13 points respectively.

This win marked Fort Valley's 28th victory in a row and sent the Green Wave to the state Class B tournament where they won the school's first state crown. Coach Bill Martin's Montezuma team, which won the third district Class C title, was runner-up in the state Class C ranks.

Consolation game: Sycamore-41, Perry-40

In the consolation game, Perry was obviously burned out from the previous night's fierce battle with Fort Valley and didn't play up to their regular standards, losing to Sycamore, 41 to 40. High scorers for Perry were James Mauldin with 17 points and Billy Powell with 13. Sycamore's Talmadge Luke ripped the chords for 17 counters; Beard canned 9, Dennim-8, Childs-6, and Holloway-5.

1954 Perry team

Members:
Billy Beckham
Ed Beckham
Billy Brock
Harvey Clarke
Percy Hardy
William Harrison
Bennett Mauldin
Franklin May
Jackie Miller
Sam Nunn
Virgil Peavy
James Scarborough
John Watts

Regular season highlights

The 1954 team began the season without the services of three All-State performers from the 1953 state championship team: Billy Powell-captain of the All-State team, and two "honorable mention" All-State players, David Gray and Joe Leverette. Returning for the 1954 season were All-State center, Billy Beckham, and "honorable mention" All-State guard, Franklin May. Aside from returnees Beckham at center and May at guard, Coach Staples started the season with three other players: Jackie Miller at guard, and Billy Brock and James Scarborough at forwards. During the season, junior William Harrison and sophomore forward Sam Nunn broke into the starting lineup on occasion. Capable reserves were Virgil Peavy, Bennett Mauldin, Harvey Clarke, John Watts, Percy Hardy, and Ed Beckham. Several of these also played on the B-team.

The 1954 Panthers won their first 14 games and owned an overall streak of 35 victories that began early in the 1953 season. The team finished the regular season with a noteworthy record of 26 wins against only four losses. All losses were against higher classification Class AA schools: Lanier of Macon, Brown High of Atlanta, and twice to North Fulton of Atlanta, the defending Class AA champions. Perry avenged its earlier loss to Lanier with a 55 to 54 victory; split with Brown, beating Brown, 43 to 42, in Atlanta; and lost its second game to North Fulton, 46 to 45, on a long range, desperation shot by Joe Delaney during the last 10 seconds of play.

The Panthers had the potential to repeat as state champions, but looming in their path was the undefeated Fort Valley five featuring the state's top player, 6' 7" Ed Beck, who was returning for his final year and being recruited heavily by college coaches across the nation.

Third District Tournament at Fort Valley

Opening game: Perry-62, Terrell County-19
Perry's 6' 3" forward Billy Brock led the Panthers with 17 points and played an outstanding game on the backboards. Billy Beckham added 13 tallies. Ace guard Franklin May, out with a sprained ankle, was replaced by William Harrison, who played an exceptional floor game in keeping Perry's high-powered offense clicking in the blow-out of Terrell County. Fulford hit for 7 for Terrell County.

Semifinals: Perry-42, Cuthbert-39
On the strength of two baskets by center Billy Beckham, the Panthers overcame a 4-point deficit in the last minute and 15 seconds to take a narrow 42 to 39 lead. Billy Beckham paced Perry with 19 points followed by Franklin May with 17. High man for Cuthbert was Jimmy Hartman with 14.

Championship game: Fort Valley-57, Perry-28
Before a jam-packed throng of 3,000 spectators, the undefeated Fort Valley Green Wave trounced the Perry Panthers by a lop-sided score of 57 to 28. Fort Valley's Ed Beck, playing sensationally in all phases of the game, tallied 27 points to lead all scorers. Richard Aultman supplemented Beck's production with 13 markers. Perry's All-State center, Billy Beckham, pumped in 17 of Perry's 28 points in a losing cause.

Perry's Franklin May was plagued with recurrent problems associated with his ankle sprain and was not at full speed. His ankle was heavily taped by Coach Frank Holland, and he limped noticeably throughout the entire game, his last as a Panther.

The championship game was Fort Valley's 27th consecutive victory. Fort Valley advanced to the state Class B tournament and came away champions for the second time in three years under Hall of Fame coach Norman Faircloth.

1955 team

Kneeling, L-R: Manager Horace "Chance" Evans, Dick Doll, Jimmy Beatty, Marvin Griffin, Percy Hardy, William Harrison, and Manager Joneal Lee. Standing, L-R: Assistant Coach Frank Holland, Sam Nunn, Harvey Clarke, Virgil Peavy, Ed Beckham, Bennett Mauldin, and Coach Eric Staples.

Regular season highlights

For the first time in school history, Perry instituted a football program. It started in early September 1954 and delayed basketball practice for almost three months. Coach Staples was into his 22nd year of coaching before football arrived.

The Panthers lost all five starters from the 1954 team, yet Coach Staples said his charges were capable of beating most any Class B team in the state. Those words from Georgia's "Mr. Basketball" meant that his 1955 Panthers would be in the title hunt. Perry, having won the state championship in 1947, 1949, and 1953, had an opportunity to win a fourth state Class B crown, a feat that no other team in Georgia had accomplished. Two other schools besides Perry had won three state titles. Vienna's "Wonder Five" captured the state Class B championship three times in a row: 1927, 1928, and 1929 and went to the national finals in Chicago each year, capturing second place in 1927. Also, Canton won three titles: 1934, 1936, and 1942.

At season end, Coach Staples had in his starting lineup William Harrison and Jimmy Beatty at guards, Virgil Peavy at center, and Sam Nunn and Bennett Mauldin at forwards. Others who vied for significant playing time were Percy Hardy, Ed Beckham, Marvin Griffin, Harvey Clarke, and Dick Doll. The team finished the regular season with an impressive record of 24 wins and four losses. Three of the four losses were to Class AA clubs: Grady of Atlanta, and Griffin High-twice.

The other loss was a 51 to 49 defeat by Pineview in the Christmas Invitational Tournament at Rochelle, Georgia. Pineview was led by one of Georgia's greatest offensive players, Walker Cook, a 6' 3" forward, who pitched in 25 points against Perry despite heavy guarding by two and sometimes three Panthers. Cook was averaging 38.4 points per game, and had scored over 50 points on occasion, including a season high of 66. Coach Staples, seeking revenge for the earlier defeat, invited coach Jim Jordan's Pineview team to play in Perry so the locals could see the fabulous Cook perform. The Pineview team, since its school burned down and the gym was converted into classrooms, had to practice on an outdoor court. The Panthers blew Pineview out of the gym with a 94 to 63 drubbing, but couldn't slow down the Walker Cook express. Cook racked up 40 points against a Panther defense expressly rigged to stop him. Cook didn't have to be close to the basket to score either. He was lethal anywhere from 30 to 40 feet of the goal.

Perry downed the Class AA Lanier Poets twice during the season: 64 to 50, led by Virgil Peavy's 23 points; and 54 to 50 as Sam Nunn racked up 21 points. In addition to Lanier, the 1955 team also beat the higher classification teams of Northside, 58-33, R.E. Lee, 72 to 53, Warner Robins, 61 to 55, and the Middle Georgia College freshmen, 77 to 51. By season's end, this team was averaging 63 points per game and only allowing 49.

Third District Tournament at Perry

Opening round: Perry-50, Hawkinsville-49
Perry had a close call, barely winning over Hawkinsville, 50 to 49, on a last second shot by Percy Hardy from mid-court that sent the Panther fans into a wild celebration. Percy had snatched victory from defeat and kept the Panthers' title hope alive. Virgil Peavy registered 19 points followed by Sam Nunn-10, Bennett Mauldin-10, Percy Hardy-5, William Harrison-4, Jimmy Beatty-1, and Ed Beckham-1. Hawkinsville's scoring was balanced: Head-14, D. Conner-12, Dunn-10, Lee-8, and Williams-5.

Semifinals: Perry-67, Fort Valley-64
Panther reserve Ed Beckham scored only one basket, but it was the most important field goal of the contest, as he broke a 64 to 64 tie to place Perry in the winner's circle. Top point maker for Perry was Virgil Peavy with 25, followed by Bennett Mauldin-17, Jimmy Beatty-12, Sam Nunn-7, and William Harrison-4. Fort Valley's scoring: Delmar Fennell-18, Butch Anthoine-16, Tommy Fagan-12, Al Hutto-12, and Henry Wheaton-6, Brand-0, and Young-0.

Championship game: Perry-68, Warner Robins-57
A standing room only crowd of 1200 fans witnessed a determined Perry team, expertly coached by Eric Staples and exploiting the wizardry of assistant coach Frank

Holland, take the lead over its Houston County neighbor, Warner Robins, and stay out front the entire game. The Panthers presented a balanced scoring attack: Bennett Mauldin-17, Virgil Peavy-15, Sam Nunn-15, and Jimmy Beatty-13. Guard William Harrison, the only senior in the lineup, added 8 tallies and played an outstanding floor game in priming the offense, setting screens and hitting the open man. Three Warner Robins' players netted 45 points: Jerry Dennard-16, Don Hardin-15, and Billy Adams-14. Further contributing to the Warner Robins' effort were Lewis-7, Willis-4, Childs-1, and Davidson-0.

Third District Class B and C Championship at Perry

Perry defeated East Crisp, the Class C third district champion, 65 to 53. Sam Nunn and Bennett Mauldin combined for 50 points: Nunn-27 and Mauldin-23. The East Crisp scoring sensation, Weyman Banks, connected for 30 to lead all scorers. C. Cape-12 and T. Cook-11 rounded out the scoring for East Crisp.

State Tournament at Macon City Auditorium

Opening round: Perry-57, Conyers-33

Virgil Peavy, who did not start the game due to a cut hand, came off the bench to rip the nets for 21 points and lead the Panthers to victory. Marvin Griffin was next high man with 12. Team co-captain, Jeff Autrey, of Conyers pitched in 16 to pace the losers.

Quarterfinals: Perry-70, Bowdon-66

Bowdon, sporting a 21-3 record, would not be a cakewalk for the Panthers. Perry forward Bennett Mauldin fouled out late in the third period. Then Virgil Peavy, Perry's center, fouled out with four minutes remaining in the fourth quarter. At that point, Coach Staples ordered delaying tactics to preserve a 7-point margin, 62 to 55, but an unrelenting Bowdon team began to whittle away at Perry's lead. With only four seconds left in the game and the score 62 to 60 in Perry's favor, Bowdon's 6' 5" Perry Styles hit one from 20 feet out to send the game into overtime.

In the overtime, Sam Nunn, who had been shooting all night as if he were equipped with radar, drilled one from the outside and canned two free throws. Jimmy Beatty and Ed Beckham each added a basket, and Perry had prevailed 70 to 66 when the final horn blew. Virgil Peavy and Sam Nunn were Perry's sharp-shooters with 24 and 20 points respectively. The "Macon Telegraph" praised the gallant efforts and gutsy play of Perry's William Harrison, Jimmy Beatty, Bennett Mauldin, Ed Beckham, Percy Hardy, and Marvin Griffin in overcoming the adversity of losing two starters and refusing to wilt under Bowdon's determined rally.

Clifford Adams with 22, Perry Styles with 18, and Wilson hitting for 14 formed a magnificent offensive trio for Bowdon.

Semifinals: Hahira-61, Perry-59

The Panthers led Hahira (27-3 record) by a 12 point margin, 39 to 27, at the half. Hahira evened the score 45 to 45, as the third quarter ended. With 45 seconds left in the game and Hahira ahead 59 to 55, Sam Nunn scored a two-pointer to move Perry within two points, 59 to 57. Hahira's Joe Kendricks quickly added a field goal making the count, 61 to 57. Nunn, not to be denied, came back down court and hit again. The score then stood 61 to 59. Seconds before the horn blew, William Harrison fired a long pass to Nunn, who shot a 25 footer that was dead on line to its target, but rimmed out. Perry had lost, but this bunch of talented Panthers with only one senior in the starting line-up would be back next year.

High men for the Panthers were Sam Nunn -18, Virgil Peavy-17, and Bennett Mauldin-10. Also scoring were William Harrison-4, Jimmy Beatty-4, Marvin Griffin-4, and Ed Beckham-2. Percy Hardy, always hustling, played an excellent and aggressive defensive game.

Hahira's forward, Briggs Tyler, shot the eyes out of the goal with a whopping 30 points to his credit. Jimmy Vickers added 14, Millirons-8, Martin -5, Boone-2, Kendricks-2, and Stalvey-0.

The winning Hahira coach, Jack Garrard, played under Perry's assistant coach, the renowned Frank Holland, when he coached at Chauncey High. After the game, when Coach Holland shook Garrard's hand to congratulate him, he said, "I should have run you off when I had you."

Lakeland grabbed the Class B state crown with a 62 to 53 victory over Hahira.

All-State:
Sam Nunn
Virgil Peavy

1957 Perry team

Members:
Jimmy Beatty
Ed Beckham
Bobby Brock
Ralph Dorsett
Terry Griffin
Roy Henson
Frank Holland, Jr.
Thomas (Boot) Hunt
Eddie Livingston
Johnny Mobley

Bill Morris
Ed Stokes

Regular season highlights

The 1957 edition of the Perry Panthers began the season at a serious disadvantage. Four starters on the 1956 state championship team were lost to graduation: All-State players Virgil Peavy, Sam Nunn and Bennett Mauldin, and honorable mention All-State Percy Hardy. Marvin Griffin, a capable and talented reserve, also graduated.

The only 1956 starter returning was guard Jimmy Beatty, an honorable mention selectee on the All-State team the previous year. He was joined by center Ed Beckham who saw considerable duty as a reserve in 1956. Rounding out the starting five were forwards Bobby Brock and Terry Griffin, and guard Eddie Livingston.

The highlight of the regular season was the Panthers' upset of the powerful Vienna quintet, 40 to 38, breaking the Cubs' 35-game winning streak. Enabling this victory was a coaching masterpiece by Coach Staples, whose charges played a slow and deliberate offensive game and employed a tight, shifting man-to-man defense. Center Ed Beckham racked up 12 markers for the Panthers while Jerry Vaughn led the Cubs with 10.

Perry also avenged an earlier 46 to 39 loss to the highly rated Class AAA Griffin team with a 41 to 38 victory.

Perry finished the season with a record of 12 wins and 12 losses. The 12 defeats were more losses than the Panthers had suffered over the last four years. Due to inexperience, there was little likelihood the Panthers would repeat as third district champions. If they did, it would take a Herculean effort.

Third District tournament at Fort Valley

Perry defeated Marion County from Buena Vista in the semifinals, 49 to 36. Ed Beckham with 19 markers and Terry Griffin with 18 set the scoring pace for the Panthers. Jimmy Roberts-14 and Stout McMickle-11 led the losers.

In the championship battle against Fort Valley, Perry overwhelmed the Green Wave team, 50 to 43, to capture the Class B Third District crown, a signal accomplishment for this determined group of Panthers.

Perry's top scorer was Jimmy Beatty with 20. Bobby Brock added 13, Ed Beckham-8, Terry Griffin-5, and Eddie Livingston-4. Boot Hunt was Perry's only reserve. For the Green Wave, Russell Vennes tossed in 15 followed by Ray Anthoine-12, Brand-10, Davis-2, Young-2, and Sutton-2.

Third District Class B and C Championship at Fort Valley

The Vienna Cubs, the Class C winner, nipped the Perry Panthers, the Class B champions, 41 to 40. Perry held a 40 to 39 lead with seven seconds remaining. The Cubs' Marcus Shipman missed a free throw, but teammate Robert Bailey grabbed the ball and tossed in a two-pointer to give Vienna a one-point lead. Before Perry could move down court for another shot, the game ended.

John Crozier led the Glenn Cassell-coached Cubs with 23 points. Ed Beckham hit 17 for the Panthers. Bobby Brock added 8, and three Panthers scored 5 points each: Terry Griffin, Jimmy Beatty, and Eddie Livingston. Reserve Boot Hunt played well in Perry's controlled offense.

Other Vienna scorers were Shipman-7, Bailey-4, Mixon-4, and Vaughn 3. Taylor was the only Vienna reserve.

State Tournament at Macon's City Auditorium

Opening round: Perry-52, Sylvester-48

An outstanding second half performance by Captain Ed Beckham kept Perry's title hopes alive. The 6'1" center scored 14 of his 18 points during the last two quarters to hold a charging Sylvester team at bay. In the rebounding department, Panther forward Bobby Brock held his own against the taller Sylvester front line, grabbing 11 key rebounds, and playing a superb defensive game.

The Sylvester Eagles forged ahead 48 to 47 on a snowbird by 6' 5" center Gates Ford. Ed Beckham then took charge, dropping in the winning basket with 1:28 left in the contest. Beckham added another two-pointer and a free throw to seal the victory.

Perry's Jimmy Beatty garnered 16 points. Terry Griffin added-6, Bobby Brock-4, Eddie Livingston-4, and Boot Hunt tossed in 4.

Sylvester was paced by Fred Adkinson-16 points, Sonny Williams-14, and Gates Ford-13. Hendrick and Anderson chipped in 3 points apiece, and Hinnant was Sylvester's only reserve.

Semifinals: Nahunta-54, Perry-45

Nahunta, coached by Harold L. Scott, was seeking revenge from last year's semifinal defeat inflicted by the Panthers. As the fourth quarter began, Nahunta was leading 36 to 35. During the torrid final quarter with 7:36 remaining, Bobby Brock tied the game 38 to 38, and added a free throw to put the Panthers ahead 39 to 38. With 5:14 remaining, Nahunta's Melvin Griffin connected on four free throws to give his team a 45 to 41 lead. From there on, it was Nahunta's game. Perry's Terry Griffin fouled out; so did Nahunta's Melvin Griffin.

Nahunta's top three offensive threats scored 42 points: Terry Allen-15, Layton Johns-14, and Melvin Griffin-13. Brooker tallied 6, Cleland-4, and William Royster-2, who saved the day for his team the previous night. In the quarterfinals against Milner, Royster hit a last second field goal to send the game into overtime. In the extra period with 12 seconds on the clock, Royster drilled another two-pointer to give Nahunta the victory.

Jimmy Beatty, hitting all over the court and sinking long range shots 30 to 40 feet from the basket, led the Panthers with 23 points. Bobby Brock, with 10 markers, was the only other Panther to hit in double figures. Brock played an outstanding defensive game and rebounded well against Nahunta's 6' 6" center, Layton Johns. Other Panthers contributing were Ed Beckham-5, Terry Griffin-4, Boot Hunt-3 and Eddie Livingston.

Stone Mountain tripped Nahunta, 44 to 43, to win the state Class B title.

All-State:
Jimmy Beatty

1958 Perry team

Members:
Derrell Davis
Terry Griffin
Frank Holland, Jr.
Thomas (Boot) Hunt
Eddie Livingston
Francis Marshall
Johnny Mobley
Bill Morris
Pierce Staples
Derry Watson
Tommy Sandefur-manager

Regular season highlights

     Lost to graduation were two starters from the 1957 team that had advanced to the state semifinals: All-State guard Jimmy Beatty and the Panthers' outstanding center and team captain, Ed Beckham. Also lost to graduation were three capable reserves: guard Ralph Dorsett, center Roy Henson, and forward Ed Stokes. Three highly-skilled veteran players were returning, however: forward Bobby Brock, guard Eddie Livingston, and forward Terry Griffin. Last year's sixth man, Boot Hunt, a rising junior, was expected to earn a starting role.

     The 1957-58 school year was the last season the Panthers used the old wooden gym, built in 1926, that had spawned four state championship teams: 1947, 1949, 1953, and 1956. The next year, they would move across town into a new gym.

     After the Panthers finished the regular season with 11 wins and nine losses, there were doubts that the 1958 team possessed the firepower to return to the state meet, but an Eric Staples-coached Panther squad could never be counted out. The old master had a knack for preparing his teams to peak at tournament time.

     The Panthers' most significant win was its upset over the Triple A Griffin High Eagles, 52 to 41. Earlier, Griffin had beaten Perry in overtime. In the first game, with three seconds left in regulation play and Perry trailing by two-points, Boot Hunt fired a 20-foot jumper to send the game into overtime. Griffin pulled away in the overtime period to squeak by, 45 to 43. But, in the return encounter, the story was entirely different. The Panthers exploded for 14 points in the third quarter, and Griffin could never catch up, losing by 11 points, 52 to 41. Boot Hunt took individual scoring honors for Perry with 21 tallies. Griffin's Butch Michael, who scored 24 points in the first game, again led his team with 21 markers.

Region 2B West tournament at Perry

Starting with the 1957-58 season, high schools in Georgia were organized into regions rather than districts. Perry, formerly in the third district, was assigned to region 2.

Semifinals: Perry-41, Wilkinson County-29
Pierce Staples and Eddie Livingston sparked the Panthers with 15 and 10 points respectively. Wilkinson County's Frank Shepard tossed in 8 for the losers.

Finals
Cochran-44, Perry-34
The Panthers led 12 to 10 after the first quarter, but the Cochran Royals gradually pulled away to win by 10 points. Perry shot miserably from the floor, hitting only 27 percent of its attempts. Billy Padgett pitched in 18 for the Royals while Terry Griffin and Boot Hunt were high men for the Panthers with 9 and 7 points respectively.

Region 2B tournament at Mount Vernon

Opening round: Perry-45, Treutlen County-33
Boot Hunt swished the nets for 18 points, 12 of them coming at crucial times during the second half to move Perry ahead, as Treutlen led, 20 to19, at halftime. Frank Holland tallied 10. Treutlen's Tommy Heath was a one-man offensive machine, scoring 27 of Treutlen's 33 points.

Quarterfinals: Cochran-50, Perry-35
Perry played without its ace forward, Boot Hunt, who was injured the previous night against Treutlen County. Billy Padgett proved again to be Perry's nemesis, hitting for 22 markers. Francis Marshall was the Panther's high man with 7 points. Cochran and Perry, as number 1 and number 2 teams, advanced to the region semifinals. Perry would play Portal and Cochran would face Glenville.

Semifinals: Perry-59, Portal-48
Perry, twice beaten by Cochran, took a first quarter lead over Portal and kept increasing the lead for the remainder of the game. Boot Hunt led all scorers with 24

points. He was followed by Terry Griffin with 15 and Frank Holland hitting for 10. Spence and Williford each scored 13 for Portal.

Cochran was eliminated by Glenville, 59 to 57. In this game, Cochran's Bob Chambers stripped the nets with a field goal that would have tied the game and sent it into overtime, but the official ruled he shot after the final horn. It took the officials 15 minutes to restore order. Police had to guard the referees and the official scorers.

Finals: Perry-47, Glenville-43

Perry took a 10 to 7 first quarter lead and led 21 to 17 at intermission. At the end of the third quarter, Glenville had narrowed the lead to 31 to 29. Perry outdistanced Glenville 16 to 14 in the final stanza to capture the region 2B Class B championship.

Boot Hunt again led the Panther offense with 21 tallies. Eddie Livingston added 11, Frank Holland-10, and Pierce Staples-5. Glenville's Gene Durrence scored 20 points followed by Adair Blocker with 14 to pace the losers.

State tournament at Macon's City Auditorium

Opening game: Perry-45, Pike County-36

Perry, without a six-footer in the starting line, played superior defense to throttle the Pike County Pirates in the opener. The Pirates, with a 22-11 record and coached by Dick Reynolds, had three players over the 6' 1" mark. Coach Staples injected more height into the game when he substituted 6' 2" center, Francis Marshall, for Pierce Staples, who committed three fouls in the first half.

Although Perry led at halftime, 24 to 16, Pike County outscored the Panthers in the third period and closed within one point, 32 to 31, as the quarter ended. The Panthers got hot in the final stanza and outscored the Pirates, 13 to 5. Contributing to this 13-point outburst were Boot Hunt-6, Eddie Livingston-4, and Terry Griffin-3.

The Panther scorebook read: Boot Hunt-14, Eddie Livingston-11, Terry Griffin-11, Frank Holland-6, Francis Marshall-2, and Pierce Staples-1. Pike County's Wayne Newton was the only Pirate to reach double figures with 18 points. Others Pike Countians figuring in the offense were Marshall-8, Mabrey-5, Goldman-4, and J. Killingsworth-1. W. Killingsworth and Mayfield also played in the game.

Semifinals: Forsyth County-37, Perry-35

Coach D. B. Carroll's Forsyth County Bulldogs had four players well over six feet tall, including 6' 5" center Harold Whitt, while all of Perry's starters were less than six feet. With Forsyth County controlling the backboards, Coach Staples, during the second quarter, sent in his 6' 2" center, Francis Marshall, as an equalizer. For the rest of the game, Marshall matched rebound-for-rebound with the taller Bulldogs, and helped the Panthers get back into the game. Perry's Pierce Staples fouled out at the beginning of the fourth quarter, and Frank Holland followed him to the bench with excessive fouls at the

3:21 mark.

Perry, trailing 23-16 at intermission, scored 8 points to Forsyth County's 5 to cut the margin to 28-24 at the third quarter mark. The Panthers continued their rally and moved within one-point, 28-27, early in the final quarter. Forsyth County then scored five unanswered points to move ahead, 33-27. The Panthers were not to be denied; however, Boot Hunt scored on a jumper, Frank Holland drove for a score, and Hunt came back with another jumper to knot the score at 33-all. Perry's Francis Marshall rebounded a missed shot under the offensive basket and put it back up to push Perry into the lead, 35-33. Forsyth County returned the favor with a two-pointer and the score was knotted again, 35-35. With two seconds on the clock, the Bulldog's Harold Whitt let fly a one-handed shot from the side of the court that made nothing but string music, and the Forsyth County Bulldogs of Cumming had nipped the Perry Panthers 37 to 35 in a thriller. Whitt led his team with 18 points. Joining Whitt in the scoring column were Gilbert-11, Rollins-6, and Martin-2. Pruitt also played an exceptional game.

Perry ace Boot Hunt paced the Panthers with 14 points. Frank Holland added 10, Terry Griffin-7, Francis Marshall-2, and Pierce Staples-2. Perry's only reserve was Derrell Davis.

Nahunta, with Layton Johns in the line-up, edged Forsyth County by one point to capture the state Class B crown. Johns later played at Auburn and was an All-SEC performer.

With three veteran starters, Boot Hunt, Frank Holland, and Pierce Staples returning as well as outstanding reserve center, Francis Marshall, the Panthers had the nucleus of a highly competitive team that would be gunning again for the unprecedented fifth state title.

All-State:
Thomas (Boot) Hunt

1960 team

Members:
Lindy Evans
Dennis Fike
Bobby Griffin
Ronnie Griffin
Pete Hunt
Wilson Martin
Dwayne Powell
Jimmy Smallwood
Pierce Staples
Larry Walker

Jerry Wilson

Sonny Wilson-manager

Regular season highlights

The 1960 season was Perry's only losing season under Coach Staples: nine wins and 11 losses during the regular season. After winning the state championship in 1959, the Panthers had expected a banner year in 1960; however, the loss of All-State player Lee Martin to a football knee injury and the transfer of two promising players, Bonny and Curtis Strom, to McRae, Georgia, significantly diminished Perry's chances of defending its 1959 state title. Wilson Martin, an outstanding guard prospect, also sustained a knee injury in football. He played sparingly for a while, but eventually had to drop out of competition. The team was plagued with injuries and sickness all season, causing Coach Staples to constantly juggle the line-up.

Staples built his team around three core players, Jimmy Smallwood and Lindy Evans at forwards, and Pierce Staples at center, but shuffled his lineup numerous times during the year. Three guards who logged significant playing time were Larry Walker, Jerry Wilson, and Pete Hunt. Top reserves were Dennis Fike, and freshman Dwayne Powell. Powell was a pleasant surprise. He established himself as a talent for the future and a deadly shooter when he came in during the second half of the Crawford County game in early January 1960 to lead Perry with 14 points, hitting seven field goals in a row from long range. John Mathews of Crawford County, one of the state's best players, led all scorers with 30 points as the powerful Crawford County five downed Perry 66 to 50.

The Panthers defeated Coach Martin Allman's Willingham Rams, 42 to 40, in two overtimes. The regulation game ended 38 to 38 and, after the first overtime, the score was knotted 40 to 40. In the sudden death overtime, Coach Staples sent in his sharpshooter, Dwayne Powell. Perry got the tip and screened for Powell at the forward position. The slender ninth grader fired a 30-footer from the corner that hit nothing but nylon, and the Panthers won a squeaker over the higher classification Macon school, 42 to 40.

Coach Staples engineered a big upset over a strong Macon County club, 52 to 49. Jimmy Smallwood led Perry with 22 points, closely followed by Pierce Staples with 18. Other Panthers in the game were Lindy Evans-10 markers, Larry Walker-2, Pete Hunt, Jerry Wilson, and Dennis Fike. Bill Martin's Macon County squad was paced by Leonard Liggin-14, and Benny Rodgers-12. Other Macon County players in the game were Floyd Rooks-8, Mack Lockerman-6, Paul Reed -4, Bill Athon-4, Bobby Lamberth-1, and Neal Bentley.

Assistant coach Frank Holland retired from coaching after the 1959-60 season. Coach Holland, before coming to Perry, had produced outstanding teams, first at Byron and then at Chauncey.

Region 2B Area 1 tournament at Dublin

For the first time in many years, the Panthers were eliminated in the first game of the sub-region tournament. They were defeated by East Laurens, 58 to 46. Although Perry was behind 40 to 32 at the end of the third period, the Panthers came to life and hit six straight points to move within two points, 38 to 40, early in the fourth quarter. At this point, East Laurens rallied and scored 17 points while Perry could garner only 6.

Leading the Perry attack were Jimmy Smallwood with 13 and Lindy Evans and Pierce Staples with 10 points each. Others Panthers scoring were reserve Dwayne Powell, who pumped in 6 tallies, Dennis Fike-4, Larry Walker-2, and Jerry Wilson-1. Pete Hunt also played.

East Laurens executed a balanced offense: Stinson-15, Watson-13, Morris-10, Ennis-10, Irby-8, and King-2.

1961 Perry team

Members:
Paul Bozeman
Ronnie Davis
Alton Ellis
Dennis Fike
Bobby Goodman
Ronnie Griffin
Lee Martin
George Nunn
Dwayne Powell
Kline Rentz
Wayne Riner
Ronnie Sanders
Gene (Butch) Skinner
Sonny Wilson-manager

Regular season highlights

The Perry Panthers opened the season on an optimistic note. All-State Lee Martin's knee had mended, and he was ready to suit up and play. He was joined by rising sophomore, Dwayne Powell, a pure shooter, who as a freshman in 1960, had gained valuable experience and could be counted on to help Martin carry the offensive load. Dennis Fike, a forward, who had started in some games last season, was a terrific rebounder and could score around the basket. George Nunn, up from the B-team, showed great promise as being a post player the team could depend upon both offensively and defensively. The fifth member of the team was Ronnie Griffin, an outstanding point guard who could move the ball around and keep the offense clicking. Capable reserves were Ronnie Sanders, Alton Ellis, Butch Skinner, Paul Bozeman, Kline Rentz, and Wayne Riner.

The Panthers finished the regular season with an admirable record of 24 wins and only six losses. Their most significant victory was ending Telfair County's 40-game winning streak. Telfair County had won the state championship in 1960 and returned virtually the same team. Telfair featured two All-State players in Everett Copeland and Bonnie Strom; the latter had moved from Perry to Telfair County in 1960. The Panthers nipped Telfair County in overtime, 64 to 60. Lee Martin led Perry with 25 points. Other Panthers contributing to the win were Dennis Fike and George Nunn with 11 apiece, Dwayne Powell-9, Ronnie Griffin-4, Alton Ellis-4, and Ronnie Sanders. Bonnie Strom and Everett Copeland pitched in 19 and 18 points respectively for Telfair County. They were followed by Best-12, Dennis-9, Batchelor-2, and Cook.

Perry also tripped the undefeated Warner Robins Demons coached by Coach Don La Blanc, a class AAA team. The Demons had beaten the Panthers twice earlier: in the finals of the Christmas tournament, 44-42, and again, 57-49, in mid-January 1961. In the third game, the Panthers squeezed by the Demons 49 to 48. The Panthers were led offensively by Dwayne Powell with 16 points, followed by Lee Martin and Dennis Fike with 12 tallies each. Other Panthers contributing to the Demons' upset were Ronnie Griffin-4, Alton Ellis-4, George Nunn-1, who played a great defensive game, and Ronnie Sanders, who came in the game at point guard and played well. The Demons played only five men: Bob Davis-32 points, Bobby Cribb-12, Buster McConnell-2, Muha-1, and Bass-1.

The good news was that the young Panthers didn't have a senior in the starting line-up, and practically all the reserves would return for another year. If the Panthers didn't make a run at the state championship in 1961, they would certainly be a power to be reckoned with in 1962.

Sub-region at Irwinton

Opening game: Perry-61, Wilkinson County-26
Dennis Fike and Dwayne Powell were Perry's offensive standouts with 20 and 14 points respectively. Lee Martin met a defense rigged to slow him and dropped in 8. Ronnie Griffin added 6, Alton Ellis-6, George Nunn-3, Ronnie Sanders-2, and Bobby Goodman-2. Butch Skinner and Ronnie Davis also played in the game. Wilkinson County's forward, Wornock, found the range for 15 points.

Finals: Perry-50, East Laurens-32
Perry hammered East Laurens 50 to 32 to win the Region 2B Area 1 tournament. Lee Martin was the game's top scorer with 21 points followed by Dennis Fike-13, Dwayne Powell-11, and George Nunn-5. Junior Irby of East Laurens led the losers' efforts with 12 markers.

Region 2B tournament at Mount Vernon

Opening round: Perry-62, Metter-40

Perry's big gun was Lee Martin with 23 markers. Dwayne Powell backed him up with 11. Other Panthers playing in the game were Dennis Fike-8 points, George Nunn-8, Ronnie Griffin-5, Butch Skinner-2, Ronnie Sanders-2, Alton Ellis-2, Paul Bozeman-1, Wayne Riner, Bobby Goodman, and Ronnie Davis. Metter got all of its scoring from Sam Sapp with 17 tallies, Chase-13, Collins-8, and Lanier-2. Hulsey also played for Metter.

Semifinals: Telfair County-48, Perry-40

Telfair County, the defending state champions, rolled over the inexperienced Panthers, 48 to 40, to advance to the region finals against Vidalia. Telfair County's two All-State players, Bonnie Strom and Everett Copeland, each scored 17 points. Rounding out Telfair's offense were Best-11, Dennis-2, and Batchelor-1. Perry's scorebook read: Lee Martin-16, George Nunn-12, and Dennis Fike-3. Sophomore Dwayne Powell was held to 9 points by Telfair's Bonnie Strom, one of Georgia's top defensive players. Perry's Ronnie Griffin, Alton Ellis, and Ronnie Sanders also played, but did not score.

Championship game:

Telfair County downed Vidalia, 61 to 50, to win the region title as the twin bombers, Bonnie Strom and Everett Copeland, hit for 20 and 19 points respectively. Jimmy Treadwell led Vidalia with 23 points followed by Otis Willis with 11.

Consolation game:

Perry won the consolation game over East Laurens, 74 to 35, to capture third place in the region. Lee Martin took individual scoring honors with 25 points. Dennis Fike added 14 and Dwayne Powell-10. Ed Irby was the only double-figure man for East Laurens with 13 tallies. This victory began a 50-game winning streak for the Panthers.

1965 Perry team

Members:
Alrie Adams
Charles Ayer
Edgar Barfield
Lynwood Barrett
Tom Clark
Ricky Cotton
Benny Dennard
Currey Gayle

David Hathaway
Joe Martin
Ed Pierce
Lee St. John
Terry Todd
David Walker
Tommy White

Regular season highlights

The 1965 team had a remarkable achievement to follow. Perry had won three state championships in a row—1962, 1963, and 1964—and, considering the 1959 championship, the Panthers had won four state championships in the last six years, a truly phenomenal run. Never was a team so decimated by the loss of experience and talent as the 1965 team. Lost to graduation were three All-State players from the 1964 state championship team: Bert Bozeman, Jimmy Dorsett, and Garold Spena. Also not returning was Alton Ellis, an outstanding front court player. The only returning starter from the 1964 state championship team was rising sophomore, Joe Martin, a prolific scorer, who showed great promise to lead Perry back to the big dance. Aside from Martin, only three returnees had logged any appreciable experience in reserve rolls: Edgar Barfield, Tommy White, and Ricky Cotton. In summary, the 1965 season would definitely be a rebuilding year.

As his team's nucleus, Coach Staples initially chose guards Joe Martin and Charles Ayer, center Edgar Barfield, and forwards Tommy White and Ricky Cotton. Forwards Terry Todd and Currey Gayle alternated in starting roles as the season progressed. Other capable reserves were Benny Dennard, Ed Pierce, Lee St. John, David Walker, David Hathaway, Lynward Barrett, Tom Clark, and Alrie Adams. Perry finished the season with 14 wins and 12 losses.

Perry defeated a number of good area teams during the year. The game scores and Perry's top three individual scorers were:

Perry-58, Dudley Hughes-33.... Joe Martin-20, Currey Gayle-10, Charles Ayer-9
Perry-58, Crawford Co.-46....Tommy White-29, Joe Martin-13, Edgar Barfield-9
Perry-52, Macon Co-26....Tommy White-18, Joe Martin-14, Charles Ayer-10
Perry-57, Butler-47....Joe Martin-30, Charles Ayer-9, Edgar Barfield-8
Perry-58, Hawkinsville-46....Joe Martin-17, Charles Ayer-16, Edgar Barfield-13
Perry-64, Northside-54....Joe Martin-21, Ricky Cotton-17, Edgar Barfield-14

Coach Staples stepped down as head basketball coach after the 1964-65 season, and Paul Hartman became Perry High's basketball coach effective with the 1965-66 season. After 32 highly successful years at Perry, Staples had produced an unprecedented 8 state championships: 1947, 1949, 1953, 1956, 1959, 1962, 1963, and 1964. He remained as principal of the Perry schools for another four years, until his retirement in May 1969.

Sub-region 2A tournament at Cochran

Opening round: Perry-52, Washington County-44

Perry trailed 27 to 19 at the half and rallied by the end of third quarter to pull ahead by one point, 37 to 36. During the final period, the Panthers exploded for 15 points while holding Washington County to only 8.

Joe Martin scorched the nets for 27 markers to account for over half of Perry's offensive production. Other Panthers producing the winning effort were Charles Ayer-9 points, Edgar Barfield-9, Tommy White-3, Ricky Cotton-2, Terry Todd-2, and Currey Gayle.

John Douglas hit a game high 28 points for Washington County. He was followed by Pate-8, Walker-5, Thomas-2, Rhodes-1, and Garner.

Finals: Cochran-64, Perry-46

The Cochran Royals pulled away from the Perry Panthers and never lost the lead. The Royals were leading 12-7 at the first quarter mark, 38-12 at halftime, and 49-30 at the end of the third stanza.

Cochran's big gun was Jimmy Padgett who stripped the nets for 21 points. Close behind were Maddox-19, and Holder-14. Rounding out Cochran's attack were Horton-6, Fair-2, Hobbs-2, Parker, Scarborough, and Sapp.

Pacing the Panthers were Joe Martin-20 points and Ricky Cotton-14. Other Panthers contributing were Benny Dennard-4 points, Charles Ayer-3, Tommy White-3, Edgar Barfield-1, Terry Todd-1, Currey Gayle, and Lee St. John.

As sub-region runner-up, Perry advanced to the region tournament, but lost on opening night to Statesboro, 49 to 45.

Cochran defeated Statesboro, 67 to 55, for the region title and advanced to the state tournament, capturing the state Class A championship in 1965.

1967 Perry team

Members:
Lynward Barrett
Bill Bryant
Marion Cloud
Eugene Graham
Ed Harley
Rodney Lowe
Jay Michael
Don Norris
Lee St. John

Terry Todd
Eddie Watson
Stephen Smith-manager
David Costlow-manager

Regular season highlights

Returning from Perry's 1966 state championship team were two All-State players, Terry Todd and Marion Cloud; however, lost through graduation was the scoring punch provided by three other All-State selectees—Joe Martin, Charles Ayer and Ed Pierce, who carried the 1966 team to a record of 31 wins and only two losses.

Also returning were Lee St. John, with extensive reserve experience in 1966, along with Ed Harley, Eddie Watson, Rodney Lowe, and Eugene Graham.

Because Perry had lost so much of its finely-tuned offense that carried the team to the state winner's circle in 1966, the Panthers struggled all season trying to find the combination that could rekindle the offensive fire power it once enjoyed.

Sub-region 1A, East tournament

Opening game: Perry-62, Cook County-44

Perry pummeled Cook County, 62 to 44, on the hot-shooting of Eddie Watson, who garnered 27 points. Terry Todd added 12, Marion Cloud-11, Ed Harley-4, and Lee St. John-2. Reserves playing were Lynward Barrett-4 points, Bill Byrant-2, Rodney Lowe, Eugene Graham, and Jay Michael.

Cook County was led by Coward with 13 points, Connell-10, Ray-9, Currington-8, Whitehurst-2, Hill-1 and Bowman-1.

Semifinal: Bacon County-62, Perry-42

Ed Harley paced the Panthers with 15 markers. Eddie Watson added 13, Terry Todd-10, Marion Cloud-2, and Eugene Graham-2. Other Panthers in the game were Lee St. John, Rodney Lowe, Jay Michael, and Lynward Barrett.

Bacon County's top scorer was Taylor with 23 tallies. Other Bacon Countians playing in the semifinal battle were McQuaig-14 points, Graham-10, Jordan-9, Jowers-4, Johnson-2, Bratcher, Head, and Tyre,

1968 Perry team

Members:
Lynward Barrett
Bill Byrant
Johnny Ellison
Eugene Graham

Steve Mayo
Gerald Norris
Bert Richards
Tommy Smith
Lee St. John
Ben Stephens-manager
David Costlow-manager

Regular season highlights

Perry lost to graduation four starters from the 1967 team: Terry Todd, Marion Cloud, Eddie Watson, and Ed Harley. Three others with considerable playing time not returning were Rodney Lowe, Jay Michael, and Don Norris.

Returnees were starting guard Lee St. John and previous year reserves Eugene Graham, Lynward Barrett, and Bill Bryant. Moving up from the B-team were Johnny Ellison, Steve Mayo, Tommy Smith, Bert Richards, and Gerald Norris.

As was the case in 1967, the 1968 team struggled without the outstanding shooters that had characterized Panthers' teams of the past, and broke even during the regular season, winning 11 games and losing 11.

Perry defeated the Class AAA Willingham Rams 45 to 44 on a 20-foot jump shot by Johnny Ellison at the final buzzer. Willingham held a 44-43 lead going into the last minute of play. With 24 seconds on the clock, Ram coach Billy Beale called timeout. His team worked the ball around a pressing Panther defense and sprung a man open for a lay-up, but his shot caromed off the glass. With only 10 seconds left, Perry rebounded and had time for last-second heroics. Ellison took the shot and the game was history. Three Panthers hit in double-figures: Ellison-12 points, Eugene Graham-11 and Tommy Smith-11. Lynward Barrett added 9 and Gerald Norris-2. Lee St. John and Bill Byrant played well in reserve roles.

Willingham's Mark Smith was the only Ram in double figures with 13 points. Other Rams contributing to the offense were Mims-9 markers, Kendricks-7, Goolsby-6, Jones-5, Beale-4, Wilson-0, and Fussell-0.

Sub-region 1A, East tournament

Opening game: Bacon County-49, Perry-39

The game was nip and tuck during the first half with Bacon County leading 22 to 21 at halftime. Perry fell behind ten points, 37 to 27, at the end of the third quarter, but failed to close the gap down the stretch. Bacon County was the team that eliminated the Panthers in sub-region play in 1967.

Lynward Barrett ripped the nets for 15 points to pace Perry's offense. Also scoring were Eugene Graham-7 tallies, Johnny Ellison-6, Lee St. John-6, and Gerald Norris-5. Reserves Tommy Smith and Bill Bryant played, but did not score.

All of Bacon County's starters were in the scoring column: Tyre-17, Jowers-15, Medders-8, Knight-5, and Salter-4. Reserve Bratcher played, but did not score.

1969 Perry team

Members:
Max Baker
Bob Cunningham
Johnny Ellison
Jimmy Hathaway
Randy Loggins
Steve Mayo
Lonnie McClintic
Gerald Norris
Wendy Pierce
Jimmy Scoggins
Bert Richards
Jerry Smith
Tommy Smith
Ben Stephens-manager
David Costlow-manager

Regular season highlights
Four members of the 1968 team returned: two starters, Johnny Ellison and Gerald Norris; and two reserves, Tommy Smith and Steve Mayo. Moving up to the varsity for the first time were Lonnie McClintic, Randy Loggins, Wendy Pierce, Bert Richards, Max Baker, Bob Cunningham, Jimmy Hathaway, Jimmy Scoggins, and Jerry Smith.

Two thrillers during the year were Perry's 32 to 30 win over Americus and its 45 to 42 upset of Unadilla. The Unadilla game was hard-fought to the final buzzer with the Panthers emerging victorious during the final minute of play. Gerald Norris tossed in 14 buckets, and Randy Loggins, an excellent future prospect, swished the nets for 12. Lonnie McClintic hit for 6 points, Johnny Ellison garnered 5, and Steve Mayo collected 4. Reserves entering the game were Max Baker, who accounted for 4 points, and Tommy Smith, who played a fine floor game.

Unadilla's big guns were Brannen-19, Mason-10, and Brooks-9. Others in Unadilla's offense were Sinnard-2, Kindley-2, and Dennard-0.

Perry's last state championship was in 1966. Three to four years are normally required to reload for another run at a championship. Either the current 1968-69 season or the next might find the Panthers back at Macon's City Auditorium. Although the Panthers didn't break even during the regular season, winning 10 games and losing 12, they possessed the potential, if they peaked at the right time, to go far in regional tournament competition and, with a little luck, advance to the state meet.

Sub-region 1A East tournament at Fitzgerald

Opening game: Perrry-67, Fitzgerald-56

Four Perry starters hit in the double figures: Johnny Ellison-17, Tommy Smith-15, Randy Loggins-13, and Gerald Norris-12. Barker led Fitzgerald with 13, followed by Moore-10, and Callaway-9.

Semifinals: Perry-50, Bacon County-40

Johnny Ellison was the top scorer in the game with 19 points. Tommy Smith added 12. Dowdy and Jowers paced Bacon County with 10 and 9 points respectively. This was sweet revenge for the Panthers, as Bacon County had eliminated Perry from the sub-region in both 1967 and 1968.

Finals: Perry-50, Center High-49

Although Perry led by 3 points with 30 seconds to play, Center High of Waycross, Georgia, drove down the court and narrowed the lead to one point. Center High quickly regained possession of the ball and moved in for the winning basket, but the Panthers' pressing defense tied-up the ball with only 6 seconds remaining. Perry controlled the tip and the game as time ran out.

Johnny Ellison, hot as a firecracker, riveted the nets for 24 points. Steve Mayo hit for 11 points, Gerald Norris-8, Randy Loggins-4, and Tommy Smith-3.

Center High of Waycross had balanced scoring throughout the game: Killens-10 markers, Dickerson-9, Moore-7, Jackson-7, Brown-6, Eason-6, Taylor-4, and Wells-0.

Region 1-A tournament at Tifton (ABAC gym)

Perry won the sub-region 1-A tournament at Fitzgerald, Georgia, and advanced to the region 1A semifinals to play Coach Tommy Whitehurst's Early County Bobcats, a team averaging 66-points a game with an impressive 23-4 season mark. The Bobcats handily disposed of the Panthers, 80 to 54, in a game whose outcome was never in doubt.

Howell was the top gunner for Early County with 25 ticks on the scoreboard. Arnold came in second with 18 counters and Earnest third with 17. Other Bobcats in the game were Brown-6 points, Hollington-6, Rickelson-4, Cannon-2, McCormick-2, and Starr-0.

All five of Perry's starters entered the scorebook. Tommy Smith collected 16 points, Johnny Ellison-14, Gerald Norris-6, Steve Mayo-10, and Randy Loggins-8. Perry had one reserve in the contest, Max Baker, who performed well on defense.

Appendix II – Perry High School Basketball Cheerleaders

V...I...C...T...O...R...Y, that's the way you spell it, here's the way you yell it... PERRY...PERRY...PERRY!"

1948 Perry High Cheerleaders. Front row, L-R: Joanne Cooper, little Kerry Strong, and Betty Connell. Directly behind Kerry Strong is Vadie Riddle. Back row, L-R: Jo Alice Moody, Jeanne Pierce, Billie Davis, June Satterfield, and Dot Ogletree

Perry High School's basketball dynasty was not the result of happenstance. The school was gifted with a great coach, and the town, over the span of four decades, produced talented players who, through their coach, developed into outstanding teams. But, the combination of a great coach and outstanding teams by themselves cannot produce a dynasty any more than flour and sugar without butter, eggs, and milk can make a cake. To produce a basketball dynasty, two other key ingredients are essential to the recipe. One is the fan and the other is the cheerleader. Fans blend the mixture of player and coach and cheerleaders give it flavor. Imagine for a moment two teams vying for a state championship with no fans or cheerleaders in the gym. Wouldn't be much of a game would it? Without question, cheerleaders have played an important role in the winning tradition that Perry High School enjoyed.

As a seventh grader, I was fascinated as much with the cheerleaders in their colorful uniforms and swirling skirts, as I was with the players. The cheerleaders were so poised and so very pretty. I was secretly in love with every one of them.

The cheerleaders worked as hard to make the cheerleading squad as the players practiced to make the varsity. There were usually 20 to 25 girls who tried out. Often judges would be brought in from other towns to select the cheerleaders for the coming season. From eight to ten individuals were normally selected.

For all Perry basketball seasons except three, only girls were selected. One of Perry's first cheerleaders was a male student—Emmett Cater, a cheerleader during the early 1940s. The 1946 squad included one male, Lorie McElheney, and the 1951 group featured four males: Charles Carter, Charles Hill, Hentz Houser, and Phillip Sledge. These four young men were chatting one day in study hall, lamenting the fact that Perry High had no male cheerleaders and suggesting that the addition of a few males would pick up the tempo and be a crowd pleaser. Word about their conversation spread back to Coach Staples. He called the four youngsters into his office and asked if they felt the cheerleading squad needed a few males. They all responded in the affirmative. Then Staples surprised and shocked them, saying, "I agree. I expect the four of you to be dressed out as cheerleaders at the game Friday night." In a few days, these four young men were faced with the daunting task of obtaining uniforms, learning the yells, and performing seamlessly with the eight female cheerleaders. They made their debut the following Friday night at the basketball game. They were met with tremendous applause by the Perry fans. They were the talk of the town.

Every year, a cheerleading coach was designated by the school to mentor the squad during the basketball season. The cheerleaders practiced anywhere they could—in the gym, the school auditorium or in private homes. Transportation to out-of-town games was usually provided by their parents. On some occasions, cheerleaders rode in the school bus to games played at other sites.

Over the decades the cheerleaders' attire changed and their skirts shortened with the fashion of the times. One Perry High cheerleader outfit that was standard issue during the late 1940s and early 1950s was a white sweater with a "P" on the front, a maroon corduroy skirt, and saddle oxfords. Later team cheerleaders wore maroon jumpers with a gold "P" on the front, a white, long-sleeved shirt, and maroon sneakers.

When the team exited the dressing room for pre-game warm-ups, cheerleaders would line the sidelines and cheer the players onto the playing floor. Just before tip-off, they led the crowd in singing the alma mater and then a rousing fight song. They cheered during time-outs and at halftime. During the game, they were continuously screaming and clapping after every basket and every clutch play to spur the Panthers to victory. The players, knowing that the cheerleaders were solidly behind them, were motivated to excel, oftentimes at the upper limits of their abilities. Nothing equaled the cheerleaders coming on the court to hug and congratulate each Panther after a win, particularly those hard fought games. Once driving down court on a fast break, I collided with my defender and was knocked out of bounds. I landed in a pile of cheerleaders sitting near the sideline. It was like falling on a soft cushion. I looked around at all that beauty and didn't want to get up.

Perry High's cheerleaders were always courteous. They greeted the opposing cheerleaders before the game and discouraged any discourteous behavior among fans. Perry had a great school spirit, one that was contagious and sometimes volatile, but through it all, Coach Staples demanded good sportsmanship, and it was the job of the cheerleaders to encourage and sustain it. It was not unusual for a cheerleader to go up in the stands and chide those making unsportsmanlike noises or gestures.

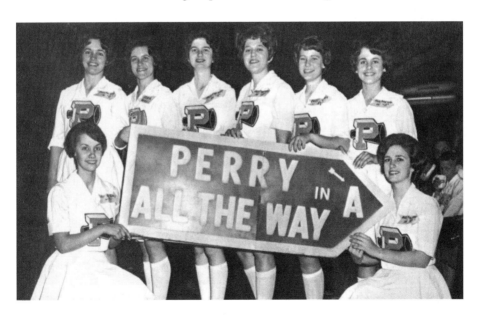

1963 Perry High Cheerleaders. Front row, L-R: Shirley Matthews and Molly Richardson. Back row, L-R: Brenda Roper, Judy Gray, Judy Smith, Jan Brown, Miriam Wheelus, and Cheryl Richards.

Before games with arch-rivals like Fort Valley, Lanier, and Warner Robins, the cheerleaders would arrive early and whip the Perry fans into a frenzy. The mood of the Perry fans took its cue from the fervor of the cheerleaders. In close games, every basket or decisive maneuver by the Panther team was met with a deafening crowd roar...a repetitive roar that crescendoed to a fever pitch, inspiring players to produce remarkable feats on the hardwood that became the difference between winning and losing.

At regional and state tournaments, where many schools were represented, Perry's cheerleaders were recognized as the cream of the crop. Their decorum was excellent and they represented their school and their community with distinction. They made all of us, players, students, and fans, proud to be called Panthers. Perry High School's cheerleaders were, indeed, one of its greatest assets.

During the mid-to-late 1930s, before there were organized cheerleaders, Perry High designated students to serve as yell and song leaders. Some of these were Evelyn Andrew, Charles Andrew, Earnest Davis, Hilda Gray, William Hunt, Betty Jane Lee, Carolyn Marshall, Courtney Mason, Hazel Nesmith, Mary Lee Peek, and James Short.

Organized cheerleading teams did not appear at Perry High School until the early 1940s. Perry's first two cheerleaders were Emmett Cater and Annie Ruth Debbins. Other 1940-1945 era cheerleaders were Lynette Eason, Betty Gooden, Louise Kezar, Mary Lewis, Carlene Ogletree, Evelyn Peed, Joyce Tolleson, Betty Boler, Lillie Brooks, Jerry Cater, Merryl Hunnicutt, Martha Ann Gordon, Annis Jean NeSmith, Bess Nunn, Jane Riley, and Barbara Whipple.

The first Perry High School yearbook was published in 1946. Since that time, the names of cheerleaders are available. Listed below are the names of Perry High School varsity basketball cheerleaders by year, from 1946 through 1969. Each of these cheerleaders deserves the gratitude of all the Perry Panthers.

1946	1947	1948	1949
Jerry Cater	Joanne Cooper	Betty Connell	Essie Claude
Helen Cawthorn	Frances Davis	Joanne Cooper	Bloodworth
Frances Davis	Mary Davis	Billie Davis	Betty Connell
Mary Davis	Naomi Kersey	Jo Alice Moody	Joanne Cooper
Helen Lewis	Betty McElheney	Dot Ogletree	Billie Davis
Betty McElheney	Dot Ogletree	Jeanne Pierce	Jo Alice Moody
Lorie McElheney	Jeanne Pierce	Vadie Riddle	Dot Ogletree
Bess Nunn	Annabelle Watts	June Satterfield	Jeanne Pierce
			Vadie Riddle
			June Satterfield
			Barbara Tolleson

1950
Bennieta Andrew
Kitty French
Evelyn Gilbert
Peggy Jo Mitchell
Mary Evelyn Mc-
Cormick
Jo Alice Moody
Betty Ann Smith
Bobbe Smith

1951
Angela Anderson
Bennieta Andrew
Geraldine Best
Charles Carter
Lula Alice Collier
Margaret Gibson
Charles Hill
Hentz Houser
Betty Jones
Mary Evelyn Mc-
Cormick
Phillip Sledge
Bobbe Smith

1952
Angela Anderson
Lula Alice Collier
Martha Cooper
Nelda Edwards
Margaret Gibson
Betty Jones
Bobbe Smith
Rosemary Tharpe

1953
Martha Cooper
Barbara Davis
Carolyn Davis
Nelda Edwards
Margaret Gibson
Betty Nunn
Sylvia Tabor
Rosemary Tharpe

1954
Carolyn Davis
Barbara Davis
Joan Hay
Betty Nunn
Dorothy Walton
Sylvia Tabor
Faye Tharpe
Rosemary Tharpe

1955
Laurie Anderson
Martha Evans
Claire Grimes
Marilyn Holland
Patsy Hughes
Marcilla Jacobs
Marjorie Nunn
Sherry Staples
Billie Smith
Theresa Williams
Faye Tharpe

1956
Marilyn Holland
Martha Evans
Laurie Anderson
Marjorie Nunn
Claire Grimes
Patsy Gail Hughes
Nancy Logue
Joan Roper
Sherry Staples
Myra Wilder

1957
Martha Evans
Claire Grimes
Helen Head
Patsy Gail Hughes
Beverly Jacobs
Barbara Langston
Jean Norman
Marjorie Nunn
Joan Roper
Sherry Staples
Myra Wilder

1958
Claire Grimes
Helen Head
Patsy Gail Hughes
Missie McCroskey
Susan McNeill
Susan Roberts
Joan Roper
Sherry Staples
Kay Tabor
Linda Tabor

1959
Georgette Austin
Mary Ellis Manship
Carole Mason
Susan McNeill
Susan Roberts
Linda Tabor

1960
Georgette Austin
Kathy Borders
Jan Brown
Kay Coleman
Jackie Harris
Betty Kersey
Carole Mason
Susan McNeill
Ann NeSmith

1961
Georgie Austin
Jayne Boles
Kathy Borders
Jan Brown
Bit Hunt
Betty Kersey
Mary Ellis Manship
Susan McNeill
Susan Roberts
Linda Tabor

1962
Kathy Borders
Jan Brown
Judy Gray
Faye Helms
Bit Hunt
Shirley Matthews
Molly Richardson
Brenda Roper

1963
Jan Brown
Judy Gray
Faye Helms
Donna Loggins
Shirley Matthews
Cheryl Richards
Molly Richardson
Brenda Roper
Judy Smith
Miriam Wheelus

1964
Cheryl Crutchfield
Judy Gray
Carol Maddox
Shirley Matthews
Molly Richardson
Brenda Roper
Linda Satterfield
Miriam Wheelus

1965
Susan Dubois
Donna Loggins
Shirley Matthews
Brenda Roper
Laurie Tolleson
Judy Wilson
Pat Wilson
Karen Wright

1966
Donna Byrant
Marianne Coley
Vaughn Cranshaw
Lynn Daniels
Donna Loggins
Julie Ogletree
Gale Weems
Miriam Wheelus
Shirley Woodruff
Karen Wright

1967
Cheryl Crutchfield
Linda Davis
Lynn Daniels
Mitzi Mills
Linda Rodgers
Beverly Roper
Linda Satterfield
Lida Smith
Martha Suber
Gale Weems
Karen Wright

1968
Lynn Daniels
Linda Davis
Jane Van Fossen
Elaine Gutzke
Mitzi Mills
Karen NeSmith
Linda Rodgers
Lida Smith
Karen Wright

1969
Sandy Forehand
Jane Van Fossen
Marsha Green
Elaine Gutzke
Deborah Parkinson
Linda Rodgers
Lida Smith
Judy St. John
Lee Warren

Appendix III – Perry High School Girls' Basketball: 1959-1969

Girls' basketball began at Perry High School during the early 1920s, but was discontinued in 1933, the same year that Coach Staples arrived in town as the new boys' basketball coach. For the next 25 years, Perry enjoyed such a dynasty in boys' basketball that no thought was given to instituting a girls' program. School officials and townspeople alike feared it might dilute the emphasis on boys' basketball. However, in 1958, a group of ladies began to clamor for reinstating girls' basketball. They initiated an aggressive campaign that resulted in 300 women petitioning Perry's school administration to reorganize girls' basketball. Consequently, the 1958-59 school year marked Perry's first return to girls' basketball in 25 years.

Perry's first girls' team in almost 30 years, the 1959 Lady Panthers: Seated, L-R: Betty Yeomans, Janice Knighton, Patsy Todd, Beverly Jacobs, Katherine Kovac, Vivian Culpepper, and Coach Earl Marshall. Back row, L-R: Sam Coby, Jerrie Lasseter, Janelle Parker, Roxie Ann McEachern, Adelaine Stocks, and Karen Harley.

Little did Earl Marshall know, when he began teaching science at Perry High School in 1951, that seven years later, he would become the coach of a new era in girls' basketball.   Earl Marshall, who played basketball for Coach Eric Staples during 1943-44, graduated from Mercer University in 1949, and took his first job as a teacher and basketball coach at Unadilla High School. Marshall arrived at Perry in 1951 and began coaching B-team basketball. He also assisted Coach Staples with the varsity. When Coach Eric Staples offered Marshall the opportunity to organize a girls' basketball program in 1958, Earl felt unqualified and was reluctant to accept the offer, but Staples convinced him to give it a try.

And try he did, for the next eleven seasons Marshall produced outstanding teams that were fundamentally sound, well-disciplined, and known for good sportsmanship. No overall won-loss records are available, but the accomplishments of Marshall's teams have been a source of lasting pride for PHS graduates and supporters. Perry's girls' teams excelled in spite of the fact that other area schools had been playing for decades, had feeder systems established at the lower grades, and had traditions to build upon.

Every Perry player brought her own unique skills to the game. Some were great scorers. Others were defensive stars, rebounding leaders, and skilled floor generals. Since basketball is a team sport, every Perry girl player was a star in her own right. Perry also boasted of outstanding team managers.

Jean Martin, 66-69   Judy Peavy, 60-62   Patsy Todd, 1959

Janice Knighton, 59-60   Faye Smallwood, 62-65   Lula Alice Collier

Beth Bennett-mgr, 67-69

Listed below by year are the Perry players from the Marshall era:

1959 team: Betty Yeomans, Janice Knighton, Patsy Todd, Beverly Jacobs, Katherine Kovac, Vivian Culpepper, Sam Coby, Jerrie Lasseter, Janelle Parker, Roxie Ann McEachern, Adelaine Stocks, and Karen Harley.

1960 team: Adelaine Stocks, Betty Yeomans, Vivian Culpepper, Janice Knighton, Sam Coby, Sandy Crumley, Karen Harley, Janice Rackley, Lanis Crooms, Judy Peavy, Jackie Dean, Roxie Ann McEachern, Margaret Bowen, and Sue Wilson.

1961 team: Adelaine Stocks, Jackie Dean, Vivian Culpepper, Judy Peavy, Karen Harley, Sam Coby, Donna Horton, Pat Ragan, Corinne Cummings, Patsy Murphy, Linda Dennard, Betty Farr, Dorothy Ratteree, and Susan Skinner-manager.

1962 team: Patsy Murphy, Corinne Cummings, Adelaine Stocks, Judy Peavy, Lanis Crooms, Sam Coby, Phyllis Taylor, Penny Brewster, Dorinda Stanley, Pat Brannin, Mary Rush, Faye Smallwood, Pat Ragan, Donna Horton, Patricia Gunn-manager, and Debbie Gayle-manager.

1963 team: Corrine Cummings, Mary Rush, Faye Smallwood, Lanis Crooms, Patsy Murphy, Pat Ragan, Donna Horton, Phyllis Taylor, Jeffy Lewis, Cheryl Cranford, Pat Brannin, Arlene Moon, Penny Brewster, Diane Walton, Susan Skinner-manager, and Linda Crooms-manager.

1964 team: Beverly Barrett, Lynn Purdom, Pat Ragan, Corinne Cummings, Penny Brewster, Faye Smallwood, Claire Brannin, Patsy Murphy, Sue Giles, Marilyn Richardson, Arlene Moon, Belinda Darity, Jeffy Lewis, Donna Horton, Phyllis Taylor, Mary Rush, Linda Graham, Linda Crooms-manager, Susan Skinner-manager, and Patricia Gunn-manager.

1965 team: Faye Smallwood, Dianne Walton, Linda Graham, Arlene Moon, Claire Brannin, Jeffy Lewis, Phyllis Taylor, Beverly Barrett, Ouida Farr, Sue Giles, Patricia Gunn-manager, Ouida Giles-manager, and Sharlyn Daniels-manager.

1966 team: Jean Martin, Linda Graham, Judy Pace, Sue Giles, Cathy Pierce, Marian Whitehurst, Beverly Barrett, Lynn Purdom, Diane Dupree, Maida Ragan, Carroll Coley, Rena Rider, Susan Adams, Joyce Avera, Beth Tabor, Claire Brannin, Peggy Simons, Jane Barrett-manager, and Lynn Purdom-manager.

1967 team: Cathy Pierce, Judy Pace, Carroll Coley, Winifred Davis, Janet Moon, Irene Culp, Jean Martin, Sue Giles, Linda Graham, Sara Williamson, Marian Whitehurst, Beth Tabor, Claire Brannin, Susan Adams, Rena Rider, Janis Ethridge-manager, Jane Barrett-manager, and Beth Bennett-manager.

1968 team: Jean Martin, Marian Whitehurst, Sara Williamson, Dianne Lamb, Irene Culp, Meredith Cloud, Judy Pace, Cathy Pierce, Rena Rider, Carroll Coley, Susan Adams, Pam Boland, Lisa Ogletree, Janis Ethridge-manager, Vikki Whelchel-manager, and Beth Bennett-manager.

1969 team: Jean Martin, Meredith Cloud, Dianne Lamb, Alycen Whiddon, Susan Adams, Lisa Ogletree, Debbie Murphy, Pam Boland, Sara Williamson, Linda Harris, Rena Rider, Beth Bennett-manager, Janis Ethridge-manager, and Becky Horton-manager.

Since girls' basketball didn't resume until the fall of 1958, there were a number of potentially great girl basketball players during the 1940-50s who never had an opportunity to don the maroon and gold. Lula Alice Collier Batchelor, a 1952 Perry graduate, was one. This writer played a lot of backyard basketball with Lula during his pre-teen years while growing up in Perry. She was an outstanding player and a deadly shooter. My only regret is that I never beat Lula in a game.

The saying "like mother like daughter" was exemplified as two Perry players had daughters who excelled locally and went on to play college basketball. Faye Smallwood Barry's daughter, Allison, was the all-time leading scorer at Westfield High School in Perry with 2056 points. Her number was retired by the school. Allison played at Georgia College in Milledgeville. Another Westfield star was Wendy, daughter of Janice Knighton Walker, a great shooter and team leader who played on the girls' varsity basketball team at the University of Georgia.

Earl Marshall was the consummate science instructor and one of Perry's most popular teachers. He was also my friend and mentor. As Coach Staples' assistant, Coach Marshall took a personal interest in me. He stressed that mental preparation is equally important as perfecting athletic skills. In 1953 the Perry team traveled to Atlanta and north Georgia to play a series of games. The weather was very cold and windy. All team members owned top coats except me. Coach Marshall loaned me one of his. I shall never forget that wonderful gesture.

Earl Marshall and his wife, Jackie, were two of Perry High School's most proficient and beloved teachers. They were the parents of three fine daughters: Daun, Laurie, and Tonda.

L-R: Daun, Earl, Tonda, Jackie, and Laurie Marshall

Commentaries on Coach Marshall

Jean Martin Davis: "Coach Marshall knew how to get the most out of every player. He knew their individual abilities and how they needed to be coached."

Faye Smallwood Barry: "Coach Marshall enjoyed coaching and loved his girls. He was a Christian man who instilled values in his players."

Janice Knighton Walker: "I really appreciated the time and effort that Mr. Earl Marshall put into organizing and coaching Perry High's girls' basketball program. Having come to Perry from Quitman where we had championship teams, I was very happy to see Perry start a program. Mr. Marshall had an easygoing manner but expected results! I enjoyed playing for him."

Beth Bennett: "Jackie Marshall was one of our strongest supporters. She is why I am where I am today. Please give Jackie a big hug for me. Coach Marshall was my mentor and teacher. He had extraordinary people skills and could read people quickly and understand what young adults held in their heart. Coach Marshall was never judgmental, always a gentleman, and did the right thing. He constantly sought ways to challenge his students and his team. He had the most sensitive objectivity of any human being that I have ever known. He believed in us and made us believe in ourselves."

Judy Peavy Raulerson: "Coach Marshall was extremely patient with his players. He always encouraged us and never berated us. He stressed fundamentals and good sportsmanship. He made the game fun and encouraged us to play our best. He let us know he was proud of all of us. Coach Marshall laughed with us and cried with us. Coach Marshall was the best of the best! He was a very influential person in my life and someone I looked up to."

Patsy Todd Jordan: "Mr. Earl Marshall was the epitome of the southern gentleman, family man, teacher, and coach. Patience was his greatest virtue. In 1959 he found himself faced with 15 somewhat talented, emotional girls who would be representing Perry's first girls' team. State championship coaches Eric Staples and Frank Holland would be watching. Coach Marshall's dedication to this task is what made him so special. Those values he instilled in us were the foundation of what Perry High School teams have always stood for. That was our beginning."

Since Perry's boys' teams always received a disproportionate share of the publicity, the intent of this chapter is to level the hardwood floor. All former students, fans, and supporters are extremely proud of Perry's girls' teams.

This chapter is dedicated in memory of Coach Earl Marshall, who passed from this life in 2004. Coach Marshall is smiling now. He is looking down from heaven with pride and admiration for every player he coached.